F

The Homebrewer's Recipe Guide

More Than 175 Original Beer Recipes,

Including Magnificent Pale Ales,

Ambers, Stouts, Lagers, and

Seasonal Brews, Plus Tips

from the Master Brewers

PATRICK HIGGINS MAURA KATE KILGORE
PAUL HERTLEIN

A FIRESIDE BOOK PUBLISHED BY SIMON & SCHUSTER

FIRESIDE
Rockefeller Center
1230 Avenue of the Americas
New York, NY 10020

Designed by Bonni Leon-Berman

Manufactured in the United States of America

1   3   5   7   9   10   8   6   4   2

Library of Congress Cataloging-in-Publication Data
Higgins, Patrick.
The homebrewer's recipe guide : more than 175 original
beer recipes, including magnificent pale ales, ambers, stouts,
lagers, and seasonal brews, plus tips from master brewers /
Patrick Higgins, Maura Kate Kilgore, Paul Hertlein.
p.   cm.
"A fireside book."
Includes index.
1. Brewing—Amateurs' manuals.
I. Kilgore, Maura Kate.
II. Hertlein, Paul.   III. Title.
TP570.H54   1996
641.8'73—dc20   96-26007
CIP
ISBN 0-684-82921-5

ACKNOWLEDGMENTS

We would like to thank all those who have contributed their time, recipes, and opinions, in the interest of good beer, especially James W. Glasheen, Eric S. Muttee, Gill Aharon, and Garth Battista. Also, Ed Lee, George "Murph" Murphy, Wayne Waananen, and everyone that put a bottle of our homebrew to their lips and lived to tell about it.

Special thanks also go to all of the guys at the New York City Beer Guide, whose tireless pursuit of good beer served as a constant inspiration to us. And most of all, thanks to homebrew guru Charlie Papazian for his contribution to our book, but most of all for teaching us how to homebrew in the first place.

Special thanks to our editor exraordinaire Becky Cabaza and her assistant Dan Lane, whose patience and humor made everything seem easy, and who believed in and supported this project from the very start (or maybe they were just pretending in order to get all that free beer).

And last but not least, thanks to our agent Philip Spitzer, who hates beer (but we're working on that), for supporting and encouraging us the entire way.

To our family and friends,

who gave us the confidence

to put our dreams ahead of our expectations

Contents

Foreword, by Charlie Papazian xvii
Introduction xix
Before You Begin xxi

Bitters, Pale Ales, and Other Regional Ales 1

Any Pub in London Bitter 3
Yippee IPA 4
 Brewer's Tip: Aerating Your Wort 5
Easy Wheat 6
Jack the Ripper British Ale 6
Affengeil Wheat Beer 7
Kölsch 8
Bitter Old Man 9
Belgian White Men Can't Jump 9
Brewtopia IPA 10
 Brewer's Tip: Priming Sugar 11
To ESB, or Not to ESB 12
Slam Dunkelweiss 12
Alt of This World 13
Ooh La La, Saison 14
Trappist House Brew 14
Bitchin' Belgian White 15
Honey Steam 16
Genuine Stunning Ale 17
Dubbel, Dubbel, Toil and Trubble 18
California Uncommon 18
 Brewer's Tip: The T-Shirt Trick 19
Mild-Mannered 20
Maura's Bride Ale 20
Crimson and Clover Ale 21
Baby's Bath Ale 22
Irving Berliner Weiss 23
Harvard Crimson 24
Pub Bitter 25

Uncle Sam's Dark Wheat   26
Brewer's Tip: Conversion and Extraction Rate   27
Too Good to ESB True   28
Euell Gibbons' Favorite Ale   28
Thomas Jefferson's Ale   29
Oak Tree IPA   30
Tripel Play   31
Hop on Pop   32
Accident-Prone Wheat   33
Vail Pale Ale   33
Louis's French Ale   34
Brewer's Tip: Culturing Yeast from a Bottle of Beer   36

Brown Ales, Porters, and Stouts   37

Basic British Brown   39
Basic American Brown   40
Ned Flanders Brown   41
Brewer's Tip: Toasted Malt   41
Honey Nut Brown   42
Uptown Brown   42
Oak Leaf Brown Ale   43
Nutty Brown   44
Tuxedo Brown   44
Basic Porter   45
Brown-Sugar Molasses Porter   46
Steamship Porter   47
Chocolate Honey Porter   48
Brewer's Tip: Gas vs. Electric   49
Mr. Hare's Porter   49
Viennese Spiced Porter   50
Brewer's Tip: Head Retention   51
Hey Porter   52
Porter #12   53
Basic Stout   54
Russian Imperial Stout   54
Brewer's Tip: High-Gravity Starters   56
Ed's Honey Oatmeal Stout   56

Canadian Imperial Stout   57
Old McDonald Drank a Stout   58
Presidential Stout   59
Cool Summer Imperial Stout   60
Java Stout   61
Jim and Gill's Barley Stout   62
Ninepin Stout   63

Lagers   65
Basic Pilsner   67
Two Lips   68
   Brewer's Tip: Clarifying Agents   69
Dingo-Ate-My-Baby Lager   70
One Helles of a Good Beer   70
Amazing Light Lager   71
Dortmunder   72
Hophead Lager   72
American Cream Ale   73
Great-Grandma's Czech Pilsner   74
Rice and Easy Does It   75
Märzen Madness   75
Golden Pils   76
In the Midnight Hour   77
   Brewer's Tip: Carbonation   78
Munich Dunkel   79
Viva Vienna!   80
Fest Haus Märzen   80
Maple Leaf   81
Feels Like the First Time   82
Eat My Schwarzbier   83
Roll-in-the-Hay Wheat Lager   83
Green Meadow Pilsner   84
Marvin's Martian Märzen   85
Snowball's Chance in Helles   85
   Brewer's Tip: Converting All-Grain to
   Extract and Vice Versa   86

Great White North   88
Red Herring   89

Bocks, Doppelbocks, Barleywines, and Strong Ales   91

Basic Helles Bock   93
Ein Bock   94
American Bock   95
   Brewer's Tip: The Three Enemies of Beer:
   Heat, Light, and Oxygen   96
Tarheel Tarwebok   97
Dunkel Bock   98
Mai Honey Bock   99
Ides of March Mai Bock   99
Doppel Your Pleasure   100
Drunk Monk Doppelbock   101
Alligator Doppelbock   101
Masterbator   103
The Bard's Barleywine   104
Blue and Gold Barleywine   105
   Brewer's Tip: Repitching Yeast   106
John Barleycorn Must Wine   107
Pewter Pot Barleywine   108
Thatched Roof Ale   109
Ye Olde Ale   109
Macbeth's Scotch MacAle   110
Sow Your Wild Oats Strong Ale   111
Coming on a Little Strong   111

Fruit, Herb, and Smoked Beers   113

Lemon Coriander Weiss   114
Tea for Brew, and Brew for Tea   114
Some Like It Hot   115
Jammin' Jamaican Jingered Ale   116
Berry Garcia   117
   Brewer's Tip: Using Fruit in Beer   118

Murph's Cranberry Wheat 119
Sweet Woodruff 119
Pineapple Pale Ale 120
Aplomb of an Ale 121
On Top of Old Smoky 122
 Brewer's Tip: Smoked Malt 123
Blue Devil Brew 123
Cardamom Stout 124
New England Cranberry Ale 125
Smoke It If You Got It 126
Cherries Jubilee 127
 Brewer's Tip: Washing Yeast 128
Peachy Keen 128
Smoky IPA 129
Cobbler Lager 130
Jimmy Carter's Peach Wit 131
Pumpernickel Rye 132

Holiday and Seasonal Beers

Holiday and Seasonal Beers 133
New Year's Lambic 135
Super Bowl Sunday Pale Ale 136
Fat Tuesday's Cajun Pepper Ale 137
Lover's Lane Valentine Stout 138
St. Patrick's Day Irish Cream Stout 139
 Brewer's Tip: Labeling 140
Easter Sunday Bitter 141
May Day Maibock 142
Watermelon Summer Lager 142
Firecracker Red 143
Apple Brown Betty Fall Ale 144
Falling Leaves Autumn Cider 145
Slidin' on Your Back Oktoberfest Lager 146
Drunk in the Streets of Cologne Oktoberfest Lager 147
Black Cat Halloween Porter 148
The Great Pumpkin Ale 149
Pilgrim Ale 150
Grandma's House Christmas Chocolate Mint Stout 151

Holiday Prowler Beer   152
Dickens' Strong Christmas Ale   153
Winter Wonderland   154
Fireside Winter Warmer   155

Brewery Copycats   157
California Cascade   159
Dublin's Finest   159
  Brewer's Tip: Quick Souring   160
Appliance-on-the-Fritz Pale Ale   161
First Stop Bitter   161
Sinner's Salvation   162
A True American Original   163
Strange Brew   164
  Brewer's Tip: Stuck Fermentation   165
If You're Down with Pete, Then You're Down with Me 165
Slate-Lined Stout   166
Britain's Favorite Brown   167
Image Is Everything   168
Merci, Pierre   168
Trademark Ale   169

Meads, Lambics, and Ciders   171
Temptation Mead   174
  Brewer's Tip: Honey   175
Here's Pyment in Your Eye   175
Mead Me in St. Louis   176
  Brewer's Tip: Acids in Mead   177
Mead and Mrs. Jones   177
Cysing up the Situation   178
Peach Glitter   178
Hippocrasic Oath   179
Dirty Sock Gueuze   180
  Brewer's Tip: Full Wort Souring   181
Kriek   181
Framboise   182

Sunset Cider   183
Apple-Pear Cider   183
Raspberry Cider   184
Holiday Cheer   184
Two of a Perfect Pear   185

Food and Beer, Beer and Food   187

Smoky Beer and Cheddar Soup   188
Roasted Beer Soup   189
Oatmeal Beer Bread   189
Smoked Basil Shrimp   190
Hop-Spiced Pickled Veggies   191
Yams à la Belgique   191
Frijoles Borrachos   192
Malted Applesauce   192
Fiesta Pork Stew   193
Cornish Game Hens in Blackberry Stout Sauce with
   Baked Apples   194
Kickin' Hot Chili   195
Maruja's Asopado de Pollo con Cerveza   196
Red Lentil Curry   197
Beer-Battered Fish   197
Spiced Sauerbraten   198
Carbonnade Flamande   199
Chicken with Roasted-Garlic Cream Sauce   200
Erin Go Bragh Stout Pie   200
Homestyle Meatloaf   201
Ginger-Beer Bratwurst   202
Red-Hot Rack of Ribs   203
Mary Bielawski's Polska Kielbasa   204
Poached Pears with Raspberry Sauce   204
Chocolate Cream Stout Cake   205
Lambic Sorbet   206
The Great Pumpkin Pie   206

Glossary   209
Building Your Own Wort Chiller   213

World Wide Web Beer and Brewing Sites   217
American Homebrewers' Association Style Guidelines 219
Index of Beers by Style   231
Index   235

FOREWORD

I love homebrew and so do you—otherwise you wouldn't have this recipe book in your collection of beer books. The nice thing about beer books is that you can't drink them dry. They forever provide guidance, direction, inspiration, and ideas for your ever-next batch of homebrewed beer. Books are a tool that you use to fashion something of your own. And that's what it's all about, isn't it? Making your own.

Take a look at what Patrick Higgins, Maura Kate Kilgore, and Paul Hertlein have compiled in *The Homebrewer's Recipe Guide*. Here you'll find a wealth of homebrewed inspiration without boundaries. Patrick, Maura, and Paul have shared with us the stories and recipes that they live by and have succeeded with. What works best for them? Relaxing, not worrying, and having a homebrew. And that's exactly what you'll be inspired to do by *The Homebrewer's Recipe Guide*.

Homebrewing is about fun, beer, and most of all people who enjoy beer and people. You can tell that these three had a few homebrewed fun times working on this project. You can tell there's a lot of creativity in these pages. And as with all things homebrew, fun and creativity tend to be contagious. You'll enjoy brewing any of the great recipes in this book. I hope to share one with you sometime, somewhere. In the meantime . . .

Relax. Don't worry. Have a homebrew.

Charlie Papazian
author of *The New Complete Joy of Home Brewing* (Avon)
and *The Homebrewer's Companion* (Avon)
Boulder, Colorado
1996

INTRODUCTION

Ale . . . stout . . . lager . . . bitter . . . the names roll off the tongue, followed immediately by visions of tall, cool glasses in sparkling shades of gold, amber, and chocolate, with rivulets of condensation rolling gently and aimlessly down each smooth side, and the inevitable desire to take a swift, greedy gulp of this cold, tingly nectar.

Yes, beer has certainly gotten a hold on us. No longer the bland, bleached-out beverage of our guzzling college days, but a gourmet smorgasbord of complex styles and variations. And, increasingly, we find we are in good company.

The "gourmet" beer industry in America has taken off in the nineties in a big way. A host of brewpubs featuring stylized in-house brews have arisen in just about every major city and many not-so-major towns. Microbreweries, technically defined as those producing less than fifteen thousand barrels a year, but loosely used to refer to any of those smaller breweries producing quality beers in nonmega batches, are reaching beyond their original regional thresholds to market their wares nationwide, and with great success. So much success, in fact, that several of the "megabreweries" are producing microbrew wannabes.

And with this rise in commercial gourmet brewing has come an equally impressive rise in homebrewing. As tastes and appreciation have expanded, so has the desire to create. For truly there is no greater triumph for the beer lover than to taste a superb brew that he has crafted with his own hands (and a large carboy, several lengths of plastic tubing, a sturdy caldron, and a large plastic bucket). But it takes more than a love of beer and the right equipment to craft a great brew. It takes great recipes— guidelines from other gourmet craftsmen who have experimented and perfected, tweaked and reworked, and finally achieved the ultimate result—an excellent beer.

Brewers have recognized this throughout the ages. For despite the recent surge in popularity, homebrewing is by no means a recent development. People have been crafting their own beers since at least 2500 B.C. and possibly as early as the late Stone Age. In fact, in between founding our nation and running their large plantations, James Madison and Thomas Jefferson exchanged beer recipes, and, of course, compared their own brews favorably with those made by the commercial brewers of the era.

Of course, tastes in brewing have changed (and diversified) since zymurgy's early days. For example, hops are now considered a staple beer ingredient, but their use was considered illegal by the Brewer's Guild in England until the late fifteenth century. The Reinheitsgebot, or the German Beer Purity Law, established in 1516, requires that beer consist of only four ingredients: water, malted barley, hops, and yeast. Although current beer trends are broad enough to include blueberry ales, coffee stouts, and garlic beers, you will certainly no longer find any recipes for cock ale, a brew from the 1600s which relied upon (you guessed it) *chicken* for its unique flavor.

Which brings us to the important question: what will you find in this recipe guidebook? Our criterion was simple: quality recipes that have worked well for us (and the many friends who enthusiastically acted as consultants and "research assistants"), encompassing the wide range of standard and unusual beers that we have come to enjoy. Whenever possible, we've included the tips we learned along the way, so that you can (hopefully) avoid some of the mistakes we've encountered. We've also included our favorite food recipes—some excellent accompaniments to beer, others made with beer or the by-products of brewing. And, we've tried to give you a taste of the enthusiasm for beer that has spanned the ages, in the form of quotes and excerpts from a few of the many notable beer enthusiasts throughout the literary world.

So pick a recipe that makes your taste buds tingle and gather your brewing buddies, because there is no better way to brew than surrounded by your favorite beer enthusiasts and, of course, your favorite homebrews. Happy brewing!

Before You Begin

We've put together this guide as a resource book for the home-brewer looking for a collection of great recipes. It is not a how-to book. If you don't know how to homebrew, you'll need to learn that first. There are a number of homebrewing books on the market that will have you brewing away in a matter of days. Our favorite, and we would venture to guess the favorite of nine out of ten brewers, is Charlie Papazian's *The New Complete Joy of Homebrewing*. In homebrew circles it is known simply as "The Bible."

As we're sure you noticed on the cover, the book is called *The Homebrewer's Recipe Guide*, not *The Homebrewer's Recipe Book*. What this means is that none of the recipes in the book are written in stone, and we encourage you to experiment. If you *do* choose to follow the recipes to the letter, you'll come away with some great brews, but as all homebrewers know, experimentation is half the fun. So if you're a big fan of honey, you may want to add three pounds instead of two to Ed's Honey Oatmeal Stout. Or if you prefer Kent Goldings hops to Hallertau in the Jack the Ripper British Ale, use Kent Goldings. In short, there is really only one rule, and that is: there are no rules, except common sense. So experiment away and make your beer your own.

However, there are a few general guidelines that we have followed in putting together the recipes in this book that we'd like to share.

ALL RECIPES ARE FOR FIVE-GALLON BATCHES

It's been our experience that the vast majority of homebrewers brew in this quantity, either in a plastic bucket or glass carboy, and so we felt this measurement would prove to be the most universal. As you know, fermentation vessels are available from homebrew stores in a variety of sizes, and the recipes found here are easily converted to those quantities. We've also had great success brewing in one-gallon batches, and you'll find that a one-gallon glass juice bottle will serve as the perfect fermenter.

MOST RECIPES ARE MADE
USING MALT EXTRACT

Around 80 percent of all homebrewers are extract brewers, so we've structured the book to reflect this. Each chapter contains a range of recipes from basic extract to all-grain. All-grain brewing allows the homebrewer the greatest range of control over the flavor of the wort. However, the added time and effort of all-grain brewing, a minimum of six hours, can be intimidating, not to mention the additional equipment. Whether we brew all-grain or extract depends upon how much time and energy we have. Excellent award-winning beers can be made using extract, so don't let anyone tell you that you're not a *real* homebrewer because you don't all-grain. Remember, there is just one goal—make good beer.

NO MASHING SCHEDULES ARE GIVEN
FOR ALL-GRAIN RECIPES

Because mashing times and temperatures will vary depending on the methods and equipment you use, we leave the mashing schedule to the discretion of the brewer. Today's malts are generally highly modified, and a single-step infusion is therefore adequate for converting your starches to fermentable sugars.

NO BEGINNING WATER
MEASUREMENTS ARE GIVEN

All recipes were made using a full wort boil. To get the highest utilization from your hops and to help to prevent your wort from caramelizing when using malt extract, as well as ensuring that the entire batch of beer is sterile, a full wort boil is a great advantage. For all-grain recipes, it is a necessity.

In order to do a full wort boil, you'll need at least a 7- to 8-gallon brew pot to avoid boilovers. Begin with 6 gallons of water if using all extract, or wort for all-grain. During the 1-hour boil, 1 gallon of water will evaporate, leaving you with the desired amount of 5 gallons.

You may not have the space or budget for a vessel this big, in which case a partial boil is adequate. When doing a partial wort boil, begin with a minimum of 1½ gallons of water, but the more you can accommodate the better. Fill the fermenter with cold water to reach the 5-gallon mark.

RECIPES WERE MADE USING LIQUID YEAST

Again, this is a matter of personal preference. We have found that liquid yeast is much fresher and more reliable and produces a much tastier beer than dry yeast. Dry yeasts may lend themselves to contamination more easily than liquid, and this contaminated yeast will cause your beer to take on some unpleasant flavors—flavors that Charlie Papazian compares to that of Band-Aids—and you'll notice as you go through the book there isn't a single recipe for Band-Aid Ale.

Another great advantage of using liquid yeast is that it gives you the ability to repitch your yeast and brew four or five batches of beer from a single packet of yeast. However, if you've had success with, or are more comfortable using dry yeast, then by all means stay with what works best for you. We do, however, recommend that dry yeast be hydrated before use for best results.

COOL THE HOT WORT WITH A WORT CHILLER

Of the beer disasters we have had (i.e., "beer that tastes as though it were brewed through a horse," to quote Mike Royko), over 60 percent can be attributed to contamination that occurred waiting for the wort to cool, which is when the wort is most susceptible. A wort chiller changed all of that.

Wort chillers are available in a variety of systems and in a variety of prices from your local homebrew store. A very effective (and cheaper) wort chiller can be made at home. Directions for making one can be found in the Appendix (see p. 213) of this book.

FERMENTATION TIMES MAY VARY

The fermentation times listed in each recipe are based on the time it took when we brewed these recipes. Since a variety of factors, such as temperature, aeration, and changes you may have made to the original recipe, will affect the fermentation time, be sure to pay close attention to your hydrometer.

SANITIZE, SANITIZE, SANITIZE

We can't say it enough. The single easiest thing you can do to ensure the quality and consistency of your beer is to keep things sanitary. If you think you're being overly careful and too obsessive, think again. You can never be too careful. It may seem tedious, but it will be well worth it when you're sitting back enjoying your brew.

And so brew away! And with a little time, and a little creativity, your friends will soon be quoting to you from Shakespeare's *Two Gentlemen of Verona:* "Blessing of your heart," they'll proclaim, "you brew good ale!"

Bitters, Pale Ales, and Other Regional Ales

From John Barleycorn *by* Jack London

I was five years old the first time I got drunk. It was on a hot day, and my father was ploughing in the field. I was sent from the house, half a mile away, to carry to him a pail of beer. And be sure you don't spill it, was the parting injunction.

It was, as I remembered it, a lard pail, very wide across the top, and without a cover. As I toddled along, the beer slopped over the rim upon my legs. And as I toddled, I pondered. Beer was a very precious thing. Come to think of it, it must be wonderfully good. Else why was I never permitted to drink of it in the house? Other things kept from me by the grown-ups I had found good. Then this, too, was good. Trust the grown-ups. They knew. And, anyway, the pail was too full. I was slopping it against my legs and spilling it on the ground. Why waste it? And no one would know whether I had drunk it or spilled it.

I was so small that, in order to negotiate the pail, I sat down and gathered it into my lap. First I sipped the foam. I was disappointed. The preciousness evaded me. Evidently it did not reside in the foam. Besides, the taste was not good. Then I remembered seeing the grown-ups blow the foam away before they drank. I buried my face in the foam and lapped the solid liquid beneath. It wasn't good at all. But still I drank it. The grown-ups knew what they were about. Considering my diminutiveness, the size of the pail in my lap, and my drinking out of it with my breath held and my face buried to the ears in foam, it was rather difficult to estimate how much I drank. Also, I was gulping it down like medicine, in nauseous haste to get the ordeal over.

I shuddered when I started on, and decided that the good taste would come afterward. I tried several times more in the course of that long half-mile. Then, astounded by the quantity of beer that was lacking, and remembering having seen stale beer made to foam fresh, I took a stick and stirred what was left till it foamed to the brim.

And my father never noticed. He emptied the pail with the wide thirst of the sweating ploughman, returned it to me, and started up the plough. I endeavored to walk beside the horses. I remember tottering and falling against their heels in front of the shining share, and that my father hauled back on the lines so violently that the horses nearly sat down on me. He told me afterwards that it was by only a matter of inches that I escaped disemboweling. Vaguely, too, I remember, my father carried me in his arms to the trees on the edge of the field, while all the world reeled and swung about me, and I was aware of the deadly nausea mingled with an appalling conviction of sin.

I slept the afternoon away under the trees, and when my father roused me at sundown it was a very sick little boy that got up and dragged wearily homeward. I was exhausted, oppressed by the weight of my limbs, and in my stomach was a harp-like vibrating that extended to my throat and brain. My condition was like that of one who had gone through a battle with poison. In truth, I had been poisoned.

In the weeks and months that followed I had no more interest in beer than in the kitchen stove after it had burned me. The grown-ups were right. Beer was not for children. The grown-ups didn't mind it; but neither did they mind taking pills and castor oil. As for me, I could manage to get along quite well without beer. Yes, and to the day of my death I could have managed to get along quite well without it. But circumstances decreed otherwise. At every turn in the world in which I lived, John Barleycorn beckoned. There was no escaping him. And it took twenty years of contact, *of exchanging greetings and passing on with my tongue in my cheek, to develop in me a sneaking liking for the rascal.*

Would I were in an alehouse in London.
—WILLIAM SHAKESPEARE, *HENRY V*

Any Pub in London Bitter

THE NAME SAYS IT ALL. This style of classic ale can be found in every pub in London. It is a very light beer that is usually served hand drawn and at cellar temperature in London pubs. Because of the absence of any specialty grains and the relatively low quantity of malt, it possesses a strong hop flavor and bouquet. Don't worry about the almost nonexistent head; that's the way it's supposed to be. So "pull" yourself a pint and sit back and wait for the next double-decker to roll by.

3⅓ POUNDS LIGHT MALT EXTRACT

2 POUNDS LIGHT DRY MALT EXTRACT

1½ OUNCES KENT GOLDINGS HOPS
  (BOILING)

1 OUNCE CASCADE HOPS
  (FINISHING)

2 TEASPOONS GYPSUM

1 TEASPOON IRISH MOSS

1 PACKAGE LONDON ALE YEAST

½ CUP CORN SUGAR (PRIMING)

Combine malt extracts, gypsum, and Kent Goldings hops in water. Boil for 1 hour. Add 1 ounce Cascade hops and Irish Moss for the last 5 minutes of the boil. Cool wort and pitch yeast. Fermentation should be complete within 10 days. Bottle, using corn sugar. Age in bottle 5 to 7 days.

OG: 1.028

Yippee IPA

THIS RECIPE FOR A VERY strong IPA is compliments of our friend Jim. This wonderful brew possesses myriad great flavors, from an initial malt bite to a wonderful hop aftertaste.

5 POUNDS LIGHT MALT EXTRACT
4 POUNDS AMBER MALT EXTRACT
1 POUND CRYSTAL MALT GRAIN
1½ OUNCES CASCADE HOPS
  (BOILING)
2 OUNCES CASCADE HOPS
  (FINISHING)

1 OUNCE CASCADE HOPS (DRY HOP)
1 TEASPOON GYPSUM
1 TEASPOON IRISH MOSS
1 PACKAGE AMERICAN ALE YEAST
¾ CUP CORN SUGAR (PRIMING)

Place crushed crystal malt in water and steep at 155 degrees for 30 minutes. Remove spent grains and add extracts, 1½ ounces Cascade hops, and gypsum. Boil for 1 hour, adding the Irish moss for the last 10 minutes. Turn off heat, add 2 ounces of Cascade hops, and steep for 10 minutes. Cool wort and pitch yeast. Ferment for 5 to 7 days. Transfer to a secondary fermenter and add 1 ounce Cascade hops. Ferment an additional 7 to 10 days. Bottle, using corn sugar. Age in bottle for 7 to 10 days.

OG: 1.065

Aerating Your Wort

In order to get your yeast off to a good start, it will need a healthy supply of oxygen. There are a number of methods that can be used to supply it, and they come in a range of prices. The easiest, and a very effective method, is to give your wort a good shake for 10 to 15 minutes. To keep things as sanitary as possible, place a sanitized rubber stopper in the carboy rather than covering it with your hand. If you're doing your primary fermentation in a plastic bucket, affix the sanitized lid.

Another method can be used when you siphon your wort from the brew pot into your fermenter. Make two small pinholes in your siphon hose, just about where it joins the racking cane. As you siphon the wort, air will be drawn in through the pinholes, thus injecting oxygen.

The most elaborate method is the use of an aeration stone. Aeration stones for fish tanks are probably your best bet. You will also need an aquarium pump to supply the oxygen.

We've also heard of lots of other methods, including the use of a hand-held beater. Sanitize the beaters and then simply stir your wort up for 5 minutes.

Easy Wheat

NOVICE BREWERS TAKE NOTE. Impress the skeptics among your friends by handing them this delicious German-style wheat beer just weeks after buying your homebrew kit. A simple all-extract approach keeps the frustration factor low your first time out, and the compliments you get will make you want to try something a little more challenging the next time around. Ready for all-grain yet?

6⅔ POUNDS WHEAT MALT EXTRACT (60/40 BLEND)
1 OUNCE TETTNANGER HOPS (BITTERING)

1 PACKAGE BAVARIAN WHEAT YEAST
¾ CUP CORN SUGAR (PRIMING)

Bring water to a boil. Add the extract and bring to a second boil. After 15 minutes, add the hops and boil for 45 minutes longer. Transfer to fermenter when cool and add enough cold water to make 5 gallons. Pitch the yeast when the wort reaches 70 degrees. Bottle, using corn sugar, when fermentation is complete (approximately 7 to 19 days). Age for at least 7 days.

OG: 1.044

This beer is good for you. This is draft beer. Stick with the beer. Let's go and beat this guy up and come back and drink some more beer.
—ERNEST HEMINGWAY, *TO HAVE AND HAVE NOT*

Jack the Ripper British Ale

THIS ALE WAS INSPIRED BY many hours spent in a pub in the Whitechapel section of London—the same pub where, rumor has it, Jack the Ripper met and left with his last victim, Mary Jane Kelley. Perhaps Jack downed ale just like this just before he committed his deadly deed. It is a generously hopped ale with a light red color and a wonderful aroma brought on by 1 ounce of dry hopped Hallertauer hops.

6⅔ POUNDS LIGHT MALT EXTRACT
¼ POUND CRYSTAL MALT (40L)
1 OUNCE HALLERTAUER HOPS
(BOILING)
½ OUNCE TETTNANGER HOPS
(AROMA)

1 OUNCE HALLERTAUER HOPS (DRY HOP)
2 TEASPOONS GYPSUM
1 TEASPOON IRISH MOSS
1 PACKAGE ENGLISH ALE YEAST
¾ CUP CORN SUGAR (PRIMING)

Place the crushed crystal malt in water and steep at 155 degrees for 30 minutes. Remove the spent grains and add the malt extract, gypsum, and 1 ounce Hallertauer hops. Boil for 1 hour. Add ½ ounce Tettnanger hops and Irish moss in the last 5 minutes of the boil. Cool wort and pitch yeast. Ferment for 1 week, then transfer to a secondary fermenter and add 1 ounce Hallertauer hops. Ferment for 1 week in secondary fermenter. Bottle, using corn sugar. Beer should be ready within 7 days.

OG: 1.043

Affengeil Wheat Beer

A TRULY DELICIOUS AND EASY German wheat beer. The name expresses how good this beer actually is, but cannot be translated here for reasons of decorum. The lemon zest gives a citrusy flavor that is more reminiscent of a Belgian wheat. In this recipe it eliminates the necessity of serving a slice of lemon with the brew as is traditional in Bavaria. Don't skimp on the yeast; it adds the banana and clove aroma that makes this style so special.

6⅔ POUNDS WHEAT MALT EXTRACT
(55/45 BLEND)
1¼ POUNDS PALE MALT EXTRACT
1 POUND MALTED WHEAT
ZEST OF ONE LEMON
1 OUNCE HALLERTAUER HOPS
(BOILING)

¼ OUNCE HALLERTAUER HOPS
(AROMA)
1 PACKAGE WEIHENSTEPHAN WHEAT
YEAST (WYEAST)
¾ CUP CORN SUGAR (PRIMING)

Place cracked wheat malt in water and steep at 155 degrees for 30 minutes. Remove the spent grains and add malt extract and 1 ounce Hallertauer hops. Boil for 45 to 60 minutes. Add lemon zest during last 5 minutes of the boil. Add ¼ ounce Hallertauer during the last 2 minutes of the boil. Cool wort and pitch yeast. Primary fermentation should be complete within 7 days. Transfer to secondary fermenter, and ferment for 7 days. Bottle, using corn sugar. Age in bottle for 7 to 10 days.

OG: 1.040–1.045

Kölsch

ASSOCIATED WITH THE CITY OF COLOGNE, Kölsch is a light, slightly fruity beer that is not readily available in the United States. Special yeast and cool fermentation temperatures in the secondary fermenter produce maximum attenuation, giving this beer a slightly winelike quality that is indicative of the style.

5½ POUNDS ALEXANDER'S PALE MALT EXTRACT
1½ POUNDS WHEAT MALT EXTRACT (55/45 BLEND)
1 OUNCE TETTNANGER HOPS (BITTERING)
½ OUNCE SPALT HOPS (FLAVORING)
½ OUNCE SAAZ HOPS (AROMA)
1 TEASPOON IRISH MOSS
1 PACKAGE GERMAN ALE YEAST
1 PACKAGE KÖLSCH YEAST
¾ CUP CORN SUGAR (PRIMING)

Bring water to a boil and add malt extracts and Tettnanger hops. Boil for 1 hour, adding the Spalt hops after 30 minutes. Add Irish moss for last 10 minutes. Turn off heat and steep Saaz hops for 10 minutes. Cool wort and pitch both yeasts. Ferment for 7 days at 65 to 70 degrees. Transfer to secondary fermenter and ferment an additional 14 days at 45 to 50 degrees. Bottle, using corn sugar. Age in bottle for 10 to 14 days.

OG: 1.038

There are more old drunks than old doctors.

—ANONYMOUS

Bitter Old Man

CAN BEER REALLY PROLONG YOUR life? The people at Guinness vote "yes" with their slogan "Guinness is good for you." And a group of five gentlemen who imbibed at the Bradford Abbas in Dorset, England, amassed a total of 434-plus years among them, downing a few good pints. So brew up batch after batch of this British bitter, consume it in liberal amounts, and you will live forever. Well, not really, but we'd like to think so.

3⅓ POUNDS LIGHT MALT EXTRACT
1½ POUNDS ALEXANDER'S PALE
   MALT EXTRACT
¼ POUND CRYSTAL MALT (40L)
1½ OUNCES KENT GOLDINGS HOPS
   (BITTERING)

½ OUNCE KENT GOLDINGS HOPS
   (AROMA)
2 TEASPOONS GYPSUM
1 TEASPOON IRISH MOSS
1 PACKAGE BRITISH ALE YEAST
½ CUP CORN SUGAR (PRIMING)

Place cracked crystal malt and gypsum in water and steep at 155 degrees for 30 minutes. Remove spent grains and add malt extract and 1½ ounces Kent Goldings hops. Boil for 1 hour, adding ½ ounce Kent Goldings hops, and Irish moss for the last 5 minutes. Cool wort and pitch yeast. Ferment for 7 to 10 days. Bottle, using corn sugar. Age in bottle 5 to 7 days.

OG: 1.033

Belgian White Men Can't Jump

BUT THEY SURE CAN BREW! This tasty take on the Wit style will have you jumping for joy and praising the genius of Belgian brewers. The refreshing flavor is excellent after a game of one-on-one, or for just kicking back in front of the TV to watch your favorite hoopsters.

6⅔ POUNDS WHEAT MALT EXTRACT
   (55/45)
½ POUND CRYSTAL MALT (10L)
½ POUND WHEAT MALT
½ POUND TORREFIED WHEAT
1 OUNCE EAST KENT GOLDINGS
   HOPS (BITTERING)

¾ OUNCE CORIANDER SEED
ZEST OF 2 ORANGES
1 PACKAGE BELGIAN WHITE ALE
   YEAST
ZEST OF 1 ORANGE
1 CUP CORN SUGAR (PRIMING)

Place crushed grains in water and steep at 155 degrees for 30 minutes. Remove spent grains and add malt extract. Bring to a boil, add East Kent Goldings hops and ¼ ounce of cracked coriander seed. Boil 1 hour. Shut off heat, and add remaining cracked coriander, and zest of 2 oranges. Steep for 10 minutes. Cool wort and pitch yeast. Ferment 7 to 10 days. Transfer to secondary fermenter. Wash orange thoroughly, peel, and clean off as much of the white pith as possible. Slice the zest into strips and add to secondary. Ferment an additional 7 to 10 days. Bottle, using corn sugar, and age 7 days.

OG: 1.039

Brewtopia IPA

HOP LOVER'S HEAVEN. You will have a transcendental experience with this beer, and if you drink enough of it, you will reach a state of nirvana. Enjoyable for quiet meditation alone, or during group sessions with friends.

8 POUNDS PALE MALT EXTRACT
½ POUND CRYSTAL MALT (10L)
½ POUND MUNICH MALT
1 TEASPOON GYPSUM
1½ OUNCES EAST KENT GOLDINGS
   HOPS (BITTERING)
2 OUNCES CASCADE HOPS (FLAVOR/
   AROMA)

1½ OUNCES CASCADE HOPS (DRY
   HOP)
1 TEASPOON IRISH MOSS
1 PACKAGE AMERICAN ALE YEAST
1¼ CUPS LIGHT DRY MALT EXTRACT
   (PRIMING)

Place crushed grains and gypsum in water and steep at 155 degrees for 30 minutes. Remove spent grains and add pale malt extract. Bring to a boil, add 1½ ounces East Kent Goldings hops.

Add 1 ounce of Cascade hops at 30 minutes. During final 10 minutes of boil, add ½ ounce Cascade hops and Irish moss. At the end of the boil, turn off heat and add ½ ounce of Cascade hops. Steep for 10 minutes. Cool wort and pitch yeast. Ferment 7 to 10 days. Transfer to secondary and add 1½ ounces Cascade hops. Ferment an additional 7 to 10 days. Bottle, using dry malt extract, and age 7 days.

OG: 1.057

Priming Sugar

The standard priming sugar for homebrewers is corn sugar. It does not impart any flavor, and it carbonates in a few days, but technically speaking it is an adjunct. Truth be told, it would be proper to prime with dry malt extract. You can expect tinier bubbles and a finer head than you will get from corn sugar; the drawback is that it may take up to three weeks for your bottles to carbonate.

Another option, and purists may say the only option, is to *kraeusen*. Kraeusening is essentially priming your beer with unfermented wort. This involves some planning. After brewing, and before pitching your yeast, set aside some wort (fully diluted) in a sterilized container. The amount needed will vary inversely with the original gravity of your recipe (OG 1.030 = 2 quarts; OG 1.040 = 1.5 quarts; OG 1.060 = 1 quart). Store the container in your refrigerator until bottling time and add like any priming sugar.

The fact is that any fermentable sugar may be used as a priming sugar. Honey, maple syrup, and molasses all work equally well while imparting their own distinct flavors to the finished beer. Indeed, molasses is a traditional priming sugar for certain British ales. Have fun, experiment.

For a quart of ale is a dish for a king.
—WILLIAM SHAKESPEARE, *A WINTER'S TALE*

To ESB, or Not to ESB

REFERENCES TO BEER ABOUND IN William Shakespeare's work. No doubt Will enjoyed a few pints as he crafted his finest works, again proving our theory that beer inspires genius.

6⅔ POUNDS LIGHT MALT EXTRACT

1 POUND CRYSTAL MALT (40L)

2 OUNCES CHOCOLATE MALT

2 OUNCES ROASTED BARLEY

2 TEASPOONS GYPSUM

2 OUNCES KENT GOLDINGS HOPS
  (BOILING)

1 OUNCE FUGGLES HOPS (AROMA)

1 OUNCE FUGGLES HOPS (DRY HOP)

1 TEASPOON IRISH MOSS

1 PACKAGE LONDON ESB YEAST

¾ CUP CORN SUGAR (PRIMING)

Place crushed crystal malt, chocolate malt, and roasted barley in water, and steep at 155 degrees for 30 minutes. Remove spent grains and add the malt extract, gypsum, and Kent Goldings hops. Boil for 1 hour. Add 1 ounce of Fuggles hops during the last 10 minutes, and Irish moss for last 5 minutes. Cool wort and pitch yeast. Ferment in primary fermenter for 7 days. Transfer to secondary fermenter and add 1 ounce Fuggles hops. Ferment for an additonal 7 days. Bottle, using corn sugar. Age for 7 days in the bottle.

OG: 1.045

Slam Dunkelweiss

THE STRONG BANANA ESTERS PRODUCED by the Weihenstephan yeast and richness from the roasted malts blend perfectly in this dark German wheat beer. Fermenting the wort at a cooler temperature will produce more of a clovelike nose instead of the banana, which occurs at warmer temperatures.

6²/₃ POUNDS WHEAT MALT EXTRACT   1 OUNCE SAAZ HOPS (BITTERING)
  (55/45 BLEND)   1 PACKAGE WEIHENSTEPHAN WHEAT
1½ POUNDS DARK MALT EXTRACT   YEAST
½ POUND CHOCOLATE MALT   ¾ CUP CORN SUGAR (PRIMING)
½ POUND ROASTED BARLEY

Place crushed chocolate malt and roasted barley in water, and steep at 155 degrees for 30 minutes. Remove spent grains and add malt extracts and Saaz hops. Bring to a boil, and boil for 1 hour. Cool wort and pitch yeast. Ferment for 10 to 14 days at temperatures between 68 and 74 degrees. Bottle, using corn sugar. Age in bottle for 10 days.

OG: 1.043

Alt of this World

BEFORE LAGERS BECAME THE SIGNATURE style of Germany, ales, more similar to Belgian and British styles, were common. Altbier, or Old Beer, refers to these old-style copper-colored ales. Secondary fermentation at cooler temperatures will drive off many of the esters and allow the malt and hop flavors to shine through.

6²/₃ POUNDS AMBER MALT EXTRACT   1 OUNCE PERLE HOPS (BITTERING)
1 POUND CRYSTAL MALT (60L)   1 PACKAGE GERMAN ALE YEAST
½ POUND CHOCOLATE MALT   ¾ CUP CORN SUGAR (PRIMING)
1 OUNCE GALENA HOPS (BITTERING)

Place crushed crystal malt and chocolate malt in water and steep at 155 degrees for 30 minutes. Remove spent grains and add malt extract and Galena hops. Bring to a boil, and boil for 1 hour, adding the Perle hops after 30 minutes. Cool the wort and pitch the yeast. Ferment for 7 days. Transfer to the secondary fermenter, and ferment an additional 10 to 14 days at 45 to 55 degrees. Bottle, using corn sugar. Age in the bottle 10 to 14 days.

OG: 1.045

Ooh La La, Saison

SAISON IS TRADITIONALLY BREWED at the end of the brewing season. Compared with other Belgian beers, this one is pretty tame. Brew it in late spring for those early summer trips to the beach or lake.

3⅓ POUNDS LIGHT MALT EXTRACT
3⅓ POUNDS AMBER MALT EXTRACT
2 POUNDS CRYSTAL MALT (40L)
½ POUND FLAKED BARLEY
2 OUNCES HALLERTAUER HOPS
(BITTERING)

½ OUNCE KENT GOLDINGS HOPS
(FLAVOR)
1 PACKAGE BELGIAN WHITE ALE
YEAST
1 CUP CORN SUGAR (PRIMING)

Steep crystal malt and flaked barley in 155-degree water for 30 minutes. Strain out spent grains, add malt extracts, and bring to a boil. Add Hallertauer hops and boil for 1 hour. Add Kent Goldings hops during the last 15 minutes of the boil. Cool wort and pitch yeast. Ferment 7 to 10 days, and transfer to secondary fermenter. Ferment an additional 7 to 10 days. Bottle, using corn sugar, and age 1 to 2 weeks.

OG: 1.050

The best beer is where the priests go to drink.
—ANONYMOUS

Trappist House Brew

BREWED WITHIN THE WALLS OF Trappist monasteries in Belgium, Trappist ales are some of the most magnificent beers in the world. They are brewed in three strengths: house, double, and triple. The term "house" means exactly what it says; it is the beer the monks brew for their own consumption. It is essential to use a yeast culture propagated from a bottle of Trappist beer to duplicate this style, and Chimay is probably the most readily available. And while you're at it, pick up some of their wonderful cheese.

4 POUNDS ALEXANDER'S PALE MALT
  EXTRACT
3⅓ POUNDS AMBER MALT EXTRACT
2 POUNDS DRY LIGHT MALT EXTRACT
2 OUNCES CHOCOLATE MALT
1 POUND BELGIAN CANDY SUGAR
  (LIGHT BROWN SUGAR MAY BE
  SUBSTITUTED)

1½ OUNCES PERLE HOPS
  (BITTERING)
1 OUNCE TETTNANGER HOPS
  (AROMA)
YEAST CULTURED FROM BOTTLE OF
  CHIMAY
¾ CUP CORN SUGAR (PRIMING)

Place crushed chocolate malt in water and steep at 155 degrees for 30 minutes. Remove spent grains and add malt extracts, candy sugar, and Perle hops. Boil for 1 hour, adding the Tettnanger hops during the last 10 minutes. Cool wort and pitch yeast culture. Ferment for 7 to 10 days. Transfer to secondary fermenter and ferment an additional 2 to 3 weeks. Bottle, using corn sugar. Age in bottle 3 to 4 weeks.

OG: 1.063

Bitchin' Belgian White

THIS IS ONE OF THE best homebrews we've ever sampled. The recipe is courtesy of our friend Elliot—a homebrewer so dedicated that he has turned the spare bedroom in his home into a brew room. It is best served very cold. A slice of lemon is a great addition.

3⅓ POUNDS WHEAT MALT EXTRACT
2 POUNDS DRY WHEAT MALT
  EXTRACT
¼ POUND WHOLE-WHEAT FLOUR
2 TEASPOONS CORIANDER SEEDS
1½ OUNCES HALLERTAUER HOPS
  (BOILING)

1½ OUNCES CASCADE HOPS (DRY
  HOP)
1 PACKAGE BELGIAN WHITE BEER
  YEAST
¾ CUP CORN SUGAR (PRIMING)

Combine malt extracts and Hallertauer hops in water. Boil for 45 minutes. Turn off heat and remove hops. Sift whole-wheat flour into wort while stirring constantly. When all flour is dissolved, add cracked coriander seeds and steep for 10 minutes. Cool wort and pitch yeast. When primary fermentation is complete, transfer to secondary fermenter and add Cascade hops. Ferment for 7 additional days. Bottle, using corn sugar. Age in bottle for 7 to 10 days.

OG: 1.036

Honey Steam

THE CALIFORNIA COMMON BEER STYLE is one of the most wide open of all beer styles, since the only real guideline is the use of lager yeast at ale fermentation temperatures. In short, you pretty much have a blank slate to work with. In this recipe, the additional sweetness from the honey is balanced nicely by the liberal hopping.

6²/₃ POUNDS LIGHT MALT EXTRACT
2 POUNDS CLOVER HONEY
1 POUND BUCKWHEAT HONEY
½ POUND CRYSTAL MALT (40L)
¼ POUND CARA-PILS MALT
2 OUNCES TETTNANGER HOPS
  (BITTERING)

1 OUNCE CASCADE HOPS (AROMA)
1 OUNCE CASCADE HOPS (DRY HOP)
1 PACKAGE CALIFORNIA LAGER
  YEAST
¾ CUP CORN SUGAR (PRIMING)

Place crushed crystal malt and Cara-Pils malt in water and steep at 155 degrees for 30 minutes. Remove spent grains and add malt extract, honeys, and Tettnanger hops. Boil for 1 hour. Turn off heat and add 1 ounce Cascade hops and steep for 10 minutes. Cool wort and pitch yeast. Ferment for 7 to 10 days at temperatures between 65 and 75 degrees. Transfer to secondary fermenter and add 1 ounce Cascade hops. Secondary-ferment an additional 10 to 14 days at temperatures between 40 and 45 degrees. Bottle, using corn sugar. Age in bottle 7 to 10 days.

OG: 1.051

"What is your best—your very best—ale a glass?"
"Two-pence-halfpenny," says the landlord, "is the
price of the Genuine Stunning Ale."
"Then," says I, producing the money, "just draw
me a glass of the Genuine Stunning, if you
please, with a good head to it."
—CHARLES DICKENS, *DAVID COPPERFIELD*

Genuine Stunning Ale

ONE CAN ONLY IMAGINE WHAT the Genuine Stunning of Dickens's
David Copperfield was like. But with such a magnificent name it
had to be great. This is what we think it was like. The addition of
the lemon zest lends a nice citrus bite. We think Charles would
approve.

6⅔ POUNDS LIGHT MALT EXTRACT

2 POUNDS DRY LIGHT MALT EXTRACT

1 POUND CRYSTAL MALT (60L)

1 POUND ROLLED OATS

2 OUNCES CASCADE HOPS (BOILING)

1 OUNCE HALLERTAUER HOPS
(AROMA)

1 OUNCE KENT GOLDINGS HOPS
(AROMA)

2 TEASPOONS GYPSUM

1 PACKAGE LONDON ALE YEAST

1 CUP DRY MALT EXTRACT (PRIMING)

Place crushed crystal malt in water and steep at 155 degrees
for 30 minutes. Remove spent grains. Add light and dry light malt
extracts, rolled oats, Cascade hops, and gypsum, and boil for 1
hour, adding the Hallertauer and Kent Goldings hops during the
last 5 minutes of the boil. Cool wort and pitch yeast. Primary
fermentation should be complete in 10 to 14 days. Bottle, using
1 cup dry malt extract. Age in bottle for 10 to 14 days.

OG: 1.056

Dubbel, Dubbel, Toil and Trubble

POSSESSING A SUBTLE ROASTINESS, THIS Belgian dubbel is guaranteed to double your pleasure. It is certainly a bewitching brew.

10 POUNDS AMBER MALT EXTRACT
1 POUND CARA-PILS MALT
1/2 POUND CRYSTAL MALT (40L)
1/2 POUND CHOCOLATE MALT
1/4 POUND ROASTED BARLEY

1 OUNCE PROGRESS HOPS
  (BITTERING)
1/2 OUNCE SAAZ HOPS (AROMA)
1 PACKAGE BELGIAN ABBEY YEAST
3/4 CUP CORN SUGAR (PRIMING)

Place crushed Cara-Pils malt, crystal malt, chocolate malt, and roasted barley in water, and steep at 155 degrees for 30 minutes. Remove spent grains, add malt extract and Progress hops, and boil for 1 hour, adding the Saaz hops for the last 5 minutes. Cool wort and pitch yeast. Ferment for 7 to 10 days. Transfer to secondary fermenter and ferment an additional 7 to 10 days. Bottle, using corn sugar. Age in bottle for 14 to 21 days.

OG: 1.071

California Uncommon

WE CREATED THIS RECIPE AS an attempt to bridge the gap between an American pilsner and a British pale ale. What we got was a unique, hoppy ale (or is it a lager?). Using lager yeast at ale temperatures, in the California common style, resulted in an uncommon character that is rather tasty.

6 2/3 POUNDS EXTRA-LIGHT MALT
  EXTRACT
1 POUND WHEAT MALT
1 OUNCE CASCADE HOPS
  (BITTERING)
1/2 OUNCE TETTNANGER HOPS
  (AROMA)

1/2 OUNCE TETTNANGER HOPS (DRY)
1/2 TEASPOON IRISH MOSS
1 PACKAGE CALIFORNIA LAGER
  YEAST
1 CUP CORN SUGAR (PRIMING)

Place crushed wheat malt in water and steep at 155 degrees for 30 minutes. Remove spent grains and add malt extract. Bring to a boil and add 1 ounce Cascade hops. Add Irish moss and ½ ounce Tettnanger hops during the last ten minutes of the boil. Transfer to secondary fermenter and add ½ ounce Tettnanger hops. Ferment an additional 7 days. Bottle, using corn sugar, and age for 7 days.

The T-Shirt Trick

In the heat of the summer, keeping your beer at an acceptable fermentation temperature can be difficult. Rather than give up brewing for three months (heaven forbid!), we've learned a few simple tricks for maintaining ale-fermentation temperatures. To avoid the addition of off-flavors, which can result from fermenting at too high a temperature, place your fermenter in a bucket or basin filled with cold water. Wet an old T-shirt and wring it out, then place it over the carboy, so that the fermentation lock protrudes through the neckhole and the bottom sits in the cool water. The T-shirt will continually draw up moisture and allow it to evaporate, thus cooling your beer by 5 to 10 degrees. An old towel kept wet will also work, but keep an eye out for developing mold.

Mild-Mannered

BRITISH MILD IS SORT OF the halfway point between a bitter and brown ale. It is soft and well mannered, with a light body and a polished finish.

4 POUNDS ALEXANDER'S PALE MALT
EXTRACT
1 POUND AMBER DRY MALT EXTRACT
2 OUNCES CRYSTAL MALT (40L)
2 OUNCES CHOCOLATE MALT
1 OUNCE FUGGLES HOPS
(BITTERING)

½ OUNCE KENT GOLDINGS HOPS
(AROMA)
1 PACKAGE BRITISH ALE YEAST
½ CUP CORN SUGAR (PRIMING)

Place cracked crystal malt and chocolate malt in water and steep for 30 minutes. Remove spent grains and add malt extracts and Fuggles hops. Boil for 1 hour, adding the Kent Goldings hops during the last 10 minutes. Cool wort and pitch yeast. Ferment for 7 to 10 days. Bottle, using corn sugar. Age in bottle 5 to 7 days.

OG: 1.037

I asked these Indians: "Do men ever make Chicha?" My question was met with gales of laughter. The women howled. Bent over in hilarity, one replied, "Men can't brew. Chicha made by men would only make gas in the belly. You are a funny man! Beer is women's work."

—ALAN EAMES

Maura's Bride Ale

IN DAYS OF YORE, WHEN brewing was done almost solely by women, a young bride would commemorate her wedding day by brewing a "bride ale" (from which we get the modern term "bridal").

The ale was then sold to increase the bride's dowry. With the resurgence of homebrewing today, it is a tradition we hope to see revived. Frankly, we could use the cash.

6⅔ POUNDS LIGHT MALT EXTRACT

1 POUND CRYSTAL MALT (20L)

½ POUND FLAKED BARLEY

1 POUND HONEY

2 OUNCES WILLAMETTE HOPS
  (BITTERING)

1 OUNCE LIBERTY HOPS
  (FLAVORING)

1 OUNCE CASCADE HOPS (AROMA)

1 OUNCE CASCADE HOPS (DRY HOP)

1 TEASPOON IRISH MOSS

1 PACKAGE IRISH ALE YEAST

1½ CUPS HONEY (PRIMING)

Steep crushed crystal malt and flaked barley in water at 155 degrees for 30 minutes. Remove spent grains. Add malt extract, honey, and Willamette hops. Boil for 1 hour, adding Liberty hops for last 30 minutes. Add Irish moss for last 5 minutes. Remove from heat, add 1 ounce Cascade hops, cover, and steep for 10 minutes. Cool wort and pitch yeast. Ferment for 7 to 10 days. Transfer to secondary fermenter, add 1 ounce of Cascade hops, and ferment for 10 to 14 days. Bottle, using honey. Age in bottle for 10 to 14 days.

OG: 1.049

Crimson and Clover Ale

SINCE THIS RECIPE CALLS FOR equal parts of malt and honey, it could be considered a pale ale–mead hybrid. The honey lends a lighter quality to what would be a traditionally maltier ale. The addition of crystal malt and roasted barley contributes the wonderful red color.

6 POUNDS LIGHT MALT EXTRACT

6 POUNDS CLOVER HONEY

½ POUND CRYSTAL MALT (40L)

2 OUNCES ROASTED BARLEY

1½ OUNCES SAAZ HOPS (BITTERING)

½ OUNCE FUGGLES HOPS (AROMA)

1 TEASPOON IRISH MOSS

1 PACKAGE IRISH ALE YEAST

¾ CUP CORN SUGAR (PRIMING)

Place crushed crystal malt and roasted barley in water and steep at 155 degrees for 30 minutes. Remove spent grains and add the malt extract, honey, and Saaz hops, and boil for 1 hour. Add the Irish moss during the last 15 minutes of the boil. Add the Fuggles hops during the last 5 minutes of the boil. Cool wort and pitch yeast. Fermentation should be complete in 10 to 14 days. Bottle, using corn sugar. Age in bottle for 7 days.

OG: 1.054

No children without sex—no drunkenness without beer.

—ANCIENT SUMERIAN PROVERB

Baby's Bath Ale

IN ENGLAND AND COLONIAL AMERICA, a "groaning ale" was prepared by an expectant mother as soon as she learned of her pregnancy. Using only of the finest ingredients, a high-gravity ale was brewed and conditioned for seven to nine months. When labor began, the midwives would tap the cask and share the special ale with the mother, to help them through the ordeal. Legend has it that the newborn would be bathed in the beer, since it was purer than the available water.

10 POUNDS LIGHT MALT EXTRACT	2 OUNCES KENT GOLDINGS HOPS
1 POUND CRYSTAL MALT (40L)	(BITTERING)
3 POUNDS HONEY	1 OUNCE FUGGLES HOPS (AROMA)
¾ POUND LIGHT OR DARK BROWN	1 PACKAGE EUROPEAN ALE YEAST
SUGAR	1 CUP MOLASSES (PRIMING)

Steep crystal malt in water at 155 degrees for 30 minutes. Remove spent grains. Add malt extract, honey, brown sugar, and Kent Goldings hops. Boil for 1 hour, adding Fuggles hops for the last 15 minutes. Cool wort and pitch yeast. Ferment in primary fermenter for 7 to 10 days. Transfer to secondary fermenter and ferment for an additional 21 to 28 days. Bottle, using molasses. Age in bottle for 10 to 14 days or until birth.

OG: 1.079

Irving Berliner Weisse

NOTED FOR THEIR PUNGENT SOURNESS, Berliner weisse beers are often mixed with liquors such as sweet woodruff syrup. You can determine the degree of sourness your beer possesses by increasing or decreasing the amount of wort you sour.

4 POUNDS GERMAN 2-ROW MALT

3 POUNDS MALTED WHEAT

¼ POUND PALE MALT (SOURING)

½ OUNCE SAAZ HOPS (BITTERING)

1 PACKAGE BAVARIAN WHEAT YEAST

2 OUNCES YEAST NUTRIENT

¾ CUP CORN SUGAR (PRIMING)

Mash grains for 60 to 90 minutes. Collect 6 gallons of wort, placing 3 gallons in a brew pot and 3 gallons in a plastic bucket. Sour the wort in the plastic bucket using ¼ pound crushed pale malt (see Brewer's Tip, p. 181). Add ¼ ounce Saaz hops to the wort in the brew pot and boil for 1 hour. Cool wort and pitch yeast. After 2 to 3 days, when the wort in the plastic bucket is soured, transfer to the brew pot and add ¼ ounce Saaz hops. Boil for 1 hour. Cool wort and combine with fermenting wort in the fermenter. Add yeast nutrient. Ferment an additional 5 days. Transfer to secondary fermenter and ferment an additional 5 to 7 days. Bottle using corn sugar. Age in bottle 10 to 14 days.

OG: 1.040

Harvard Crimson

BELIEVE IT OR NOT, BEER played a major part in the early (and, we're sure, the present) history of America's most distinguished university. In 1674 Harvard actually opened a brewery on campus, and Harvard's first head, Nathaniel Eaton, was fired from his job in large part because he failed to provide enough beer for the student body. In fact, beer was such a prized commodity in colonial times that Harvard students were actually able to pay their tuition in barley. Sounds like a fair trade to us.

8 POUNDS PALE 2-ROW BARLEY
1 POUND CRYSTAL MALT (60L)
¼ POUND ROASTED BARLEY
1½ OUNCES LIBERTY HOPS
  (BITTERING)
1½ OUNCES CASCADE HOPS
  (AROMA)

2 TEASPOONS GYPSUM (FOR SOFT
  WATER)
1 TEASPOON IRISH MOSS
1 PACKAGE AMERICAN ALE YEAST
¾ CUP CORN SUGAR (PRIMING)

Mash grains with gypsum for 60 to 90 minutes. Collect 6 gallons of wort. Add Liberty hops, and boil for 1 hour. Add Irish moss for last 5 minutes. Remove from heat, add Cascade hops, and allow to steep for 10 minutes. Cool wort and pitch yeast. Ferment for 7 to 10 days. Bottle, using corn sugar. Age in bottle 7 days.

OG: 1.056

A glass of bitter or pale ale, taken with the principal meal of the day, does more good and less harm than any medicine the physician can prescribe.

—Doctor Carpenter, 1750

Pub Bitter

This British bitter-style beer is an ideal recipe for the first-time all-grain brewer. It produces a wonderful session beer that will leave you wondering why you didn't step up to all-grain sooner.

5½ pounds British 2-row malt
½ pound crystal malt (20L)
1½ ounces Kent Goldings hops (bittering)
1 ounce Kent Goldings hops (aroma)

1 teaspoon Irish moss
1 package London ale yeast
¾ cup corn sugar (priming)

Mash grain for 60 to 90 minutes. Collect 6 gallons of wort. Bring to a boil and add 1½ ounces Kent Goldings hops. Boil for 1 hour, adding 1 ounce Kent Goldings and Irish moss during the last 5 minutes. Cool wort and pitch yeast. Ferment for 7 to 10 days. Bottle, using corn sugar. Age in bottle 5 to 7 days.

OG: 1.034

Uncle Sam's Dark Wheat

MANY OF THE BEERS BREWED in early colonial America were made with wheat as the base rather than barley. This dark wheat beer is made with only American-grown ingredients, which will earn you extra points in the patriotism department. Brew this up for your Fourth of July barbecue, or brew up a batch for election night to drown your sorrows should Newt Gingrich ever be elected president.

5 POUNDS 2-ROW AMERICAN
  KLAGES MALT
3 POUNDS WHEAT MALT
1 POUND TOASTED WHEAT MALT
½ POUND CHOCOLATE MALT

1½ OUNCES CASCADE HOPS
  (BITTERING)
1 OUNCE CASCADE HOPS (AROMA)
1 PACKAGE AMERICAN ALE YEAST
¾ CUP CORN SUGAR (PRIMING)

Mash grains for 60 to 90 minutes. Collect 6 gallons of wort. Add 1½ ounces Cascade hops and boil for 1 hour. Remove from heat and add 1 ounce Cascade hops and steep for 10 minutes. Cool wort and pitch yeast. Ferment for 10 to 14 days. Bottle, using corn sugar. Age in bottle 7 to 10 days.

OG: 1.043

Conversion and Extraction Rate

When all-grain brewing, you're going to want to check a couple of things. First is conversion. To do this, place a sample of your mash water onto a white plate. Place a drop of iodine in the sample. If the color of the iodine stays the same, conversion is complete. If the color turns to a dark blue or black, starches are still present and conversion is not complete.

Second, you'll want to check your extraction rate. To do this, first take a hydrometer reading of your wort. Then apply this formula:

$$\frac{(\text{GRAVITY} - 1) \times 1000 \times \text{GALLONS OF WORT}}{\text{POUNDS OF GRAIN}} = \text{POINTS PER POUND}$$

Example:

Gravity reading: 1.044

.044 × 1000 × 6 gallons = 264

264 ÷ 8.2 pounds of grain = 32.19 points per pound

Your extraction rate should be around 30, but anything above 28 is acceptable.

Too Good to ESB True

THIS ESB IS IN THE true British tradition. Well-balanced malt and hops make this an excellent session beer. The corn syrup lends additional body and a slight residual sweetness.

8 POUNDS PALE 2-ROW MALT
3/4 POUND CRYSTAL MALT (40L)
1 POUND TORREFIED WHEAT
1 OUNCE CHOCOLATE MALT
1 POUND LIGHT CORN SYRUP
1 1/2 OUNCES FUGGLES HOPS
  (BITTERING)
1 OUNCE PROGRESS HOPS
  (FLAVORING)

1/2 OUNCE KENT GOLDINGS HOPS
  (AROMA)
1 OUNCE KENT GOLDINGS HOPS
  (DRY HOP)
1 TEASPOON IRISH MOSS
1 PACKAGE BRITISH ALE YEAST
3/4 CUP CORN SUGAR (PRIMING)

Mash grains for 60 to 90 minutes. Collect 6 gallons of wort. Add corn syrup and bring to a boil, add Fuggles hops, and boil for 1 hour, adding the Progress hops after 30 minutes and the Irish moss for the last 10 minutes. Remove from heat, add 1/2 ounce Kent Goldings hops, and steep for 10 minutes. Cool wort and pitch yeast. Ferment for 5 to 7 days. Transfer to secondary fermenter and add 1 ounce Kent Goldings hops. Ferment an additional 7 to 10 days. Bottle, using corn sugar. Age in bottle 7 to 10 days.

OG: 1.061

Euell Gibbons' Favorite Ale

FOR THOSE OF YOU THAT weren't watching TV in the early seventies, Euell was a grain enthusiast who pitched Grape-Nuts cereal on TV by informing us that many parts of a tree were edible. While this recipe doesn't call for you to boil any parts of a tree in the wort, it does call for a variety of adjuncts that make this a wonderfully unusual brew.

6 POUNDS 2-ROW KLAGES MALT
2 POUNDS RICE (CRUSHED AND
  SOAKED OVERNIGHT IN COLD
  WATER)
1 POUND RYE MALT
1 POUND OATMEAL
½ POUND FLAKED BARLEY
1 CUP MOLASSES

1 TEASPOON IRISH MOSS
1 ½ OUNCES NORTHERN BREWER
  HOPS (BITTERING)
1 OUNCE CASCADE HOPS (AROMA)
1 PACKAGE AMERICAN ALE YEAST
1 ¼ CUPS DRY MALT EXTRACT
  (PRIMING)

Mash grains for 60 to 90 minutes (protein rest recommended). Collect 6 gallons of wort. Add molasses and Northern Brewer hops, and boil for 1 hour, adding Irish moss for the last 10 minutes. Remove from heat, add Cascade hops, and steep 10 minutes. Cool wort and pitch yeast. Ferment for 5 to 7 days. Transfer to secondary fermenter and ferment an additional 5 to 7 days. Bottle, using malt extract. Age in bottle 2 to 3 weeks.

OG: 1.052

It puts eloquence in an orator, it will make the philosopher talk profoundly . . . it is a great friend to the truth . . . it will put courage in a coward . . . it is the seal to a bargain . . . it is the nourisher of mankind.

—JOHN TAYLOR

Thomas Jefferson's Ale

ALONG WITH WRITING THE Declaration of Independence, inventing the dumbwaiter, and founding the University of Virginia, Thomas Jefferson was also an accomplished homebrewer, and his beers were considered among the finest in the colonies. And like every great homebrewer, he compared his beers favorably to the commercial breweries of the time. In a letter to fellow homebrewer and neighbor James Madison, Jefferson wrote, "We brew 100 gallons of ale in the fall and 100 gallons in the spring, taking 8 gallons only from a bushel of wheat, the public brewers take 15 which makes their liquor meager and often vapid." Some things never change.

6 POUNDS PALE 2-ROW BARLEY	1 OUNCE KENT GOLDINGS HOPS
4 POUNDS MALTED WHEAT	(AROMA)
1 POUND MOLASSES	1 PACKAGE AMERICAN ALE YEAST
1½ OUNCES KENT GOLDINGS HOPS	1 CUP DRY MALT EXTRACT (PRIMING)
(BITTERING)	

Mash grains for 60 to 90 minutes. Collect 6 gallons of wort, add molasses and 1½ ounces Kent Goldings hops, and boil for 1 hour, adding 1 ounce of Kent Goldings hops during the last 10 minutes. Cool wort and pitch yeast. Ferment for 10 to 14 days. Bottle, using malt extract. Age in bottle for 7 to 10 days.

OG: 1.060

Oak Tree IPA

AS WITH ANY IPA, THE hops dominate the flavor here. The oak chips present a faint woodiness that must have been present in the original IPAs, since they had spent the long jouney to India in oak casks. Unlike the British soldiers stationed in India, you won't have to wait eight months for this one. Enjoy it in the comfort of your own home, or in the backyard under that big old oak tree.

9 POUNDS BRITISH PALE MALT	1½ OUNCES CASCADE HOPS (DRY
½ POUND CARA-PILS MALT	HOP)
¾ POUND CRYSTAL MALT (80L)	2 OUNCES OAK CHIPS
2 TEASPOONS GYPSUM	1 TEASPOON IRISH MOSS
1½ OUNCES KENT GOLDINGS HOPS	1 PACKAGE AMERICAN ALE YEAST
(BITTERING)	¾ CUP CORN SUGAR (PRIMING)
1½ OUNCES KENT GOLDINGS HOPS	
(AROMA)	

Mash grains with gypsum for 90 minutes. Collect 6 gallons of wort and bring to a boil. Add 1½ ounces Kent Goldings hops and boil for one hour. Add Irish moss during the last 20 minutes of the boil. Add 1½ ounces of Kent Goldings during the last 15 minutes of the boil. Cool wort and pitch yeast. Ferment 7 to 10 days. Transfer to secondary fermenter and add Cascade hops. Boil oak chips in water for 10 minutes to sanitize, drain the water, and add the oak chips to the secondary fermenter. Ferment an additional 7 to 10 days. Bottle, using corn sugar. Age an additional week.

OG: 1.059

Tripel Play

THIS STRONG BELGIAN TRAPPIST ALE will benefit from the use of a true Trappist ale yeast cultured from a bottle of Orval, Westmale, or Chimay (see Brewer's Tip, p. 36). Clear Belgian candy sugar should be used to recreate the style, but if you are unable to find it, turbinado sugar may be used as a substitute. Table sugar can be substituted for the invert sugar, in a pinch.

13 POUNDS 2-ROW PILSNER MALT
2 POUNDS CLEAR BELGIAN CANDY
  SUGAR
2 OUNCES FUGGLES HOPS
  (BITTERING)

1 OUNCE SAAZ HOPS (FLAVORING)
1 OUNCE SAAZ HOPS (AROMA)
2 PACKAGES BELGIAN ABBEY YEAST
⅔ CUP INVERT SUGAR (PRIMING)

Mash grains for 60 to 90 minutes. Collect 6 gallons of wort. Add candy sugar and Fuggles hops, and boil for 1 hour, adding 1 ounce Saaz hops after 30 minutes and 1 ounce Saaz after 45 minutes. Cool wort and pitch one package yeast. Ferment for 10 to 14 days. Rack to secondary fermenter, add second yeast packet, and ferment an additional 10 to 14 days. Bottle using invert sugar. Age in bottle 14 to 21 days. Beer will improve with age.

OG: 1.075

We like to hop.
We like to hop
on top of Pop.
—DR. SEUSS,
HOP ON POP

Hop on Pop

BEER HERE
We like beer, now listen here. We like beer, it should be clear.

HOPS TOPS
We like hops, hops are tops. The tops of hops are conelike mops.

BEER HERE
Now it should be clear, brew this beer, there's hops in here.

6 POUNDS PALE 2-ROW AMERICAN MALT
1 POUND CRYSTAL MALT (10L)
1½ TEASPOONS GYPSUM
2 OUNCES TETTNANGER HOPS (BITTERING)
1 OUNCE CENTENNIAL HOPS (BITTERING)

2 OUNCES LIBERTY HOPS (FLAVORING)
2 OUNCES WILLAMETTE HOPS (DRY HOP)
1 TEASPOON IRISH MOSS
1 PACKAGE AMERICAN ALE YEAST
¾ CUP CORN SUGAR (PRIMING)

Mash grains with gypsum for 60 to 90 minutes. Collect 6 gallons of wort. Bring to a boil. Add Tettnanger hops and Centennial hops. Boil for 1 hour, adding Liberty hops after 30 minutes. Add Irish moss for last 5 minutes. Cool wort and pitch yeast. Ferment in primary fermenter for 7 to 10 days. Transfer to secondary fermenter, add Willamette hops, and ferment an additional 7 to 10 days. Bottle, using corn sugar. Age in bottle 7 to 10 days.

OG: 1.040

Accident-Prone Wheat

OUR FRIEND JIM GLASHEEN IS a true Renaissance man. He's an exceptional homebrewer, a brilliant scientist, a loving husband, an avid mountain biker, and an all-round athlete. However—he can't seem to accomplish any of these feats without injuring himself at every turn. Thanks for all the great recipes you've contributed, Jim, and be careful!

5 POUNDS GERMAN WHEAT MALT
5 POUNDS BELGIAN PILSNER MALT
¼ POUND CARA-PILS MALT
1 OUNCE KENT GOLDINGS HOPS
2 TEASPOONS GYPSUM

½ OUNCE KENT GOLDINGS HOPS
(FLAVORING)
1 PACKAGE AUSTRALIAN ALE YEAST
1½ CUPS HONEY (PRIMING)

Mash grains for 90 minutes. Collect 6 gallons of wort. Add 1 ounce Kent Goldings hops and gypsum and boil for 1 hour, adding ½ ounce Kent Goldings hops after 30 minutes. Cool wort and pitch yeast. Ferment for 8 to 10 days. Bottle, using honey. Age in bottle for 10 to 14 days.

OG: 1.052

Vail Pale Ale

WAYNE WAANANEN BEGAN HIS HOMEBREWING career in 1980 after his first taste of Boulder Beer. He won his first awards in 1985 in a national competition, where he met that year's homebrewer of the year, Russ Scherer. In 1990 when Scherer left the Wyncoop Brewing Company, he recommended Wayne for the job as brewer. In his four years there Wayne took five medals at the Great American Beer Festival, including two golds for the IPA. In February of 1995, he was hired as the brewer of The Sand Lot Brewery at Coors Field, where in his first year he took two medals at the 1995 Great American Beer Festival. This recipe for his Vail Pale Ale has won a number of homebrewing awards at competitions around the country, and he was nice enough to let us put it in the book.

10 POUNDS 2-ROW BRITISH MALT	1½ OUNCES CASCADE HOPS
1 POUND CRYSTAL MALT (60L)	(AROMA)
1½ OUNCES CENTENNIAL HOPS	1½ OUNCES CASCADE HOPS (DRY
(BITTERING)	HOP)
1½ OUNCES CENTENNIAL HOPS	1 PACKAGE AMERICAN ALE YEAST
(FLAVORING)	¾ CUP CORN SUGAR (PRIMING)
1½ OUNCES CASCADE HOPS	
(FINISHING)	

Mash grains for 90 minutes. Collect 6 gallons of wort. Add 1½ ounces Centennial hops and boil for 90 minutes, adding 1½ ounces Centennial hops after 30 minutes and 1½ ounces of Cascade hops after 80 minutes. Turn off heat, add 1½ ounces Cascade hops, and let steep for 5 minutes. Cool wort and pitch yeast. Ferment for 5 days and then transfer to secondary fermenter. Add 1½ ounces Cascade hops and allow to ferment an additional 3 weeks. Bottle, using corn sugar. Age in bottle 7 to 10 days.

OG: 1.068

Ale—not beer—in a pewter mug was comme il faut, the only thing for a gentleman of letters, worthy of the name, to drink.

—GUY DE MAUPASSANT, "TWELVE MEN"

Louis's French Ale

LOUIS PASTEUR IS USUALLY ASSOCIATED with dairy products. The chemist's work with bacterial control has benefited that industry the most. The fact is, Louis was a beer brewer trying to control the fermentation process. This strong, pale French ale was created in his honor, but is unpasteurized, as all good ales should be.

4 POUNDS AMERICAN 2-ROW MALT
4 POUNDS BELGIAN PILSNER MALT
3 POUNDS MUNICH MALT
1 POUND CRYSTAL MALT (10L)
1 OUNCE SAAZ HOPS (BITTERING)
1 OUNCE CASCADE HOPS
  (FLAVORING)

YEAST CULTURE FROM BOTTLE OF
JENLAIN (SEE BREWER'S TIP,
P. 36)
¾ CUP CORN SUGAR (PRIMING)

Mash grains for 60 to 90 minutes. Collect 6 gallons of wort. Add Saaz hops and boil for 1 hour, adding Cascade hops after 45 minutes. Cool wort and pitch yeast. Ferment for 10 to 14 days. Rack to secondary fermenter and ferment an additional 10 to 14 days. Bottle, using corn sugar. Age in bottle 7 to 14 days.

OG: 1.063

Culturing Yeast from a Bottle of Beer

Certain beers, like Belgian Trappiste brews, benefit greatly from the use of a yeast culture propagated from the actual brewery yeast strain.

Propagating yeast from a bottle-conditioned beer is incredibly easy. Five or six days before you're going to brew, prepare 6 ounces of wort by combining 6 ounces water with 1 tablespoon dry malt extract. Boil for 10 minutes and then cool to 75–78 degrees. When the wort has cooled, decant all but the last half inch of beer from your chosen bottle, being careful not to decant the yeast on the bottom. If you're beginning to feel a little stressed, drink half of the beer at this point. Pour the 6 ounces of wort into the bottle, attach an airlock, and agitate the bottle for 2 or 3 minutes. Set bottle in a cool, dark spot. Drink remainder of beer.

After two or three days, the culture should be active. At this point prepare a 1-quart starter using 3 ounces of dry malt extract. Boil wort for 10 minutes and then cool to 75–78 degrees. Add wort to your starter jug. Remove airlock from the bottle and flame the mouth using rubbing alcohol or 180-proof vodka. Swirl the contents of the bottle around and pitch into the 1-quart starter. Attach an airlock and agitate the bottle for 2 or 3 minutes. After 2 or 3 days, when fermentation is active, remove the airlock and flame the mouth of the jar. Swirl the contents around and pitch into the fermenter.

Brown Ales, Porters, *and* Stouts

From Rip Van Winkle *by Washington Irving*

On nearer approach he was still more surprised at the singularity of the stranger's appearance. He was a short square-built old fellow, with thick bushy hair, and a grizzled beard. His dress was of the antique Dutch fashion—a cloth jerkin strapped round the waist—several pair of breeches, the outer one of ample volume, decorated with rows of buttons down the sides, and bunches at the knees. He bore on his shoulder a stout keg, that seemed full of liquor, and made signs for Rip to approach and assist him with the load. Though rather shy and distrustful of this new acquaintance, Rip complied with his usual alacrity; and mutually relieving one another, they clambered up a narrow gully, apparently the dry bed of a mountain torrent. As they ascended, Rip every now and then heard long rolling peals, like distant thunder, that seemed to issue out of a deep ravine, or rather cleft, between lofty rocks, toward which their rugged path conducted. He paused for an instant, but supposing it to be the muttering of one of those transient thunder-showers which often take place in mountain heights, he proceeded. Passing through the ravine, they came to a hollow, like a small amphitheatre, surrounded by perpendicular precipices, over the brinks of which impending trees shot their branches, so that you only caught glimpses of the azure sky and the bright evening cloud. During the whole time Rip and his companion had labored on in silence; for though the former marvelled greatly what could be the object of carrying a keg of liquor up this wild mountain, yet there was something strange and incomprehensible about the unknown, that inspired awe and checked familiarity.

On entering the amphitheatre, new objects of wonder were to be seen. On a level spot in the center was a company of odd-looking persons playing at nine-pins. They were dressed in a quaint outlandish fashion; some wore short doublets, others jerkins, with long knives in their belts, and most of them had enormous breeches, of similar style with that of the guide's. Their visages, too, were peculiar: one had a large beard, broad face, and small piggish eyes: the face of another seemed to consist entirely of nose, and was surmounted by a white sugar-loaf hat, set off with a little red cock's tail. They all had beards, of various shapes and colors. There was one who seemed to be the commander. He was a stout old gentleman, with a weather-beaten countenance; he wore a laced doublet, broad belt and hanger, high crowned hat and feather, red stockings, and high-heeled shoes, with roses in them. The whole group reminded Rip of the figures in an old Flemish painting, in the parlor of Dominic Van Shaick, the village parson, and which had been brought over from Holland at the time of the settlement.

What seemed particularly odd to Rip was that though these folks were evidently amusing themselves, yet they maintained the gravest faces, the most mysterious silence, and were, withal, the most melancholy party of pleasure he had ever witnessed. Nothing interrupted the stillness of the scene but the noise of the balls, which, whenever they were rolled, echoed along the mountains like rumbling peals of thunder.

As Rip and his companion approached them, they suddenly desisted from their play, and stared at him with such fixed statue-like gaze, and such strange, uncouth lack-lustre countenances, that his heart turned within him, and his knees smote together. His companion now emptied the contents of the keg into large flagons; and made signs to him to wait upon the company. He obeyed with fear and trembling; they quaffed the liquor in profound silence, and then returned to their game.

By degrees Rip's awe and apprehension subsided. He even ventured, when no eye was fixed upon him, to taste the beverage, which he found had much of the flavor of excellent Hollands. He was naturally a thirsty soul, and was soon tempted to repeat the draught. One taste provoked another; and he reiterated his visits to the flagon so often that at length his senses were overpowered, his eyes swam in his head, his head gradually declined, and he fell into a deep sleep.

When schoolboy friends meet once again, who have not met for years.
Say, over what will they sit down and talk of their careers,
Your "whishy-washy" wines won't do, and fiery spirits fail,
for nothing blends the hearts of friends than good old English ale.

—J. CAXTON

Basic British Brown

THIS IS A BASIC BROWN in the traditional style of northern England. It relies on a blend of malts to achieve its characteristic toasty flavor. Low hop bitterness and fruity yeast are also essential.

3 1/3 POUNDS AMBER MALT EXTRACT
3 1/3 POUNDS DARK MALT EXTRACT
1 POUND CARA-PILS MALT
1 POUND CRYSTAL MALT (80L)
2 OUNCES CHOCOLATE MALT
1 1/2 OUNCES KENT GOLDINGS HOPS
   (BITTERING)
1 CUP LIGHT BROWN SUGAR

1/2 OUNCE FUGGLES HOPS
   (FLAVORING)
1/2 OUNCE KENT GOLDINGS HOPS
   (AROMA)
1 TEASPOON GYPSUM
1 PACKAGE BRITISH ALE YEAST
1 CUP LIGHT OR DARK BROWN SUGAR
   (PRIMING)

Place crystal malt, Cara-Pils malt, amber malt, and chocolate malt in water, and steep at 155 degrees for ½ hour. Add gypsum and bring water to a boil and remove spent grains. Add malt extracts, 1½ ounces Kent Goldings hops, and brown sugar. Boil for 1 hour, adding the Fuggles hops after 30 minutes and ½ ounce Kent Goldings for the last 5 minutes. Cool the wort and pitch the yeast. Ferment for 7 to 10 days. Bottle, using 1 cup brown sugar. Age in bottle for 7 days.

OG: 1.048

Basic American Brown

THIS STYLE OF BROWN ALE was developed by American homebrewers and microbrewers in the 1980s. It is somewhat darker and much hoppier than its British counterpart.

6⅔ POUNDS LIGHT MALT EXTRACT	1 OUNCE LIBERTY HOPS
1 POUND CRYSTAL MALT 40L	(FLAVORING)
½ POUND CARA-PILS MALT	1 OUNCE CASCADE HOPS (AROMA)
¼ POUND CHOCOLATE MALT	1 TEASPOON GYPSUM
2 OUNCES NORTHERN BREWER HOPS	1 PACKAGE AMERICAN ALE YEAST
(BITTERING)	¾ CUP CORN SUGAR (PRIMING)

Place gypsum, crystal malt, Cara-Pils malt, and chocolate malt in water, and steep at 155 degrees for ½ hour. Remove spent grains and bring water to a boil. Add malt extract and 2 ounces Northern Brewer hops. Boil for 1 hour, adding the Liberty hops after 30 minutes and Cascade hops for the last 5 minutes. Cool the wort and pitch the yeast. Ferment for 7 to 10 days. Bottle, using corn sugar. Age in bottle for 7 days.

OG: 1.050

Ned Flanders Brown

FLANDERS IS A REGION IN Belgium where this style originated. It is a sweet, malty brown ale that is slightly sour. The special yeast strain used here adds enough sourness without your having to sour the wort. This version is scrump-diddley-icious. Okley-dokley?

6²/₃ POUNDS AMBER MALT EXTRACT	¹/₂ OUNCE TETTNANGER HOPS
¹/₂ POUND CRYSTAL MALT (60L)	(FLAVORING)
¹/₂ POUND TOASTED MALT (SEE	1 PACKAGE BRETTANOMYCES
BREWER'S TIP, BELOW)	BRUXELLENSIS YEAST
¹/₄ POUND CHOCOLATE MALT	2 TEASPOONS LACTIC ACID
1 ¹/₂ OUNCES HALLERTAUER HOPS	³/₄ CUP CORN SUGAR (PRIMING)
(BITTERING)	

Steep grains in 155-degree water for 30 minutes. Strain out spent grains, add malt extract, and bring to a boil. Add Hallertauer hops 15 minutes into the boil. Add Tettnanger 45 minutes into the boil. Cool wort and pitch yeast culture. Ferment 7 to 10 days, and transfer to secondary fermenter. Ferment an additional 7 to 10 days. Bottle, using corn sugar and lactic acid. Age 1 to 2 weeks.

OG: 1.045

Toasted Malt

Toasted malt or amber malt adds a wonderful nuttiness without the roasted or burnt flavors associated with roasted malts. Toasted malt is very easy to make at home in your oven. Preheat oven to 275 degrees. Spead pale malt on a cookie sheet and place in the oven for 60 minutes. Raise the temperature to 350 degrees, and toast an additional 30 minutes. Allow malt to cool and then use as you would any malt.

Honey Nut Brown

THIS BROWN ALE IS QUITE smooth. The combination of crystal and chocolate malts lends the nutty flavors, while the honey contributes a distinct sweetness. Try a flavored honey to add your own accent.

6 POUNDS AMBER MALT EXTRACT
2 POUNDS HONEY
½ POUND CRYSTAL MALT (20 L)
¼ POUND CHOCOLATE MALT
1 TEASPOON GYPSUM
1 ½ OUNCES NORTHERN BREWER
  HOPS (BITTERING)

½ OUNCE WILLAMETTE HOPS
  (FLAVORING)
½ TEASPOON IRISH MOSS
1 PACKAGE BRITISH ALE YEAST
¾ CUP CORN SUGAR (PRIMING)

Steep grains in 155-degree water for 30 minutes. Remove spent grains, add malt extract, gypsum, and honey, and bring to a boil. Add Northern Brewer hops and boil for 1 hour. Add Willamette hops during the last 15 minutes of the boil. Add Irish moss for last 5 minutes. Cool wort and pitch yeast. Ferment 7 to 10 days, and transfer to secondary fermenter. Ferment an additional 7 to 10 days. Bottle, using corn sugar, and age 1 to 2 weeks.

OG: 1.045

Uptown Brown

YOU DON'T HAVE TO HAVE a big kitchen or a spacious cellar to be a homebrewer. City dwellers can make beer just like anyone else. You just have to plan your use of space a little better. This British Brown adds a touch of class to even the most cramped studio apartment. Here's to moving up in the world.

6⅔ POUNDS AMBER MALT EXTRACT
½ POUND CRYSTAL MALT (40L)
½ POUND MUNICH MALT
¼ POUND CHOCOLATE MALT
1 TEASPOON GYPSUM
3 OUNCES FUGGLES HOPS
  (BITTERING)

½ OUNCE FUGGLES HOPS (AROMA)
½ TEASPOON IRISH MOSS
1 PACKAGE BRITISH ALE YEAST
1 CUP CORN SUGAR (PRIMING)

Place crushed grains and gypsum in water and steep at 155 degrees for 30 minutes. Remove spent grains and add malt extract. Bring to a boil and add 3 ounces Fuggles hops; boil 1 hour. Add ½ ounce Fuggles and the Irish moss during final 15 minutes of boil. Cool wort and pitch yeast. Ferment 7 to 10 days. Transfer to secondary fermenter and ferment an additional 7 days. Bottle, using corn sugar, and age for 7 days.

OG: 1.044

Oak Leaf Brown Ale

THIS BROWN ALE IS SIMILAR in style to the brown ales of southern and western England. The addition of a pound of dark brown sugar lends color and a subtle sweetness.

6⅔ POUNDS LIGHT MALT EXTRACT
1 POUND CRYSTAL MALT
  (80L OR HIGHER)
½ POUND CHOCOLATE MALT
1 POUND DARK BROWN SUGAR

1 OUNCE KENT GOLDINGS HOPS
  (BITTERING)
½ OUNCE PERLE HOPS (FLAVORING)
1 PACKAGE BRITISH ALE YEAST
¾ CUP CORN SUGAR (PRIMING)

Place crystal malt and chocolate malt in water and steep at 155 degrees for 30 minutes. Remove spent grains and bring water to a boil. Add malt extract, brown sugar, and Kent Goldings hops. Boil for 1 hour, adding the Perle hops after 30 minutes. Cool the wort and pitch the yeast. Ferment for 7 to 10 days. Bottle, using corn sugar. Age in bottle for 7 days.

OG: 1.044

Shoulder the sky, my lad, and drink your ale.
— A. E. Housman, *A Shropshire Lad*

Nutty Brown

THIS IS A REALLY GOOD everyday drinking beer. Light in body and nut brown in color, it goes down easy, almost too easy.

7 POUNDS PALE 2-ROW MALT	½ OUNCE WILLAMETTE HOPS
½ POUND CHOCOLATE MALT	(AROMA)
½ POUND CRYSTAL MALT (90L)	½ TEASPOON IRISH MOSS
⅛ POUND BLACK PATENT MALT	1 TEASPOON GYPSUM
1 OUNCE WILLAMETTE HOPS	1 PACKAGE WHITBREAD ALE YEAST
(BITTERING)	1 CUP CORN SUGAR (PRIMING)
1 OUNCE PERLE HOPS (FLAVORING)	

Mash grains with gypsum for 90 minutes. Collect 6 gallons of wort and bring to a boil. Add Willamette hops and boil 1 hour. Add Perle hops at 30 minutes. Add Irish moss during final 10 minutes. Turn off the heat, add the ½ ounce of Willamette, and steep for 10 minutes. Cool wort and pitch yeast. Ferment 7 to 10 days. Transfer to secondary fermenter and ferment an additional 7 days. Bottle, using corn sugar. Age for 1 week.

OG: 1.046

Tuxedo Brown

THIS BROWN ALE IS A very good first time all-grain recipe. Bottling with brown sugar will lend a flavor that is typical of British browns.

6 POUNDS PALE 2-ROW MALT	1 OUNCE KENT GOLDINGS HOPS
½ POUND TOASTED MALT	(BITTERING)
(SEE BREWER'S TIP, P. 41)	½ OUNCE CASCADE HOPS (AROMA)
½ POUND CRYSTAL MALT (60L)	1 PACKAGE BRITISH ALE YEAST
½ POUND CRYSTAL MALT (120L)	1 CUP LIGHT OR DARK BROWN SUGAR
2 OUNCES CHOCOLATE MALT	(PRIMING)

Mash grains for 60 to 90 minutes. Collect 6 gallons of wort. Add Kent Goldings hops and boil for 1 hour. Remove from heat, add Cascade hops, cover, and steep for 10 minutes. Cool wort and pitch yeast. Ferment for 7 to 10 days. Bottle, using brown sugar. Age in bottle 7 to 10 days.

OG: 1.046

> *Make the long night shorter,*
> *Forgetting not,*
> *Good stout old English Porter.*
> —R. H. MESSENGER, "GIVE ME THE OLD"

Basic Porter

THIS EASY RECIPE IS TYPICAL of the traditional sharp-flavored British porters. While the process is quite simple, the flavors are anything but. This is a very good recipe for the beginning brewer, with results that are sure to impress.

6²/₃ POUNDS AMBER MALT EXTRACT	1½ OUNCES KENT GOLDINGS HOPS
1½ POUNDS ALEXANDER'S AMBER	(BITTERING)
MALT EXTRACT	½ OUNCE LIBERTY HOPS (AROMA)
½ POUND BLACK PATENT MALT	1 PACKAGE ENGLISH ALE YEAST
½ POUND CRYSTAL MALT (60L)	¾ CUP CORN SUGAR (PRIMING)
1 TEASPOON GYPSUM	

Place crushed black patent and crystal malt in water and steep at 155 degrees for 30 minutes. Remove spent grains and add malt extract, gypsum, and Kent Goldings hops. Boil for 1 hour. Add Liberty hops for the last 5 minutes of the boil. Cool wort and pitch yeast. Ferment for 10 to 14 days. Bottle, using corn sugar. Age for 10 days.

OG: 1.055

Brown-Sugar Molasses Porter

THE HOMESPUN AROMAS FROM THIS wort bring back childhood memories of Grandma's kitchen, which seem somehow sweeter when mixed with the heavenly scent of toasty malt and spicy hops. The resulting flavors are subtle but sweet.

3⅓ POUNDS LIGHT MALT EXTRACT	1 TEASPOON GYPSUM
3⅓ POUNDS AMBER MALT EXTRACT	½ TEASPOON IRISH MOSS
1 POUND CRYSTAL MALT	1 OUNCE LIBERTY HOPS (BITTERING)
½ POUND CHOCOLATE MALT	½ OUNCE CASCADE HOPS (AROMA)
¼ POUND BLACK PATENT MALT	1 PACKAGE AMERICAN ALE YEAST
2 CUPS DARK BROWN SUGAR	1¼ CUPS DRY MALT EXTRACT
½ CUP BLACKSTRAP MOLASSES	(PRIMING)

Place crushed crystal malt, chocolate malt, and black patent malt in water and steep at 155 degrees for 30 minutes. Remove spent grains, add malt extracts, brown sugar, molasses, gypsum, and Liberty hops, and boil for 1 hour. Add Irish moss for the last 5 minutes of the boil. Remove from heat, add Cascade hops, and steep for 15 minutes. Cool wort and pitch yeast. Ferment for 5 to 7 days and then transfer to the secondary fermenter and ferment an additional 5 to 7 days. Secondary fermentation is optional in this recipe. If you choose to do single stage, ferment for 8 to 14 days in the primary. Bottle, using dry malt extract. Age in bottle 10 to 14 days. Beer will be best after 3 to 4 weeks.

OG: 1.052

They don't mind it; it's a regular holiday to them — all porter and skittles.

—CHARLES DICKENS, *THE PICKWICK PAPERS*

Steamship Porter

WHILE PORTERS ARE TRADITIONALLY ALES, we decided to brew one in the steam beer tradition. The bitter quality of the steam beer style is balanced nicely by the malt sweetness.

3⅓ POUNDS LIGHT MALT EXTRACT
3⅓ POUNDS AMBER MALT EXTRACT
1 POUND CRYSTAL MALT (40L)
½ POUND CHOCOLATE MALT
2 OUNCES BLACK PATENT MALT
2 OUNCES WILLAMETTE HOPS
  (BITTERING)

1 OUNCE CASCADE HOPS (AROMA)
1 PACKAGE CALIFORNIA LAGER
  YEAST
¾ CUP CORN SUGAR (PRIMING)

Place crushed crystal malt, chocolate malt, and black patent malt in water and steep at 155 degrees for 30 minutes. Remove spent grains and add malt extracts and Willamette hops. Boil for 1 hour. Remove from heat, add Cascade hops, and let steep for 10 minutes. Cool wort and pitch yeast. Ferment for 5 to 7 days at temperatures between 65 to 75 degrees. Transfer to secondary fermenter, and ferment an additional 14 to 21 days at temperatures between 40 and 45 degrees. Bottle, using corn sugar. Age in bottle 7 to 10 days.

OG: 1.051

Chocolate Honey Porter

WHILE BREWING THIS BEER, OUR friend John DaSilva commented, "Life is a struggle, but the rewards are worth it." In a way, this is a wonderful metaphor for homebrewing. Keeping the mash at the right temperature, getting the correct alkalinity in your water, calculating the right HBUs, the *cleanup . . .* but in the end, when you taste a beer like this, you realize it really is worth it.

3 1/3 POUNDS AMBER MALT EXTRACT
3 1/3 POUNDS DARK MALT EXTRACT
1 POUND CRYSTAL MALT
1/4 POUND ROASTED BARLEY
1/4 POUND BLACK PATENT MALT
1/2 POUND TORREFIED WHEAT
3 POUNDS HONEY
6 OUNCES UNSWEETENED BAKING CHOCOLATE

1/2 OUNCE HALLERTAUER HOPS (BITTERING)
1/2 OUNCE FUGGLES HOPS (BITTERING)
1/2 OUNCE FUGGLES HOPS (AROMA)
1 PACKAGE IRISH ALE YEAST
1 OUNCE SLICED GINGERROOT
3/4 CUP CORN SUGAR (PRIMING)

Place crushed crystal malt, black patent malt, torrefied wheat, and roasted barley in water, and steep at 155 degrees for 30 minutes. Remove spent grains and add malt extracts, honey, and bittering hops, and boil for 30 minutes. Add melted chocolate (2 minutes in the microwave works best) and boil an additional 30 minutes. Add aroma hops for the last 5 minutes of the boil. Cool wort and pitch yeast. Ferment for 5 to 7 days, then transfer to the secondary fermenter, and add 1 ounce of sliced gingerroot. Ferment for an additional 7 days. Bottle, using corn sugar. Age for 10 to 14 days. Beer will be best after aging in the bottle for at least 4 to 6 weeks.

OG: 1.063

Gas vs. Electric

Any cook will tell you that gas is better than electric. Brewers will tell you this too. Heat is much easier to control on a gas stove and you are less likely to caramelize the wort on the bottom of your pot. If you have no other choice than an electric stove, buy a heat diffuser. Found in any camping store, a heat diffuser keeps your brew pot off the heating element. If you can't find a heat diffuser, bend a wire hanger into a 4-point-star pattern to create a small airspace between the heating element and your brew pot. Don't forget to stir often.

I use no porter . . . in my family, but such as is made in America: both these articles may now be purchased of an excellent quality.

—GEORGE WASHINGTON

Mr. Hare's Porter

GEORGE WASHINGTON WAS A BIG fan of good beer, his favorite being a porter produced by Mr. Robert Hare of Philadelphia. In 1790, Washington directed his secretary to dictate the following letter: "Will you be so good as to desire Mr. Hare to have, if he continues to make the best porter in Philadelphia, 3 gross of his best put up for Mount Vernon as the President means to visit that place in the recess of Congress and it is probable there will be a large demand for Porter at that time." We're sure every president since knew just how George must have felt. This is our version of what it may have been like.

3⅓ POUNDS AMBER MALT EXTRACT
3⅓ POUNDS DARK MALT EXTRACT
1½ CUPS MOLASSES
¾ POUND CRYSTAL MALT (80L)
½ POUND BLACK PATENT MALT
¼ POUND CHOCOLATE MALT

1½ OUNCES NORTHERN BREWER
  HOPS (BITTERING)
1½ OUNCES CASCADE HOPS
  (AROMA)
1 PACKAGE AMERICAN ALE YEAST
¾ CUP CORN SUGAR (PRIMER)

Place crushed crystal malt, black patent malt, and chocolate malt in water, and steep at 155 degrees for 30 minutes. Remove spent grains, add malt extracts, molasses, and Northern Brewer hops, and boil for 1 hour. Remove from heat, add Cascade hops, and let steep for 10 minutes. Cool wort and pitch yeast. Ferment for 10 to 14 days. Bottle, using corn sugar. Age in bottle 10 to 14 days.

OG: 1.052

Viennese Spiced Porter

THE COMBINATION OF VANILLA AND almond is a great Viennese favorite. We stumbled across this flavor combination while flipping through *Joy of Cooking* and knew immediately that it would make a great beer. We were right. The spicy flavors add a lively note to this rich, creamy porter.

6⅔ POUNDS DARK MALT EXTRACT
½ POUND CHOCOLATE MALT
¼ POUND BLACK PATENT MALT
1 POUND ROLLED OATS
2 OUNCES MOUNT HOOD HOPS
  (BITTERING)

½ OUNCE FUGGLES HOPS (AROMA)
1 PACKAGE AMERICAN ALE YEAST
1 VANILLA BEAN
2 TEASPOONS ALMOND EXTRACT
¾ CUP CORN SUGAR (PRIMING)

Place the crushed black patent malt and chocolate malt in water and steep at 155 degrees for 30 minutes. Remove spent grains. Add malt extract, oats, and Mount Hood hops, and boil for 1 hour, adding the Fuggles hops for the last 5 minutes. Cool wort and pitch yeast. Ferment for 5 to 7 days and then transfer to the secondary fermenter and add the vanilla bean. Ferment an additional 10 days. Add almond extract, and bottle, using corn sugar. Age in bottle 10 to 14 days.

OG: 1.048

Head Retention

There are many reasons why your beer may not have a rich, creamy head when you pour it. The first thing to do is check your glass. If the glasses you are using haven't been rinsed properly, soap residue will break down the bubbles instantly, resulting in a very unimpressive beer. The next thing to check is your carbonation: if bubbles are flowing steadily from the bottom of your glass, this is not your problem.

Certain proteins develop during the mashing process that will inhibit heading in any beer. There are many ways to battle these proteins (see Brewer's Tip, p. 69), but this may not be enough. If you simply can't get a good head, it may be time to take the offensive. Your homebrew supplier may stock a variety of artificial heading agents, but you can maintain the purity of your recipe and get a boost in head retention by using wheat malt. When used at a ratio of about 5 percent of the total recipe, it will not alter your flavor profile significantly. Torrefied wheat, basically an un-malted puffed wheat, is harder to find, but does not affect your original gravity when used in amounts similar to that of malted wheat, above.

Hey Porter, hey porter, can you tell me the time?
How long is it until I cross the Mason-Dixon
line?

—JOHNNY CASH

Hey Porter

YEAH, WE KNOW WHAT TIME it is. It's time for another beer. And we think this porter would be just the thing.

7 POUNDS PALE 2-ROW MALT
1 POUND DEXTRINE MALT
1 POUND CRYSTAL MALT (60L)
½ POUND FLAKED BARLEY
½ POUND CHOCOLATE MALT
¼ POUND BLACK PATENT MALT
2 OUNCES LIBERTY HOPS
   (BITTERING)

1 OUNCE WILLAMETTE HOPS
   (AROMA)
½ TEASPOON GYPSUM
1 PACKAGE AMERICAN ALE YEAST
1 CUP MOLASSES (PRIMING)

Add gypsum and mash grains for 60 to 90 minutes. Collect 6 gallons of wort. Add Liberty hops and boil for 1 hour, adding the Willamette hops during the last 10 minutes. Cool wort and pitch yeast. Ferment for 7 to 10 days. Transfer to secondary fermenter and ferment an additional 5 days. Bottle, using molasses. Age in bottle 10 to 14 days.

OG: 1.049

I have received delegations of working men who come, apparently speaking of the utmost sincerity, have declared that they would regard it as a genuine hardship to be deprived of their beer.

—WOODROW WILSON

Porter #12

WE FIRST BREWED THIS BEER on December 12, and as it turned out, our brewing schedule was 12 days for primary, 12 days in the secondary, and 12 days in the bottle. We bottled in 12-ounce bottles, and this batch yielded 4 12-packs. Why Porter #12? Why not?

6 POUNDS PALE 2-ROW MALT
2 POUNDS MUNICH MALT
1 POUND TORREFIED WHEAT
1 POUND CRYSTAL MALT (40L)
½ POUND CHOCOLATE MALT
½ POUND BLACK PATENT MALT

2 OUNCES CASCADE HOPS
  (BITTERING)
1 OUNCE CASCADE HOPS (AROMA)
1 PACKAGE BRITISH ALE YEAST
¾ CUP CORN SUGAR (PRIMING)

Mash grains for 60 to 90 minutes. Collect 6 gallons of wort. Add 2 ounces of Cascade hops and boil for 1 hour. Remove from heat and add 1 ounce Cascade hops and steep for 10 minutes. Cool wort and pitch yeast. Ferment for 12 days. Transfer to secondary fermenter and ferment an additional 12 days. Bottle, using corn sugar. Age in bottle 12 days.

OG: 1.050

Such power hath beer. The heart which grief hath one unfailing remedy—The tankard.

—CHARLES STUART CALVERLEY

Basic Stout

DRY STOUT IS ONE OF the most popular styles of beer (thank you, Mr. Guinness). It is also one of the most rewarding homebrews. A bottle of this thick, rich brew is a wonderful sight in your refrigerator on a cold winter evening.

6²/₃ POUNDS DARK MALT EXTRACT
1 POUND CRYSTAL MALT (40L)
1 POUND ROASTED BARLEY
¹/₂ POUND CHOCOLATE MALT
¹/₂ POUND MALTO-DEXTRIN POWDER

1¹/₂ OUNCES BULLION HOPS
  (BITTERING)
1 OUNCE IRISH ALE YEAST
1¹/₄ CUPS DRY MALT EXTRACT
  (PRIMING)

Place crushed crystal malt, roasted barley, and chocolate malt in water and steep at 155 degrees for 30 minutes. Remove spent grains, add malt extract, malto-dextrin, and Bullion hops, and boil for 1 hour. Cool wort and pitch yeast. Ferment for 10 to 14 days. Bottle, using 1¹/₄ cups dry malt extract. Age for 7 to 10 days.

OG: 1.052

Russian Imperial Stout

THIS IS A STRONGER VERSION of dry stout. Like India Pale Ale, this stout was brewed with a high alcohol content and high hop rate to endure long sea voyages. This particular style became very popular with the Empress of Russia, and she ordered it to be supplied to her imperial court, hence the name, Russian Imperial Stout.

6⅔ POUNDS DARK MALT EXTRACT
6⅔ POUNDS AMBER MALT EXTRACT
¾ POUND ROASTED BARLEY
½ POUND CRYSTAL MALT
½ POUND CHOCOLATE MALT
1 OUNCE GALENA HOPS (BITTERING)
2 OUNCES GALENA HOPS (FLAVOR)

1 OUNCE WILLAMETTE HOPS
(AROMA)
1 PACKAGE IRISH ALE YEAST
(MAKES 2-QUART STARTER)
1¼ CUPS DRY MALT EXTRACT
(PRIMING)

Place crushed roasted barley, crystal malt, and chocolate malt in water and steep at 155 degrees for 30 minutes. Remove spent grains and add malt extracts and 1 ounce of Galena hops. Boil for 1 hour, adding 1 ounce of Galena after 20 minutes and the last ounce after 40 minutes. Turn off the heat and add the Willamette hops and allow to steep for 15 minutes. Cool wort and pitch yeast. Ferment for 10 to 14 days and then transfer to the secondary fermenter for an additional 10 to 14 days. Because of the high malt content and the variance of your yeast starter, pay special attention to your hydrometer readings with this beer, as fermentation time will vary. Bottle, using dry malt extract. Age for a minimum of 2 months. This beer ages very well and will continue to improve and develop some interesting complexities. It can be aged up to 2 years with great results.

OG: 1.090

High-Gravity Starters

When using liquid yeast with a malt nutrient (i.e., smack pack) it is possible to add it directly to your primary fermenter with great success, provided that the yeast packet and the wort are both well aerated. However, when brewing a high-gravity beer, like an imperial stout or barleywine, making a starter is essential to ensure that the yeast won't poop out before fermentation is complete. Two or three days before you brew, sterilize a ½-gallon or 1-gallon bottle, a stopper that fits securely, and an airlock. Boil 1 quart of water and 3 ounces of dried malt extract for 10 minutes. Cool the wort (placing the covered pan in the refrigerator works nicely). Transfer to the sterilized bottle, add the yeast, and insert the stopper and airlock. Aerate very well. Let sit for 2 to 3 days until fermentation is active. Swirl the bottle to loosen the sediment. Remove the airlock and flame the mouth of the jar (and fermenter if using a glass carboy) with rubbing alcohol or high-proof vodka. Pitch the entire contents into the primary fermenter. A starter also helps the yeast to begin working more quickly and is considered by many homebrewers to be advantageous for all brews.

Ed's Honey Oatmeal Stout

AFTER DECANTING THE FIRST BOTTLE of this stout we were pleased to see that it was just what we were shooting for, jet black in color with a thick tan head. Just then, Patrick's Siamese cat, Ed, jumped up on the table and took a seat next to the pint. Not one to miss out on free food of any kind, Ed decided to take a few licks from the head. To our surprise, he liked it, not to mention his coloring matched the pint exactly. And so without another thought, this brew became Ed's Honey Oatmeal Stout.

3⅓ POUNDS AMBER MALT EXTRACT
3⅓ POUNDS DARK MALT EXTRACT
2 POUNDS BUCKWHEAT HONEY
1 POUND CRYSTAL MALT (60L)
½ POUND CHOCOLATE MALT
¾ POUND ROASTED BARLEY
¼ POUND BLACK PATENT MALT

1 POUND ROLLED OATS
1½ OUNCES CASCADE HOPS
  (BITTERING)
1 OUNCE LIBERTY HOPS (AROMA)
1 PACKAGE IRISH ALE YEAST
1¼ CUPS DRY MALT EXTRACT
  (PRIMING)

Place crushed crystal malt, chocolate malt, black patent malt, and roasted barley in water and steep at 155 degrees for 30 minutes. Remove spent grains and add malt extracts, honey, oats, and Cascade hops. Boil for 1 hour. Turn off heat, add Liberty hops, and steep for 15 minutes. Cool wort and pitch yeast. Ferment for 10 to 14 days. Bottle, using dry malt extract. Age in bottle 2 to 3 weeks.

OG: 1.051

Canadian Imperial Stout

ALTHOUGH CANADA NEVER HAD A royal court of its own, we think this is what Their Majesties would have drunk had They existed. This Imperial Stout draws character from pure Canadian maple syrup. The 1 quart called for in the recipe is barely discernible, so feel free to use more, but be prepared to pour the brew on pancakes if you add too much.

10 POUNDS AMBER MALT EXTRACT
1 QUART PURE CANADIAN MAPLE
  SYRUP
1 POUND ROASTED BARLEY
½ POUND CRYSTAL MALT
  (40L OR GREATER)
¼ POUND CHOCOLATE MALT
¼ POUND BLACK PATENT MALT
½ TEASPOON GYPSUM

4 OUNCES NORTHERN BREWER HOPS
  (BITTERING)
4 OUNCES FUGGLES HOPS (FLAVOR)
1 OUNCE CASCADE HOPS (AROMA)
½ TEASPOON IRISH MOSS
1 PACKAGE IRISH ALE YEAST
1½ CUPS PURE MAPLE SYRUP
  (PRIMING)

Place crushed grains and gypsum in water and steep at 155 degrees for 30 minutes. Remove spent grains, add malt extract and one half quart of the maple syrup. Bring to a boil, add Northern Brewer hops. Add Fuggles hops after 30 minutes. Add Cascade hops, Irish moss, and the remainder of the maple syrup for the last 10 minutes of the boil. Cool wort and pitch yeast. Ferment 10 to 14 days. Transfer to secondary fermenter and ferment an additional 10 to 14 days. Bottle, using 1½ cups maple syrup, and age 1 month minimum.

OG: 1.079

I have fed purely upon ale; I have ate my ale, and I always sleep upon ale.
—GEORGE FARQUHAR, *THE BEAUX' STRATAGEM*

Old McDonald Drank a Stout

IN BRITAIN, SWEET STOUTS ARE often referred to as farm stouts. They possess a sweet malty character and lack the roasty quality of their dry cousins. These are often served as after-dinner drinks.

6⅔ POUNDS DARK MALT EXTRACT
1 POUND CRYSTAL MALT (80L)
½ POUND CHOCOLATE MALT
¼ POUND ROASTED BARLEY
1 OUNCE NORTHERN BREWER HOPS
  (BITTERING)

1 PACKAGE LONDON ALE YEAST
¾ POUND LACTOSE
1¼ CUPS DRY MALT EXTRACT
  (PRIMING)

Place crushed crystal malt, chocolate malt, and roasted barley in water and steep at 155 degrees for 30 minutes. Remove spent grains, add dark malt extract and Northern Brewer hops, and boil for 1 hour. Cool wort and pitch yeast. Ferment for 5 to 7 days. Transfer to secondary fermenter and ferment an additional 7 to 10 days. Bottle, using dry malt extract and lactose. Age in bottle 7 to 10 days.

OG: 1.048

Presidential Stout

THIS AMERICANIZED VERSION OF RUSSIAN Imperial Stout retains the high alcohol content and intense bitterness, but aroma hops are added as well, in accordance with the growing trend at small American breweries, where this style has experienced a rebirth. We have taken ours one step further with the addition of dry hopping.

6⅔ POUNDS LIGHT MALT EXTRACT
6⅔ POUNDS AMBER MALT EXTRACT
1 POUND ROASTED BARLEY
1 POUND CRYSTAL MALT
½ POUND BLACK PATENT MALT
¼ POUND CHOCOLATE MALT
2 OUNCES PERLE HOPS (BITTERING)
1½ OUNCES PERLE HOPS
  (FLAVORING)

1 OUNCE LIBERTY HOPS (AROMA)
1½ OUNCES CHALLENGER HOPS
  (DRY HOP)
1 PACKAGE AMERICAN ALE YEAST
  (MAKE 2-QUART STARTER)
1¼ CUPS DRY MALT EXTRACT
  (PRIMING)

Place crushed roasted barley, crystal malt, chocolate malt, and black patent malt in water and steep at 155 degrees for 30 minutes. Remove spent grains and add malt extracts and 2 ounces of Perle hops. Boil for 1 hour, adding 1 ounce of Perle hops after 20 minutes and the last ½ ounce after 40 minutes. Remove from heat, add the Liberty hops, and allow to steep for 15 minutes. Cool wort and pitch yeast. Ferment for 5 to 7 days, then transfer to the secondary fermenter and add the Challenger hops. Ferment an additional 10 to 14 days. Because of the high malt content and the variance of your yeast starter, pay special attention to your hydrometer readings with this beer, as fermentation time will vary. Bottle, using dry malt extract. Age for a minimum of 2 months. This beer ages very well and will continue to improve and develop some interesting complexities. It can be aged up to 2 years with outstanding results.

OG: 1.092

A large blackboard, announcing in white letters to an enlightened public that there were 500,000 barrels of double stout in the cellars of the establishment, left the mind in a state of not unpleasing doubt and uncertainty as to the precise direction in the bowels of the earth, in which this mighty cavern might be supposed to extend.

—CHARLES DICKENS, *THE PICKWICK PAPERS*

Cool Summer Imperial Stout

WHO WOULD WANT TO BREW a stout in the summer? We would, of course. As much as we love pale ales, we need something to make those black-and-tans with. And besides, there is nothing that goes better with a juicy steak fresh off the grill than a delicious stout. If you don't have a cool basement or air-conditioned apartment to let this ferment, see Brewer's Tip (p. 19) for some methods of keeping your fermenting wort cool.

4½ POUNDS DARK MALT EXTRACT
5¾ POUNDS LIGHT MALT EXTRACT
½ POUND CHOCOLATE MALT
½ POUND ROASTED BARLEY
4 OUNCES CHINOOK HOPS
   (BITTERING)

1½ OUNCES CASCADE HOPS
   (AROMA)
1 PACKAGE IRISH ALE YEAST
1 OUNCE CASCADE HOPS (DRY HOP)
1¼ CUPS DARK DRY MALT EXTRACT
   (PRIMING)

Place crushed chocolate malt and roasted barley in water and steep at 155 degrees for 30 minutes. Remove spent grains and add dark and light malt extracts. Bring to a boil and add Chinook hops. Add 1½ ounces Cascade hops after 30 minutes, and boil for an additional 30 minutes. Cool wort and pitch yeast. Ferment for 10 days and transfer to secondary fermenter. Add 1 ounce Cascade and ferment an additional 10 to 14 days. Bottle, using dark dry malt extract. Age at least 2 weeks at room temperature, 1 to 3 months at cellar temperatures.

OG: 1.072

Java Stout

THE ADDITION OF COFFEE ADDS a strong quality, similar to the addition of roasted malts, but with an unmistakable, yet smooth, coffee flavor. Adjust the amount of coffee to your taste. And so, you ask, is this a morning beer? In our opinion, any beer is a morning beer.

6⅔ POUNDS DARK MALT EXTRACT
½ POUND CRYSTAL MALT (40L)
½ POUND CHOCOLATE MALT
¼ POUND ROASTED BARLEY
½ CUP GOOD-QUALITY GROUND
  COFFEE
1½ OUNCES FUGGLES HOPS
  (BITTERING)

1 OUNCE TETTNANGER HOPS
  (AROMA)
1 PACKAGE IRISH ALE YEAST
1¼ CUPS DARK DRY MALT EXTRACT
  (PRIMING)

Place crushed crystal malt, chocolate malt, and roasted barley in water and let steep at 155 degrees for 30 minutes. Remove spent grains, add dark malt extract and Fuggles hops. Boil for 1 hour, adding the Tettnanger hops for the last 10 minutes. Remove from heat and add coffee. Let steep for 15 minutes. Cool wort and pitch yeast. Ferment for 5 to 7 days. Transfer to secondary fermenter and ferment an additional 7 to 10 days. Bottle, using dry malt extract. Age in bottle 7 to 10 days.

OG: 1.048

Of doctors and medicines we have more than enough. What you may, for the love of God, send is some large quantity of beer.
—MESSAGE FROM NEW SOUTH WALES, AUSTRALIA, 1854

Jim and Gill's Barley Stout

THIS IS YET ANOTHER RECIPE from our friends Jim Glasheen and Gill Aharon—brewers extraordinaire. If you like your stouts a little roastier, you may want to increase the chocolate and roasted barley for this recipe.

8 POUNDS BRITISH 2-ROW MALT
1 ½ POUNDS FLAKED BARLEY
½ POUND DEXTRINE MALT
½ POUND CRYSTAL MALT (60L)
½ POUND CHOCOLATE MALT
½ POUND ROASTED BARLEY

1 OUNCE CLUSTER HOPS
 (BITTERING)
½ OUNCE CASCADE HOPS (AROMA)
1 PACKAGE IRISH ALE YEAST
½ POUND LACTOSE
1 CUP DRY MALT EXTRACT (PRIMING)

Mash grains for 90 minutes. Collect 6 gallons of wort. Add Cluster hops and boil for 1 hour. Turn off heat, add Cascade hops, and steep for 10 minutes. Cool wort and pitch yeast. Ferment for 10 to 14 days. Add lactose to bottling bucket, and bottle, using dry malt extract. Age in bottle for 10 to 14 days.

OG: 1.062

They who drink beer will think beer.
— WASHINGTON IRVING

Ninepin Stout

WHAT WAS THE MAGIC ALE that threw Rip Van Winkle into a forty-year sleep? Was it this? Brew up a batch and find out.

7 POUNDS PALE 2-ROW MALT
1 POUND CRYSTAL MALT (60L)
¾ POUND ROASTED BARLEY
½ POUND MALTED WHEAT
½ POUND FLAKED BARLEY
½ POUND CHOCOLATE MALT
1½ OUNCES KENT GOLDINGS HOPS
  (BITTERING)

1 OUNCE TETTNANGER HOPS
  (AROMA)
1 PACKAGE IRISH ALE YEAST
½ POUND LACTOSE
1¼ CUPS DRY MALT EXTRACT
  (PRIMING)

Mash grains for 60 to 90 minutes. Collect 6 gallons of wort. Add Kent Goldings hops and boil for 1 hour, adding the Tettnang-erer hops during the last 5 minutes. Cool wort and pitch yeast. Ferment for 7 to 10 days. Transfer to secondary fermenter and ferment an additional 5 to 7 days. Bottle, using lactose and dry malt extract. Age in bottle 10 to 14 days.

OG: 1.051

Lagers

From The Old House at Home
by Joseph Mitchell

McSorley's occupies the ground floor of a red-brick tenement at 15 Seventh Street, just off Cooper Square, where the Bowery ends. It was opened in 1854 and is the oldest saloon in New York City. In 88 years it has had four owners—an Irish immigrant, his son, a retired policeman, and his daughter—and all of them have been opposed to change. It is equipped with electricity, but the bar is stubbornly illuminated with a pair of gas lamps, which flicker fitfully and throw shadows on the low, cobwebby ceiling each time someone opens the street door. There is no cash register. Coins are dropped in soup bowls—one for nickels, one for dimes, one for quarters, and one for halves—and bills are kept in a rosewood cash box. It is a drowsy place; the bartenders never make a needless move, the customers nurse their mugs of ale, and the three clocks on the walls have not been in agreement for many years. The clientele is motley. It includes mechanics from the many garages in the neighborhood, salesmen from the restaurant-supply houses on Cooper Square, truck-drivers from Wanamaker's, interns from Bellevue, students from Cooper Union, and clerks from the row of second-hand bookshops just north of Astor Place. The *backbone of the clientele, however, is a rapidly thinning group of crusty old men, predominantly Irish, who have been drinking there since they were youths and now have a proprietary feeling about the place. Some of them have tiny pensions, and are alone in the world; they sleep in Bowery hotels and spend practically all their waking hours in McSorley's. A few of these veterans clearly remember John McSorley, the founder who died in 1910 at the age of 87. They refer to him as Old John, and they like to sit in rickety armchairs around the big belly stove which heats the place, gnaw on the stems of their pipes, and talk about him.*

Old John was quirky. He was normally affable but was subject to spells of unaccountable surliness during which he would refuse to answer when spoken to. He went bald in early manhood and began wearing scraggly, patriarchal sideburns before he was forty. Many photographs of him are in existence, and it is obvious that he had a lot of unassumed dignity. He patterned his saloon after a public house he had known in his hometown of Ireland— Omagh, in County Tyrone—and originally called it the Old House at Home; around 1908 the signboard blew down, and when he ordered a new one he changed the name to Mcsorley's Old Ale House. That is still the official name; customers never have called it anything but McSorley's. Old John believed it impossible for men to drink with tranquillity in the presence of women; there is a fine back room in the saloon, but for many years a sign was nailed on the street door, saying, "NOTICE, NO BACK ROOM IN HERE FOR LADIES." In McSorley's entire history, the only woman customer ever willingly admitted was an addled old peddler called Mother Fresh-Roasted, who claimed her husband died from the bite of a lizard in Cuba during the Spanish-American War and who went from saloon to saloon of the lower East Side for a couple of generations hawking peanuts, which she carried in her apron. On warm days, Old John would sell her an ale, and her esteem for him was such that she embroidered him a little American flag and gave it to him one Fourth of July; he had it framed and placed it on the wall above his brass-bound ale pump, and it is still there. When other women came in, Old John would hurry forward, make a bow, and say, "Madame, I'm sorry, but we don't serve ladies." If a woman insisted, Old John would take her by the elbow, head her toward the door, and say, "Madame, please don't provoke me. Make haste and get yourself off the premises, or I'll be obliged to forget you're a lady." This technique, pretty much word for word, is still in use.

I think this would be a good time for a beer.
—FRANKLIN D. ROOSEVELT

Basic Pilsner

THIS IS THE MOST STRAIGHTFORWARD of lagers, the German Pils. Aggressively hopped with German noble hops (Spalt and Saaz), it is light and dry and refreshing. It is the most popular style of beer consumed in Germany.

6⅔ POUNDS LIGHT MALT EXTRACT
2½ OUNCES SPALT HOPS
   (BITTERING)
1 OUNCE SAAZ HOPS (AROMA)

1 TEASPOON IRISH MOSS
1 PACKAGE MUNICH LAGER YEAST
¾ CUP CORN SUGAR (PRIMING)

Bring water to a boil and add malt extract and Spalt hops. Boil for 1 hour, adding the Saaz hops and Irish moss for the last 10 minutes. Cool wort and pitch yeast. Primary-ferment at 50 to 55 degrees for 5 to 7 days. Transfer to secondary fermenter. Lager for 3 to 4 weeks. Bottle, using corn sugar. Age in bottle for 7 to 10 days.

OG: 1.040

Two Lips

HEINEKEN HAS ESTABLISHED ITSELF AS one of the premier world brewers. Their export lager is the most widely consumed beer in the world. Our version of a Dutch lager is similar to the domestic style. Dutch malt extract lends authenticity.

4 POUNDS LAAGLANDER LIGHT MALT EXTRACT

2 POUNDS DRY LIGHT MALT EXTRACT

1½ OUNCES SAAZ HOPS (BITTERING)

½ OUNCE SAAZ HOPS (FLAVORING)

1 TEASPOON IRISH MOSS

1 PACKAGE DANISH LAGER YEAST

¾ CUP CORN SUGAR (PRIMING)

Boil malt extracts and 1½ ounces Saaz hops in water for 1 hour. Add the other ½ ounce of Saaz hops during the last 30 minutes of the boil, and Irish moss for last 5 minutes. Cool wort and pitch yeast. Primary-ferment at 50 to 55 degrees for 5 to 7 days. Transfer to secondary fermenter. Lager for 2 to 3 weeks. Bottle, using corn sugar. Age in bottle 7 to 10 days.

OG: 1.043

Clarifying Agents

Problem: you pour out a glass of tasty homebrew, hold it up to check the color, and it just looks cloudy. While not the end of the world, it can be annoying when you are showcasing your craft to your friends, or it can cost you some points in a contest. Basically, there are two things that cause haziness in a beer: suspended proteins and suspended yeast.

Protein haze is the most common clarity problem home-brewers will encounter. There are several ways to coax proteins out of your brew. You may have noticed that many of our recipes call for the addition of Irish moss at the end of the boil. This product is derived from seaweed and has a net negative charge that attracts the positive charge of the proteins in your wort. Together, they settle out as hot break. The use of a wort chiller (see Appendix) will further reduce proteins by encouraging coagulation, or cold break, during cooling. The most difficult protein haze to fight is chill haze. This is caused by further coagulation of protein when you cool your beer to drinking temperatures. While the process of lagering allows these proteins to settle during the weeks your brew sits in the fridge, most ales do not fare as well. There is a product called Polyclar that will reduce chill haze when added to the fermenter during the last few days of fermentation.

Suspended yeast is most often caused by pouring your beer too fast, thus stirring up the sediment at the bottom of the bottle. Since yeast is essential to bottle-conditioned homebrew, it would be unwise to eliminate it. But, if you have a kegging system, and would like to have your beer as clear as possible, there is a solution. Isinglass finings can be obtained from most homebrew suppliers. Though you probably don't want to know where this comes from (okay, it's fish bladders), its positive charge attracts negatively charged yeast cells quite nicely when it is added to the secondary fermentation at least one day prior to kegging.

Dingo-Ate-My-Baby Lager

KNOWN FOR THEIR LIGHT REFRESHING character, Australian lagers are crisp and cool. They have to be to stand up to hot, dry Australian summers. Australian malt extract and Pride of Ringwood hops, grown in Australia, are essential to maintain the authenticity.

6$\frac{2}{3}$ POUNDS AUSTRALIAN MALT
  EXTRACT
1 POUND LIGHT DRY MALT EXTRACT
2 OUNCES PRIDE OF RINGWOOD
  HOPS (BITTERING)

$\frac{1}{2}$ OUNCE PRIDE OF RINGWOOD
  HOPS (FLAVORING)
1 TEASPOON IRISH MOSS
1 PACKAGE PILSEN LAGER YEAST
$\frac{3}{4}$ CUP CORN SUGAR (PRIMING)

Bring water to a boil. Add the malt extracts and 2 ounces Pride of Ringwood hops. Boil for 1 hour, adding $\frac{1}{2}$ ounce Pride of Ringwood hops for the last 30 minutes, and Irish moss for last 5 minutes. Cool wort and pitch yeast. Primary-ferment at 50 to 55 degrees for 5 to 7 days. Transfer to secondary fermenter. Lager for 3 to 4 weeks. Bottle, using corn sugar. Age in bottle 10 to 14 days.

OG: 1.052

*The mouth of a perfectly happy man
is filled with beer.*
—ANCIENT EGYPTIAN PROVERB

One Helles of a Good Beer

THE MUNICH HELLES STYLE IS the king of German session beers. It is similar in ways to American lagers, possessing a crisp, clean quality, but because of the strict Reinheitsgebot law, this brew contains no adjuncts at all.

7 POUNDS ALEXANDER'S PALE MALT
  EXTRACT
1$\frac{1}{2}$ OUNCES HALLERTAUER HOPS
  (BITTERING)

$\frac{1}{2}$ OUNCE HALLERTAUER HOPS
  (AROMA)
1 PACKAGE MUNICH LAGER YEAST
$\frac{3}{4}$ CUP DRY MALT EXTRACT (PRIMING)

Combine Alexander's pale malt extract and 1½ ounces Hallertauer hops in water. Boil for 1 hour, adding ½ ounce Hallertauer hops for the last 10 minutes. Cool wort and pitch yeast. Primary-ferment at 50 to 55 degrees for 5 to 7 days. Transfer to secondary fermenter. Lager for 3 to 4 weeks. Bottle, using dry malt extract. Age in bottle 7 to 10 days.

OG: 1.040

Amazing Light Lager

WHEN WE INFORMED OUR PARENTS that we had decided to walk away from the chosen fields we had studied in college and devote ourselves to the beer business, we were met with something less than enthusiasm. Maura's mom became a little more enthused when one of her colleagues, Ed Lee, told her that he himself was a homebrewer and that the beer business was perhaps the hottest trend in America today. Ed gave us this recipe for the book. Thanks, Ed, for the recipe and the encouragement.

5 POUNDS LIGHT MALT EXTRACT	1 OUNCE SAAZ HOPS (DRY HOP)
1 POUND PALE 6-ROW MALT	1 TEASPOON IRISH MOSS
1 POUND FLAKED BARLEY	1 TEASPOON ASCORBIC ACID
1 OUNCE CASCADE HOPS	1 PACKAGE AMERICAN LAGER YEAST
(BITTERING)	¾ CUP CORN SUGAR (PRIMING)
1 OUNCE FUGGLES HOPS (AROMA)	

Place flaked barley and pale 6-row malt in water and steep at 155 degrees for 30 minutes. Remove spent grains, add malt extract and Cascade hops, and boil for 1 hour, adding the Irish moss for the last 10 minutes. Remove from heat, add Fuggles hops, and let steep for 10 minutes. Cool wort and pitch yeast. Ferment at 50 to 55 degrees for 3 to 5 days. Transfer to secondary fermenter and lager for 2 to 3 weeks, adding the Saaz hops for the last 7 days. Bottle, using ascorbic acid and corn sugar. Age in bottle 5 to 7 days.

OG: 1.038

*Give me a woman who truly loves beer,
and I will conquer the world.*

—KAISER WILHELM II

Dortmunder

THE DORTMUNDER STYLE IS NAMED after, you guessed it, the city of Dortmund in Germany. Its style falls somewhere between a Munich helles and a pilsner. It is less malty but hoppier than the Helles, and more malty and less bitter than a pilsner.

4 POUNDS ALEXANDER'S PALE MALT
  EXTRACT
3⅓ POUNDS LIGHT MALT EXTRACT
2 OUNCES HALLERTAUER HOPS
  (BITTERING)

1 OUNCE TETTNANGER HOPS
  (AROMA)
1 TEASPOON IRISH MOSS
1 PACKAGE BOHEMIAN LAGER YEAST
¾ CUP CORN SUGAR (PRIMING)

Add malt extracts and Hallertauer hops to boiling water and boil for 1 hour, adding Tettnanger hops and Irish moss during the last 10 minutes. Cool wort and pitch yeast. Primary-ferment at 50 to 55 degrees for 5 to 7 days. Transfer to secondary fermenter. Lager for 3 to 4 weeks. Bottle, using corn sugar. Age in bottle 7 to 10 days.

OG: 1.040

Hophead Lager

MANY OF OUR BEER-GUZZLING FRIENDS, whose fondness runs toward complex malt profiles, find our obsession with hops worthy of ridicule. What can we say, you are what you are. And so we wear the badge of their taunting proudly. Yes, we are indeed hopheads. Light and refreshing, this deep golden lager really lets the hops shine through.

6⅔ POUNDS LIGHT MALT EXTRACT
½ POUND CRYSTAL MALT (10L)
½ POUND CRYSTAL MALT (20L)
1½ OUNCES CENTENNIAL HOPS
  (BITTERING)
1 OUNCE HALLERTAUER HOPS
  (FLAVORING)

1 OUNCE CASCADE HOPS (DRY HOP)
1 OUNCE SAAZ HOPS (DRY HOP)
1 TEASPOON IRISH MOSS
1 PACKAGE CALIFORNIA LAGER
  YEAST
¾ CUP CORN SUGAR (PRIMING)

Place the crushed crystal malt in water and steep at 155 degrees for 30 minutes. Remove the spent grains and add the malt extract and Centennial hops. Boil for 1 hour, adding the Hallertauer hops at 30 minutes and the Irish moss for the last 10 minutes of the boil. Cool wort and pitch yeast. Primary-ferment at 50 to 55 degrees for 5 to 7 days. Transfer to secondary fermenter. Lager for 2 to 3 weeks, adding Cascade and Saaz hops for the last 7 to 10 days. Bottle, using corn sugar. Age in bottle 7 to 10 days.

OG: 1.046

'Twas a woman who drove me to drink,
and I never had the courtesy to thank her for it.
—W. C. FIELDS

American Cream Ale

DON'T LET THE TERM "ALE" fool you. The cream ale style at one time was brewed by combining beers that were fermented with ale and lager yeast, but today it is almost exclusively brewed as a lager. If you're feeling adventurous, try splitting the batch in two and fermenting one half with a lager yeast and one half with an ale yeast and then recombining them in a secondary fermenter.

5½ POUNDS ALEXANDER'S PALE
  MALT EXTRACT
2 POUNDS DRY MALT EXTRACT
½ POUND CRYSTAL MALT (20L)
1 OUNCE CASCADE HOPS
  (BITTERING)

1 OUNCE CASCADE HOPS
  (FLAVORING)
1 TEASPOON IRISH MOSS
1 PACKAGE AMERICAN LAGER YEAST
¾ CUP CORN SUGAR (PRIMING)

Place the crushed crystal malt in water and steep at 155 degrees for 30 minutes. Remove spent grains, add malt extracts, and bring to a boil. Add 1 ounce Cascade hops and boil for one hour. Add 1 ounce Cascade hops 30 minutes into the boil, and Irish moss for last 5 minutes. Cool wort and pitch yeast. Primary-ferment at 50 to 55 degrees for 5 to 7 days. Transfer to secondary. Lager for 3 to 4 weeks. Bottle, using corn sugar. Age in bottle 10 to 14 days.

OG: 1.048

Great-Grandma's Czech Pilsner

DURING PROHIBITION, HOMEBREW RIVALED BATHTUB gin as the most popular forbidden drink. If you look up your family tree, it is quite likely you will find a decent recipe or two in the branches. This recipe was created in memory of Paul's great-grandmother, Filomena Svihura, who was born near Prague and was known for her pilsner. Although her original recipe is lost, we have created an extract recipe that she would have appreciated.

6²/₃ POUNDS EXTRA PALE MALT
 EXTRACT
¹/₂ POUND MUNICH MALT
¹/₄ POUND CRYSTAL MALT
2¹/₂ OUNCES SAAZ HOPS (BITTERING)
1³/₄ OUNCES SAAZ HOPS
 (FLAVORING)

¹/₂ TEASPOON IRISH MOSS
1 PACKAGE CZECH PILS LAGER
 YEAST
³/₄ CUP CORN SUGAR (PRIMING)

Place crushed grains in water and steep at 155 degrees for 30 minutes. Remove spent grains and add malt extract. Bring to a boil, add 2¹/₂ ounces Saaz hops 15 minutes into the boil. Add 1³/₄ ounces Saaz hops 45 minutes into the boil. Add Irish moss for the last 10 minutes of the boil. Cool wort and pitch yeast. Primary-ferment at 50 to 55 degrees for 5 to 7 days. Transfer to secondary. Lager 2 to 3 weeks. Bottle, using corn sugar, and age 1 week.

OG: 1.043

*What's made Milwaukee famous
made a loser out of me.*
—JERRY LEE LEWIS

Rice and Easy Does It

RICE IS ONE OF THE most common adjuncts that go into beer. Examples range everywhere, from Tsing Tao in China, to Kirin in Japan, to Budweiser in St. Louis. Rice beer is a very smooth, light beer that finishes very cleanly.

4 POUNDS ALEXANDER'S PALE MALT
   EXTRACT
3 POUNDS RICE EXTRACT
1 OUNCE KENT GOLDINGS HOPS
   (BITTERING)

½ OUNCE CASCADE HOPS (AROMA)
1 ½ TEASPOONS IRISH MOSS
1 PACKAGE AMERICAN LAGER YEAST
¾ CUP CORN SUGAR (PRIMING)

Combine malt extract, rice extract, and Kent Goldings hops in water. Boil for 1 hour. Add Cascade hops and Irish moss during the last 5 minutes of the boil. Cool wort and pitch yeast. Primary-ferment at 50 to 55 degrees for 5 to 7 days. Transfer to secondary fermenter. Lager for 3 to 4 weeks. Bottle, using corn sugar. Age in the bottle 7 days.

OG: 1.039

Märzen Madness

THIS MÄRZEN IS RICH AND satisfying, despite its mad departure from the Reinheitsgebot, or German beer purity law. The deep, glowing orange color is a result of the Munich malt and the translucence of honey.

3⅓ POUNDS LIGHT MALT EXTRACT
3⅓ POUNDS AMBER MALT EXTRACT
2 POUNDS ORANGE-BLOSSOM HONEY
½ POUND MUNICH MALT
½ POUND CRYSTAL MALT (40L)
1½ OUNCES SAAZ HOPS (BITTERING)

½ OUNCE SAAZ HOPS (AROMA)
1 TEASPOON IRISH MOSS
1 PACKAGE MUNICH LAGER YEAST
1 CUP ORANGE-BLOSSOM HONEY
  (PRIMING)

Place the crushed grains in water and steep at 155 degrees for 30 minutes. Remove spent grains and add malt extracts, honey, and 1½ ounces Saaz hops. Boil for 1 hour. Add ½ ounce Saaz hops and Irish moss for the last 10 minutes of the boil. Cool wort and pitch yeast. Primary-ferment at 50 to 55 degrees for 5 to 7 days. Transfer to secondary fermenter. Lager for 2 to 3 weeks. Bottle, using 1 cup honey. Age in bottle 10 to 14 days.

OG: 1.050

*Mike Hammer drinks beer
because I can't spell Cognac.*
—MICKEY SPILLANE

Golden Pils

THE ADDITION OF BROWN SUGAR to the pilsner style produces a beer that is less dry than the classic pilsner. Light brown sugar is recommended to maintain the correct color for the pilsner style.

8 POUNDS ALEXANDER'S PALE MALT
  EXTRACT
½ POUND CRYSTAL MALT (20L)
1 POUND LIGHT OR DARK BROWN
  SUGAR
1 OUNCE HALLERTAUER HOPS
  (BITTERING)

1 OUNCE TETTNANGER HOPS
  (FLAVORING)
1½ OUNCES SAAZ HOPS (AROMA)
1 TEASPOON IRISH MOSS
1 PACKAGE PILSEN LAGER YEAST
¾ CUP CORN SUGAR (PRIMING)

Place the crushed crystal malt in water and steep at 155 degrees for 30 minutes. Remove spent grains, add malt extract and brown sugar, and bring to a boil. Add Hallertauer hops and boil for 1 hour. Add Tettnanger hops 30 minutes into the boil. Add Saaz hops and Irish moss for the last 10 minutes of the boil. Cool wort and pitch yeast. Primary-ferment at 50 to 55 degrees for 5 to 7 days. Transfer to secondary fermenter. Lager for 3 to 4 weeks. Bottle, using corn sugar. Age in bottle 10 to 14 days.

OG: 1.049

In the Midnight Hour

THIS GERMAN BLACK BEER, OR Schwarzbier, is perhaps the darkest of all lagers. Schwarzbier, however, does not possess the deep roasted flavor usually associated with dark beers. It is low in bitterness and very drinkable—more of a session beer than its dark counterparts.

6²/₃ POUNDS DARK MALT EXTRACT
1 POUND CRYSTAL MALT (120 L)
¹/₄ POUND BLACK PATENT MALT
2 OUNCES CHOCOLATE MALT
2 OUNCES HALLERTAUER HOPS
 (BITTERING)

¹/₂ OUNCE NORTHERN BREWER HOPS
 (AROMA)
1 PACKAGE BAVARIAN LAGER YEAST
1 ¹/₄ CUPS DRY MALT EXTRACT
 (PRIMING)

Place crushed crystal malt, black patent malt, and chocolate malt in water and steep at 155 degrees for 30 minutes. Remove spent grains, add dark malt extract and Hallertauer hops, and boil for 1 hour, adding Northern Brewer hops for the last 10 minutes. Cool wort and pitch yeast. Primary-ferment at 50 to 55 degrees for 5 to 7 days. Transfer to secondary fermenter. Lager for 3 to 4 weeks. Bottle, using dry malt extract. Age in bottle 2 to 3 weeks.

OG: 1.045

Carbonation

Most carbonation problems can be attributed to the improper amount of priming sugar. If this isn't your problem, and you're sure you used the right amount, there are other contributing factors.

To prevent overcarbonation, make sure your beer has fully fermented. Beer that is not finished will continue to ferment in the bottle and produce additional carbonation. Yeast infections can also cause overcarbonation, so keep things sanitary. If overcarbonation is a consistent problem, check the levels of iron in your water.

Undercarbonation is almost always attributed to underpriming your beer. The most common cause, other than underpriming, is an improper seal on your caps. Be sure not to overboil your caps when sterilizing and be sure your capper is providing you with a proper seal. Cold storage temperatures may inhibit ale yeast, leaving it dormant and unable to carbonate. Long lagering may also leave you without enough viable yeast to carbonate.

And in my innocence, I once thought that beer drinking in England was carried to excess, but I was mistaken, English men are in the infant class —in the ABCs in acquiring a German's education in the practice of beer drinking.

—HENRY RUGGLES

Munich Dunkel

MUNICH IS THE CAPITAL OF Bavaria, a state in southeastern Germany, and the birthplace of lagering. This beer is simply known as *Dunkel* in Germany, but we wanted to pay tribute to one of the greatest cities in the history of beer. Nothing can compare to the beer gardens and beer halls of Munich, where beer is not just a beverage but a way of life. Drink deeply of this dunkel, close your eyes, and listen carefully. Is that an oompah band I hear?

7 POUNDS AMBER MALT EXTRACT
1 POUND DRY MALT EXTRACT
½ POUND CHOCOLATE MALT
½ POUND CRYSTAL MALT (80L)
1½ OUNCES CENTENNIAL HOPS
(BITTERING)

½ OUNCE CENTENNIAL HOPS
(AROMA)
1 PACKAGE MUNICH LAGER YEAST
1¼ CUPS DARK DRY MALT EXTRACT
(PRIMING)

Spread grains on a cookie sheet and toast in a 350-degree oven for 10 minutes. Crush grain. Place grains in water and steep at 155 degrees for 30 minutes. Remove spent grains, add extracts, and bring to a boil. Add 1½ ounces Centennial hops 15 minutes into the boil. Add ½ ounce during the last 10 minutes. Cool wort and pitch yeast. Primary-ferment at 50 to 55 degrees for 5 to 7 days. Transfer to secondary fermenter. Lager 2 to 3 weeks. Bottle, using dark dry malt extract. Age in bottle 7 to 10 days.

OG: 1.048

Viva Vienna!

THOUGH ORIGINATING IN VIENNA, THIS style lives on only in Mexico, of all places, most notably with Dos Equis and Negra Modelo. While this style is a dying breed, it is a very easy and satisfying homebrew.

6⅔ POUNDS AMBER MALT EXTRACT

½ POUND CRYSTAL MALT (40L)

½ POUND CHOCOLATE MALT

1 OUNCE PERLE HOPS (BITTERING)

½ OUNCE TETTNANGER HOPS
   (AROMA)

1 PACKAGE MUNICH LAGER YEAST

1¼ CUPS DRY MALT EXTRACT
   (PRIMING)

Place crushed crystal malt and chocolate malt in water and steep at 155 degrees for 30 minutes. Remove spent grains and add amber malt extract and Perle hops. Boil for 1 hour, adding Tettnanger hops for the last 15 minutes. Cool wort and pitch yeast. Primary-ferment at 50 to 55 degrees for 5 to 7 days. Transfer to secondary fermenter. Lager for 3 to 4 weeks. Bottle, using dry malt extract. Age in bottle for 2 to 3 weeks.

OG: 1.044

*The Puritanical nonsense of excluding children —
and therefor to some extent women — from pubs
has turned these places into mere boozing
shops instead of the family gathering places
they ought to be.*
— GEORGE ORWELL

Fest Haus Märzen

TRADITIONALLY BREWED IN MARCH AND often served at Oktoberfest, Märzen is sweet and malty, with a rich orange color. This recipe uses a partial mash in order to get the authentic color from the Munich malt.

3 POUNDS MUNICH MALT

2 POUNDS PILSNER MALT

½ POUND CRYSTAL MALT (40L)

3⅓ POUNDS LIGHT MALT EXTRACT

1½ OUNCES HALLERTAUER HOPS
  (BITTERING)

1 OUNCE SAAZ HOPS (AROMA)

1 PACKAGE BAVARIAN LAGER YEAST

¾ CUP CORN SUGAR (PRIMING)

Mash crushed Munich malt, pilsner malt, and crystal malt for 60 to 90 minutes. Collect 3 gallons of wort. Add 3 gallons of water, malt extract, and Hallertauer hops, and boil for 1 hour. Add the Saaz hops during the last 15 minutes of the boil. Cool wort and pitch yeast. Primary-ferment at 50 to 55 degrees for 5 to 7 days. Transfer to secondary fermenter. Lager for 3 to 4 weeks. Bottle, using corn sugar. Age in bottle for 7 to 10 days.

OG: 1.052

Maple Leaf

DON'T EVEN THINK OF USING Log Cabin for the maple syrup in this Canadian lager. The preservatives in artificial syrup will wreak havoc on your yeast. The addition of the syrup late in the boil adds sweetness and body without overpowering.

6 POUNDS CANADIAN 2-ROW PALE
  MALT

1 POUND MUNICH MALT

1 POUND TORREFIED WHEAT

2 CUPS PURE MAPLE SYRUP

1½ OUNCES FUGGLES HOPS
  (BITTERING)

1 OUNCE FUGGLES HOPS
  (FLAVORING)

1 PACKAGE AMERICAN LAGER YEAST

1½ CUPS PURE MAPLE SYRUP
  (PRIMING)

Mash crushed grains for 60 to 90 minutes. Collect 6 gallons of wort. Add 1½ ounces Fuggles hops and boil for 1 hour, adding 1 ounce Fuggles hops 30 minutes into the boil. Add 2 cups maple syrup during the last 10 minutes of the boil. Cool wort and pitch yeast. Primary-ferment at 50 to 55 degrees for 5 to 7 days. Transfer to secondary fermenter. Lager for 2 to 3 weeks. Bottle using 1½ cups maple syrup. Age in bottle 7 to 10 days.

OG: 1.050

A woman is a lot like a beer.
They smell good, they look good, and
you'd step over your own mother to get one.
—HOMER SIMPSON

Feels Like the First Time

THE ONE THING THAT MOST American beer aficionados have in common is that their first beer-drinking experience was with one variety or another of common American lager. An option for this recipe is to tape one beechwood chip to the outside of your secondary fermenter for 1 hour at some point during fermentation. Why one chip? Why only one hour? Why taped to the outside? Well, we thought that as a homebrewer you would like to enjoy all of the benefits from beechwood aging that the pros do. Enjoy the stroll down memory lane.

4 POUNDS PILSEN MALT
4 POUNDS WHITE RICE (SOAKED IN
   COLD WATER FOR 24 HOURS)
2 OUNCES FLAKED MAIZE
1 OUNCE SAAZ HOPS (BITTERING)

½ OUNCE CASCADE HOPS (AROMA)
1 TEASPOON IRISH MOSS
1 PACKAGE PILSEN LAGER YEAST
¾ CUP CORN SUGAR (PRIMING)

Mash crushed grains for 60 to 90 minutes. Collect 6 gallons of wort. Bring to a boil and add Saaz hops. Boil for 1 hour, adding the Cascade hops and Irish moss during the last 5 minutes. Cool wort and pitch yeast. Ferment for 5 to 7 days at 50 to 55 degrees. Transfer to secondary fermenter and lager for 2 to 3 weeks. Bottle, using corn sugar. Age in bottle 5 to 7 days.

OG: 1.040

Eat My Schwarzbier

DARK AND TOASTY, YET LIGHT and refreshing. It's easy to understand why this simple yet satisfying style, seldom available commercially in the United States, has captured the attention of homebrewers.

7 POUNDS PILSNER MALT

1 POUND CRYSTAL MALT (80L)

½ POUND BLACK PATENT MALT

½ POUND MUNICH MALT

¼ POUND CHOCOLATE MALT

¼ POUND ROASTED BARLEY

1 CUP MOLASSES

1¼ OUNCES PERLE HOPS
  (BITTERING)

½ OUNCE PERLE HOPS (FLAVORING)

½ OUNCE PERLE HOPS (AROMA)

1 PACKAGE MUNICH LAGER YEAST

1¼ CUPS DRY MALT EXTRACT
  (PRIMING)

Mash crushed grains for 60 to 90 minutes. Collect 6 gallons of wort. Add molasses and 1¼ ounces Perle hops and boil for 1 hour, adding ½ ounce Perle hops 30 minutes into the boil. Remove from heat, add ½ ounce Perle hops, cover, and steep for 15 minutes. Cool wort and pitch yeast. Primary-ferment at 50 to 55 degrees for 5 to 7 days. Transfer to secondary fermenter. Lager for 2 to 3 weeks. Bottle, using dry malt extract. Age in bottle 7 to 10 days.

OG: 1.054

Up to the age of forty, eating is beneficial; after forty, drinking.

—THE TALMUD

Roll-in-the-Hay Wheat Lager

FOR THAT GROUP OF FRIENDS that we all have—you know, the ones that "like light beers"—here is a recipe that is sure to please. None of the flavors come through as overpowering, but flavorless it's not. This is an ideal summer beer.

4 POUNDS 2-ROW KLAGES MALT

3 POUNDS MALTED WHEAT

1 POUND TORREFIED WHEAT

1 1/2 OUNCES PERLE HOPS
  (BITTERING)

1 OUNCE LIBERTY HOPS (FLAVOR)

1 PACKAGE AMERICAN LAGER YEAST

3/4 CUP CORN SUGAR (PRIMING)

Mash crushed grains for 60 to 90 minutes. Collect 6 gallons of wort. Add Perle hops and boil for 1 hour, adding Liberty hops after 30 minutes. Cool wort and pitch yeast. Lager for 2 to 3 weeks. Bottle, using corn sugar. Age in bottle 7 to 10 days.

OG: 1.044

Green Meadow Pilsner

THE TOWN OF PLZEN, OR Green Meadows, in Czechoslovakia was the home of the first pilsners. This lager, characterized by a golden color, creamy, dense head, and the bitterness of Saaz hops, is brewed in the Bohemian tradition.

8 POUNDS PILSNER MALT

1/2 POUND CARA-PILS MALT

1/4 POUND FLAKED BARLEY

2 OUNCES CRYSTAL MALT (20L)

2 OUNCES SAAZ HOPS (BITTERING)

1 OUNCE SAAZ HOPS (AROMA)

1 TEASPOON IRISH MOSS

1 PACKAGE CZECH PILS YEAST

1 1/4 CUPS DRY MALT EXTRACT

Mash crushed grains for 60 to 90 minutes. Collect 6 gallons of wort and bring to a boil. Add 2 ounces of Saaz hops and boil for 1 hour, adding 1 ounce of Saaz hops and Irish moss during the last 10 minutes. Cool wort and pitch yeast. Primary-ferment at 50 to 55 degrees for 5 to 7 days. Transfer to secondary fermenter. Lager for 3 to 4 weeks. Bottle, using dry malt extract. Age in bottle 2 to 3 weeks.

OG: 1.055

*They're drinkin' home brew from a wooden cup,
The folks were dancin' there got all shook up.*
—CHUCK BERRY, *ROCK 'N' ROLL MUSIC*

Marvin's Martian Märzen

WHY DID WE CALL THIS recipe Marvin's Martian Märzen? Simple, so we could tell you that this all-grain märzen is *out of this world.* Okay, now that you've stopped groaning, go brew a batch of this beer!

6 POUNDS GERMAN 2-ROW
  PALE MALT
2 POUNDS MUNICH MALT
1½ POUNDS CRYSTAL MALT (40L)
1 POUND TOASTED MALT (SEE
  BREWER'S TIP, P. 41)
1½ OUNCES SPALT HOPS
  (BITTERING)

½ OUNCE TETTNANGER HOPS
  (FLAVORING)
½ OUNCE TETTNANGER HOPS
  (AROMA)
1 PACKAGE GERMAN LAGER YEAST
¾ CUP CORN SUGAR (PRIMING)

Mash crushed grains for 60 to 90 minutes. Collect 6 gallons of wort. Add Spalt hops and boil for 1 hour, adding ½ ounce Tettnanger hops after 30 minutes. At the end of the boil, shut off heat, add ½ ounce Tettnanger hops, and steep for 10 minutes. Cool wort and pitch yeast. Primary-ferment at 50 to 55 degrees for 5 to 7 days. Transfer to secondary fermenter. Lager for 2 to 3 weeks. Bottle, using corn sugar. Age in bottle 7 to 10 days.

OG: 1.054

Snowball's Chance in Helles

ACTUALLY, THE ODDS ARE that this beer will turn out pretty good. Never tried all-grain? Never tried lagering? Jump in with both feet and go for it with this one.

6 POUNDS PALE GERMAN 2-ROW MALT

2 POUNDS GERMAN MUNICH MALT

1 TEASPOON GYPSUM

1 1/2 OUNCES HALLERTAUER HOPS (BITTERING)

1/2 OUNCE SPALT HOPS (FLAVORING)

1/2 TEASPOON IRISH MOSS

1 PACKAGE MUNICH LAGER YEAST

3/4 CUP CORN SUGAR (PRIMING)

Mash crushed grains with gypsum for 90 minutes. Collect 6 gallons of wort and bring to a boil. Add Hallertauer hops after the first 15 minutes of the boil. Add Spalt hops after 45 minutes. Add Irish moss during final 10 minutes of boil. Cool wort and pitch the yeast. Primary-ferment at 50 to 55 degrees for 5 to 7 days. Transfer to secondary fermenter. Lager 3 to 4 weeks. Bottle, using corn sugar. Age for 1 week.

OG: 1.043

BREWER'S TIP

Converting All-Grain to Extract and Vice Versa

It is fairly simple to convert recipes from all-grain to extract and vice versa. It is not an exact science or an exact formula but it will put you in the ballpark.

A couple of simple formulas will give you the conversion for fermentables, but not specialty grains. When using a malt extract, a percentage of specialty grains is added to the mash from which the extract is produced. Unfortunately, the extract producers fail to give you the proportions of specialty grains added, so there is some experimentation and guesswork involved.

When converting all-grain to extract, a good rule of thumb is always to use pale or light malt extract, which will allow you to keep your specialty grains basically the same. Using a dark or amber extract will leave you with some guesswork in terms of how much to cut back on the specialty grains.

When going the other way, from extract to all-grain, it gets a little trickier. For example, if the recipe calls for dark malt extract, you'll have to add an extra half pound or so of dark specialty malt to your grain bill to give you the proper color. Black patent will give you color without the roast flavor, but if you'd like a little extra roastiness, add chocolate or roasted barley. Or, if the recipe calls for amber malt extract, you'll have to add some extra crystal malt or a small amount of chocolate malt. In short, it's up to you and will take some trial and error.

Below is a listing of conversions to go both ways.

ALL-GRAIN TO EXTRACT
Amount of pale malt × .8125 = amount of liquid malt extract
(example: 8 lbs. pale malt × .8125 = 6.5 lbs. liquid malt extract)
Amount of pale malt × .6875 = amount of dry malt extract
(example: 8 lbs. pale malt × .6875 = 5.5 lbs. dry malt extract)
Amount of wheat malt × .937 = amount of liquid wheat malt extract
(example: 6.5 lbs. wheat malt × .937 = 6.1 lbs. liquid malt extract)

EXTRACT TO ALL-GRAIN
Amount of liquid malt extract × 1.23 = amount of pale malt
(example: 6.6 lbs. liquid malt extract × 1.23 = 8.1 lbs. pale malt)
Amount of dry malt extract × 1.45 = amount of pale malt
(example: 5 lbs. dry malt extract × 1.45 = 7.25 lbs. pale malt)
Amount of liquid wheat extract × 1.07 = amount of wheat malt
(example: 6.6 lbs. wheat extract X 1.07 = 7 lbs. wheat malt)

Listening to someone who brews their own beer is like listening to a religious fanatic talk about the day he saw the light.

— ROSS MURRAY, *MONTREAL GAZETTE*

Great White North

BEFORE THE MICROBREW REVOLUTION TOOK hold, Canadian lagers like Moosehead and Molson were considered "the good stuff." Possessing a more interesting hop profile than the lagers produced by their neighbors south of the border, Canadian-style lagers are crisp, refreshing, and very drinkable.

6 POUNDS CANADIAN 2-ROW MALT
½ POUND FLAKED BARLEY
1 ½ OUNCES PRIDE OF RINGWOOD HOPS (BITTERING)

1 OUNCE KENT GOLDINGS HOPS (FLAVOR)
1 PACKAGE AMERICAN LAGER YEAST
¾ CUP CORN SUGAR (PRIMING)

Mash crushed grains for 60 to 90 minutes. Collect 6 gallons of wort. Add Pride of Ringwood hops and boil for 1 hour, adding Kent Goldings hops for the last 30 minutes. Cool wort and pitch yeast. Primary-ferment at 50 to 55 degrees for 5 to 7 days. Transfer to secondary fermenter. Lager for 2 to 3 weeks. Bottle, using corn sugar. Age in bottle 10 to 14 days.

OG: 1.040

Red Herring

THIS RED LAGER IS A premium version of the familiar commercial variety. No adjuncts are added and more specialty grains are used, resulting in a light pilsner with some real flavor, not just a touch of red color.

6 POUNDS 2-ROW PALE MALT
½ POUND CRYSTAL MALT (20L)
1 OUNCE ROASTED BARLEY
1 OUNCE KENT GOLDINGS HOPS
 (BITTERING)

½ OUNCE WILLAMETTE HOPS
 (FLAVOR)
1 TEASPOON IRISH MOSS
1 PACKAGE AMERICAN LAGER YEAST
¾ CUP CORN SUGAR (PRIMING)

Mash crushed grains for 60 to 90 minutes. Collect 6 gallons of wort. Add Kent Goldings hops and boil for 1 hour, adding ½ ounce Willamette hops 30 minutes into the boil. Add Irish moss during the last 10 minutes of the boil. Cool wort and pitch yeast. Primary-ferment at 50 to 55 degrees for 5 to 7 days. Transfer to secondary fermenter. Lager for 2 to 3 weeks. Bottle, using corn sugar. Age in bottle 7 to 10 days.

OG: 1.039

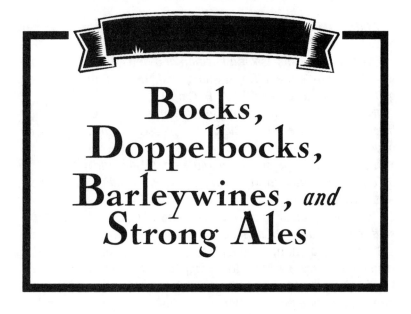

Bocks, Doppelbocks, Barleywines, and Strong Ales

From 1984, by George Orwell

Hurriedly, lest he should have time to become frightened, he descended the steps and crossed the narrow street. It was madness, of course. As usual, there was no definite rule against talking to proles and frequenting their pubs, but it was far too unusual an action to pass unnoticed. If the patrols appeared he might plead an attack of faintness, but it was not likely that they would believe him. He pushed open the door, and a hideous cheesy smell of sour beer hit him in the face. As he entered the din of voices dropped to about half its volume. Behind his back he could feel everyone eyeing his blue overalls. A game of darts which was going on at the other end of the room interrupted itself for perhaps as much as thirty seconds. The old man whom he had followed was standing at the bar, having some kind of altercation with the barman, a large, stout, hook-nosed young man with enormous forearms. A knot of others, standing round with glasses in their hands, were watching the scene.

"I arst you civil enough, didn't I?" said the old man, straightening his shoulders pugnaciously. "You telling me you ain't got a pint mug in the 'ole bleeding boozer?"

"And what in the hell's name is a pint?" said the barman, leaning forward with the tips of his fingers on the counter.

" *'Ark at 'im! Calls 'isself a barman and don't know what a pint is! Why, a pint's the 'alf of a quart, and there's four quarts to a gallon. 'Ave to teach you the A, B, C next."*

"Never heard of 'em," said the barman shortly. *"Litre and half-litre—that's all we serve. There's the glasses on the shelf in front of you."*

"I likes a pint," persisted the old man. *"You could'a drawed me off a pint easy enough. We didn't 'ave these bleeding litres when I was a young man."*

"When you were a young man we were all living in the treetops," said the barman, with a glance at the other customers.

There was a shout of laughter, and the uneasiness caused by Winston's entry seemed to disappear. The old man's white-stubbled face had flushed pink. He turned away, muttering to himself, and bumped into Winston. Winston caught him gently by the arm.

"May I offer you a drink?" he said.

"You're a gent," said the other, straightening his shoulder again. He appeared not to have noticed Winston's blue overalls. *"Pint!"* he added aggressively to the barman. *"Pint of wallop."*

The barman swished two half-litres of dark-brown beer into thick glasses which he had rinsed in a bucket under the counter. Beer was the only drink you could get in prole pubs. The proles were supposed not to drink gin, though in practice they could get hold of it easily enough. The game of darts was in full swing again, and the knot of men at the bar had begun talking about lottery tickets. Winston's presence was forgotten for a moment. There was a deal table under the window where he and the old man could talk without fear of being overheard. It was horribly danger-ous, but at any rate there was no telescreen in the room, a point he had made sure of as soon as he came in.

" *'E could'a drawed me off a pint,"* grumbled the old man as he settled down behind his glass. *"A 'alf-litre ain't enough. It don't satisfy. And a 'ole litre's too much. It starts my bladder running. Let alone the price."*

"You must have seen great changes since you were a young man," said Winston tentatively.

The old man's pale blue eyes moved from the darts board to the bar, and from the bar to the door of the Gents, as though it were in the bar-room that he expected the changes to have occurred.

"The beer was better," he said finally. "And cheaper! When I was a young man, mild beer—wallop, we used to call it—was fourpence a pint. That was before the war, or course."

"Which war was that?" said Winston.

"It's all wars," said the old man vaguely. He took up his glass, and his shoulders straightened again. " 'Ere's wishing you the very best of 'ealth!"

In his lean throat the sharp-pointed Adam's apple made a surprisingly rapid up-and-down movement, and the beer vanished. Winston went to the bar and came back with two more half-litres. The old man appeared to have forgotten his prejudice against drinking a full litre.

Beer was not made to be moralized about, but to be drunk.

—THEODORE MAYNARD

Basic Helles Bock

THIS IS A VERY GOOD beginner recipe that packs an impressive wallop. An ideal late-fall, early-winter brew.

8 POUNDS ALEXANDER'S PALE MALT
   EXTRACT
½ POUND CRYSTAL MALT (40L)
¼ POUND CRYSTAL MALT (80L)
2 OUNCES HALLERTAUER HOPS
   (BITTERING)

1 TEASPOON IRISH MOSS
1 PACKAGE BAVARIAN LAGER YEAST
¾ CUP CORN SUGAR (PRIMING)

Place crushed crystal malts in water and steep at 155 degrees for 30 minutes. Remove spent grains and add malt extract and Hallertauer hops. Boil for 1 hour, adding Irish moss for last 10 minutes. Cool wort and pitch yeast. Primary-ferment at 50 to 55 degrees for 5 to 7 days. Transfer to secondary fermenter. Lager for 4 to 6 weeks. Bottle, using corn sugar. Age in bottle 7 to 10 days.

OG: 1.059

Ein Bock

IT IS THOUGHT THAT THE original bock beers came from Einbeck, Germany. This recipe is our attempt to recreate those beers. In the 1200s, when the style is thought to have been developed, wheat malt was widely used and lagering had not yet been invented. We thought a 60/40 wheat malt extract to barley malt extract ratio, and German ale yeast would be the best approximation.

6⅔ POUNDS IREKS WHEAT MALT EXTRACT (100 PERCENT)
4 POUNDS AMBER MALT EXTRACT
½ POUND GERMAN PALE 2-ROW MALT
½ POUND CHOCOLATE MALT
1 OUNCE HALLERTAUER HOPS (BITTERING)

½ OUNCE HALLERTAUER HOPS (FLAVORING)
1 PACKAGE GERMAN ALE YEAST
1¼ CUPS DARK DRY MALT EXTRACT (PRIMING)

Place crushed grains in water and steep at 155 degrees for 30 minutes. Remove spent grains and add Ireks and amber malt extract. Bring to a boil and add 1 ounce Hallertauer hops. Add ½ ounce Hallertauer hops 30 minutes into the boil. Cool wort and pitch yeast. Ferment 10 to 14 days. Transfer to secondary fermenter and ferment an additional 7 to 10 days. Bottle, using dark dry malt extract. Age 10 to 14 days.

OG: 1.068

Keep your libraries, keep your penal institutions, keep your insane asylums . . . give me beer. You think man needs rule, he needs beer. The world does not need morals, it needs beer. It does not need your lectures and charity. The souls of men have been fed with indigestibles, but the soul could make use of beer.

—HENRY MILLER, "MAKE BEER FOR MAN"

American Bock

AS WITH MANY AMERICANIZED VERSIONS of other beer styles, one of the most notable characteristics of American bock is the addition of more hops. As with the German Dunkel bock, any toasted quality from the roasted malt is almost nonexistent. Many commercially available American dark beers fall into this category.

6⅔ POUNDS LIGHT MALT EXTRACT

2 POUNDS DARK DRY MALT EXTRACT

1 POUND CRYSTAL MALT (40L)

2 OUNCES CHOCOLATE MALT

2 OUNCES TETTNANGER HOPS
  (BITTERING)

1 OUNCE CASCADE HOPS (AROMA)

1 PACKAGE AMERICAN LAGER YEAST

¾ CUP CORN SUGAR (PRIMING)

Place crushed crystal malt and chocolate malt in water and steep at 155 degrees for 30 minutes. Remove spent grains and add malt extracts and Tettnanger hops. Boil for 1 hour, adding the Cascade hops for the last 10 minutes. Cool wort and pitch yeast. Primary-ferment at 50 to 55 degrees for 5 to 7 days. Transfer to secondary fermenter. Lager for 3 to 4 weeks. Bottle, using corn sugar. Age in bottle for 7 to 10 days.

OG: 1.063

The Three Enemies of Beer: Heat, Light, and Oxygen

If stored properly, most homebrew will keep up to 12 months (or longer for high-gravity beers). Use common sense. Don't leave a case of homebrew in your garage until the Fourth of July barbecue and expect it to be as good as when you brewed it in March. If you have a cellar, store it there. Cool temperatures of 50 to 60 degrees are fine. If you don't have a cellar, store your beer in a cool closet, or better yet the refrigerator.

To combat light, brown bottles are best. Green and clear bottles allow light to react with certain hop compounds to produce what has been described as a skunklike odor and flavor. Exposure for as little as one hour can produce unpleasant results. If you use clear or green glass bottles, store your beer in well-darkened areas. (If you are hooked on Grölsch swing-top bottles, look for Fischer d'Alsace. These brown bottles also have swing tops, and they are bigger than the green Grölsch bottles.)

The last enemy, oxygen, is the hardest to battle. There is very little you can do to prevent oxidation, which will result in a stale-tasting beer. Fill your bottles as much as you can. The less air space, the less oxygen there is to harm your beer (zero air space will inhibit carbonation, so find a happy medium). For those extremely concerned about oxidation, oxygen-absorbent caps can be used.

Tarheel Tarwebok

NOT TO BE OUTDONE BY their Tobacco Road rivals (see Blue Devil Brew, p. 123), the University of North Carolina won the NCAA Men's Basketball Championship in 1993. In consideration of equal time, this Dutch wheat bock was created to commemorate the Tarheels' achievement. Why a bock? Well, *bock* means "goat," and their mascot is sort of like one. . . .

4 POUNDS AMBER MALT EXTRACT
3 POUNDS IREKS WHEAT MALT
  EXTRACT (100 PERCENT)
1 POUND CRYSTAL MALT (20L)
½ POUND CHOCOLATE MALT
1 TEASPOON GYPSUM

2 OUNCES FUGGLES HOPS
  (BITTERING)
½ TEASPOON IRISH MOSS
1 PACKAGE MUNICH LAGER YEAST
¾ CUP CORN SUGAR (PRIMING)

Place crushed grains and gypsum in water and steep at 155 degrees for 30 minutes. Remove spent grains and add malt extracts. Bring to a boil, add Fuggles hops. Add Irish moss for the last 10 minutes of the boil. Cool wort and pitch yeast. Primary-ferment at 50 to 55 degrees for 2 to 3 weeks. Transfer to secondary fermenter. Lager for 2 weeks. Bottle, using corn sugar, and age another week.

OG: 1.050

For when the lepers she nursed implored her for beer and there was none to be had, she changed the water which was used for the bath into an excellent beer, by the sheer strength of her blessing, and dealt it out to the thirsty in plenty.
—FROM *THE LIFE OF ST. BRIGID*

Dunkel Bock

THE DARK VERSION OF BOCK beer differs from other dark beers in that it contains little or no trace of the toasted or burnt flavor from the roasted malts. Hops character is also very low.

6⅔ POUNDS AMBER MALT EXTRACT
2 POUNDS DARK DRY MALT EXTRACT
1 POUND CRYSTAL MALT (80L)
½ POUND MUNICH MALT
2 OUNCES CHOCOLATE MALT
2 OUNCES BLACK PATENT MALT
1 OUNCE PERLE HOPS (BITTERING)

½ OUNCE HALLERTAUER HOPS
   (FLAVOR)
½ OUNCE HALLERTAUER HOPS
   (AROMA)
1 PACKAGE PILSEN LAGER YEAST
1¼ CUPS DRY MALT EXTRACT
   (PRIMING)

Place crushed grains in water and steep at 155 degrees for 30 minutes. Remove spent grains, and add amber malt extract, dark dry malt extract, and Perle hops. Boil for 1 hour, adding ½ ounce of Hallertauer hops after 30 minutes and ½ ounce Hallertauer hops after 50 minutes. Cool wort and pitch yeast. Primary-ferment at 50 to 55 degrees for 5 to 7 days. Transfer to secondary fermenter. Lager for 5 to 8 weeks. Bottle, using dry malt extract. Age in bottle 2 to 3 weeks.

OG: 1.069

Mai Honey Bock

MAI BOCKS ARE TRADITIONALLY HOPPIER than standard bocks, and can even be dry-hopped and still remain within the style. The addition of honey is untraditional but contributes some wonderful flavors.

3 POUNDS MUNICH MALT
2 POUNDS VIENNA MALT
4 POUNDS ALEXANDER'S PALE MALT EXTRACT
2 POUNDS WILDFLOWER HONEY
2 OUNCES HALLERTAUER HOPS (BITTERING)
1 OUNCE TETTNANGER HOPS (FLAVORING)

1 OUNCE HALLERTAUER HOPS (AROMA)
1 OUNCE HALLERTAUER HOPS (DRY HOP)
1 TEASPOON IRISH MOSS
1 PACKAGE BAVARIAN LAGER YEAST
¾ CUP CORN SUGAR (PRIMING)

Mash crushed grains for 60 to 90 minutes. Collect 6 gallons of wort. Add malt extract, honey, and 2 ounces Hallertauer hops. Boil for 1 hour, adding Tettnanger hops after 30 minutes and 1 ounce Hallertauer and Irish moss after 50 minutes. Cool wort and pitch yeast. Primary-ferment at 50 to 55 degrees for 5 to 7 days. Transfer to secondary fermenter. Lager for 3 to 4 weeks, adding 1 ounce Hallertauer hops for the last 5 to 7 days. Bottle, using corn sugar. Age in bottle 10 to 14 days.

OG: 1.062

Ides of March Mai Bock

MAI BOCK, OR MAY BOCK, is traditionally brewed in October to warm the bones between March and May as winter gives way to spring. While we're big on tradition, this style is simply too good to enjoy only three months out of the year.

7 POUNDS 2-ROW KLAGES MALT

2 POUNDS VIENNA MALT

1 POUND MUNICH MALT

1 POUND CARA-PILS MALT

½ POUND CRYSTAL MALT (40L)

1 OUNCE LIBERTY HOPS (BITTERING)

1 OUNCE LIBERTY HOPS (AROMA)

1 TEASPOON IRISH MOSS

1 PACKAGE MUNICH LAGER YEAST

¾ CUP CORN SUGAR (PRIMING)

Mash crushed grains for 60 to 90 minutes. Collect 6 gallons of wort. Add 1 ounce of Liberty hops and boil for 1 hour, adding 1 ounce Liberty hops and Irish moss during the last 10 minutes. Cool wort and pitch yeast. Primary-ferment at 50 to 55 degrees for 5 to 7 days. Transfer to secondary fermenter. Lager for 4 to 6 weeks. Bottle, using corn sugar. Age in bottle 2 to 3 weeks.

OG: 1.065

Doppel Your Pleasure

THE USE OF HONEY AND molasses as fermentables gives this doppelbock a unique character. Feel free to add even more of each to create something completely different.

8 POUNDS ALEXANDER'S PALE MALT
   EXTRACT

3 POUNDS BUCKWHEAT HONEY

1 POUND BLACKSTRAP MOLASSES

1½ POUNDS CRYSTAL MALT (20L)

2 OUNCES CHOCOLATE MALT

1½ OUNCES PRIDE OF RINGWOOD
   HOPS (BITTERING)

1 PACKAGE BAVARIAN LAGER YEAST
   (STARTER RECOMMENDED)

1¼ CUPS DRY MALT EXTRACT
   (PRIMING)

Place crushed crystal malt and chocolate malt in water and steep at 155 degrees for 30 minutes. Remove spent grains and add Alexander's pale malt extract, honey, molasses, and Pride of Ringwood hops. Boil for 1 hour. Cool wort and pitch yeast. Primary-ferment at 50 to 55 degrees for 5 to 7 days. Transfer to secondary fermenter. Lager for 4 to 6 weeks. Bottle, using dry malt extract. Age in bottle 3 to 4 weeks.

OG: 1.066

*The selling of bad beer is a crime against
Christian love.*
—THIRTEENTH-CENTURY LAW FROM THE CITY OF AUGSBURG

Drunk Monk Doppelbock

BREWED AS A FORM OF liquid bread to sustain monks during Lent, the doppelbock may be the only beer in history that was first brewed by special permission of the Pope. We have a theory that it was this brew that gave birth to the Easter Bunny. Because, believe us, after consuming nothing but this beer for forty days straight, you'd start to see giant egg-toting bunnies too!

10 POUNDS PALE 2-ROW MALT
2 POUNDS CARA-PILS MALT
2 POUNDS MUNICH MALT
1 POUND CRYSTAL MALT (60L)
½ POUND CHOCOLATE MALT
¼ POUND BLACK PATENT MALT
1 CUP BLACKSTRAP MOLASSES
1 POUND DARK BROWN SUGAR

2 OUNCES TETTNANGER HOPS
  (BITTERING)
1 OUNCE SAAZ HOPS (AROMA)
1 PACKAGE MUNICH LAGER YEAST
  (1 PINT STARTER RECOMMENDED)
1¼ CUPS DRY MALT EXTRACT
  (PRIMING)

Mash crushed grains for 60 to 90 minutes. Collect 6 gallons of wort. Add molasses, brown sugar, and Tettnanger hops, and boil for 1 hour, adding the Saaz hops for the last 5 minutes. Cool wort and pitch yeast. Primary-ferment at 50 to 55 degrees for 5 to 7 days. Transfer to secondary fermenter. Lager for 6 to 8 weeks. Bottle, using dry malt extract. Age in bottle 3 to 4 weeks.

OG: 1.080

Alligator Doppelbock

PAUL BREWED THIS AMAZING BEER with our friend the Lizard Man of Costa Rica (aka Lagarto Hombre) his first time out. Although the partial mash is not recommended for novices, it is a great transition to all-grain brewing. You get a feel for the mash techniques without requiring the array of equipment. Paul never realized how true to style this beer was until he tasted a real German doppelbock years later. A heavy beer with a roasty nose and a chocolate aftertaste, this is the perfect dessert beer. The use of California lager yeast allows lagering at ale temperatures. If you have the capability to lager, by all means substitute an appropriate German lager yeast.

6⅔ POUNDS BIERKELLER GERMAN
   DARK MALT EXTRACT
2 POUNDS DARK DRY MALT EXTRACT
½ POUND CRYSTAL MALT (40L OR
   HIGHER)
½ POUND CHOCOLATE MALT
1 POUND MUNICH MALT
1¾ OUNCES TETTNANGER HOPS
   (BITTERING)

½ OUNCE HALLERTAUER HOPS
   (AROMA)
1 PACKAGE CALIFORNIA LAGER
   YEAST
1¼ CUPS DARK DRY MALT EXTRACT
   (PRIMING)

Spread crystal, chocolate, and Munich malts on a cookie sheet and toast in a 350-degree oven for 10 minutes. Bring 3 quarts of water to 130 degrees. Crush the grains and add to water. Hold mash at 120 to 122 degrees for 30 minutes. Add 2 quarts boiling water to raise the temperature to 150 degrees and hold for an additional 10 minutes. Raise the temperature to 158 degrees and hold for 40 minutes. Sparge the grains with about 3 quarts 170-degree water, and bring the wort to a boil. Add the Bierkeller and 2 pounds dark dry malt extract and bring to a second boil. Add the Tettnanger hops and boil for 1 hour. Add the Hallertauer hops for the last 5 minutes of the boil. Cool wort and pitch yeast. Ferment for 7 days and transfer to secondary fermenter. Ferment an additional 7 to 10 days. Bottle, using 1¼ cups dark dry malt extract. Age another 7 to 10 days.

OG: 1.071

Masterbator

AS WITH MOST THINGS IN LIFE, homebrewing is more fun with a partner, but there is no shame in doing it by yourself. Everybody does it. This doppelbock was created for the lone brewer. Easy and straightforward, this all-extract recipe will keep you from going blind with confusion. Once you get the hang of it, you will find yourself brewing alone more often. There is no reason to make arrangements with your partner. When it is convenient for you, lock yourself in and make a beer. This one is so good you will want to keep it all to yourself. By the way, did we mention monks invented doppelbock?

10 POUNDS AMBER MALT EXTRACT

2 POUNDS DARK MALT EXTRACT

1 POUND MUNICH MALT

½ POUND CRYSTAL MALT (60L)

½ POUND CHOCOLATE MALT

2 OUNCES BLACK PATENT MALT

2 OUNCES NORTHERN BREWER HOPS (BITTERING)

1 PACKAGE BAVARIAN LAGER YEAST

1 ¼ CUPS DRY MALT EXTRACT (PRIMING)

Place crushed Munich malt, crystal malt, chocolate malt, and black patent malt in water and steep at 155 degrees for 30 minutes. Remove spent grains, add amber malt and dark malt extracts and Northern Brewer hops. Boil for 1 hour. Cool wort and pitch yeast. Primary-ferment at 50 to 55 degrees for 5 to 7 days. Transfer to secondary fermenter. Lager for 6 to 8 weeks. Bottle, using dry malt extract. Age in bottle 3 to 4 weeks.

OG: 1.077

I'll make it felony to drink small beer.
—WILLIAM SHAKESPEARE, *HENRY VI, PART 2*

The Bard's Barleywine

THE INTENSE WINELIKE QUALITY OF the barleywine style makes it a beer to be sipped and savored. This beer is an ideal candidate to brew in smaller batches, since it is not a beer you're going to be downing one after another.

12 POUNDS ALEXANDER'S PALE MALT EXTRACT

2 POUNDS DRY LIGHT MALT EXTRACT

4 OUNCES GALENA HOPS (BITTERING)

2 OUNCES LIBERTY HOPS (AROMA)

1 PACKAGE IRISH ALE YEAST (STARTER RECOMMENDED)

¾ CUP CORN SUGAR (PRIMING)

Combine malt extracts and Galena hops in water and boil for 1 hour, adding the Liberty hops for the last 10 minutes. Cool wort and pitch yeast. Ferment for 7 to 10 days. Transfer to a secondary fermenter and ferment an additional 3 to 4 weeks. Bottle, using corn sugar. Age in bottle 6 to 8 weeks. This beer will improve greatly with age.

OG: 1.090

Blue and Gold Barleywine

OUR FRIEND EOGHAN McGILL IS the biggest Notre Dame fan we know, followed closely by Patrick. One autumn, we all made a journey to South Bend to see a game, and we brewed this to spice up our tailgate party before the big event. It was the perfect way to warm up a chilly November day in Indiana.

8 POUNDS ALEXANDER'S PALE MALT
  EXTRACT
3⅓ POUNDS LIGHT MALT EXTRACT
2 POUNDS DRY MALT EXTRACT
4 OUNCES CHALLENGER HOPS
  (BITTERING)

3 OUNCES CASCADE HOPS (AROMA)
1 PACKAGE IRISH ALE YEAST
  (STARTER RECOMMENDED)
1 CUP CLOVER HONEY (PRIMING)

Combine malt extracts and Challenger hops in water and boil for 1 hour, adding the Cascade hops during the last 5 minutes. Cool wort and pitch yeast. Ferment for 10 to 14 days. Transfer to secondary fermenter and ferment an additional 3 to 4 weeks. Bottle, using honey. Age in bottle 2 to 3 months.

OG: 1.092

Repitching Yeast

Using liquid yeast rather than dry yeast gives the ability to produce beers that are professional-quality, if not even better. Using liquid yeast also gives you the ability to repitch the same yeast for 5 or 6 batches. We've even heard stories of brewers repitching yeast for up to 12 batches. Repitching your yeast is incredibly easy.

When you're ready to transfer your wort from the primary fermenter, sterilize a glass jar, including the lid. (A mason jar is ideal.) Siphon all but the last 1 inch of beer from your fermenter. Swirl around the slurry and remaining beer in the bottom of the fermenter and then sterilize the mouth of the fermenter. Pour the contents of the fermenter into the sanitized jar. Replace the lid, leaving it a bit loose to allow any gases to escape, and then place the jar in the refrigerator.

When you're ready to pitch the yeast for your next batch, take the jar out of the refrigerator and allow it to come to room temperature. Remove the lid, pour off the top layer of beer, and flame the mouth of the jar. Swirl around the contents and pour it into your fermenter. Yeast that is being repitched should be used within two weeks to ensure good quality.

A couple of things to remember: First, keep things sanitary. The yeast is still very susceptible to infection. Second, repitch only liquid yeast. Though you can repitch dry yeast, the chance of infection is increased each time you do, so it's just not worth risking your batch of beer.

Repitching your liquid yeast will actually make it cheaper than using dry yeast. So go ahead and give it a try.

John Barleycorn Must Wine

BARLEYWINE HAS CARVED ITS NICHE as the strongest of British ales. By barleywine standards, this one is rather mild, but it still packs a wallop. If you are looking to drown your sorrows, this ale will certainly do the trick. Owing to its strength, this ale should be allowed to age for quite some time. By the time you do begin to enjoy it, you will have forgotten how much you spent on the ingredients.

13¼ POUNDS BRITISH PALE MALT
  EXTRACT
½ POUND CRYSTAL MALT (40L)
¼ POUND BLACK PATENT MALT
¼ POUND CHOCOLATE MALT
5 OUNCES KENT GOLDINGS HOPS
  (BITTERING)

3½ OUNCES FUGGLES HOPS
  (FLAVOR AND AROMA)
1 TABLESPOON GYPSUM
1 PACKAGE LONDON ALE YEAST
1 CUP MOLASSES (PRIMING)

Place crushed grains and gypsum in water and steep at 155 degrees for 30 minutes. Remove spent grains and add malt extract. Bring to a boil and add Kent Goldings hops. Add Fuggles hops 45 minutes into the boil. Cool wort and pitch yeast. Ferment 10 to 14 days. Transfer to secondary fermenter and ferment an additional 10 to 14 days. Bottle, using molasses. Age at least 1 month. Flavor will peak in 6 to 12 months.

OG: 1.095

*Ale, man, ale's the stuff to drink
For fellows whom it hurts to think;
Look into the pewter pot
To see the world as the world's not.*
— A. E. HOUSMAN, *A SHROPSHIRE LAD*

Pewter Pot Barleywine

BARLEYWINE IS A HIGH-GRAVITY, and thus high-alcohol, intensely flavored beer that is not for the meek of palate. If you can find them, 8-ounce bottles would be perfect for packaging this brew. It should be enjoyed in small quantities, as an aperitif. In fact, there is so much alcohol that the yeast typically dies off before all the sugars can be fermented. Pitching champagne yeast, which is more alcohol tolerant than ale yeast, a few days prior to bottling can aid carbonation for those who fear flat beer.

6⅔ POUNDS LIGHT MALT EXTRACT
5 POUNDS BRITISH 2-ROW PALE MALT
1 POUND CARA-PILS MALT
1 POUND FLAKED BARLEY
½ POUND ROASTED BARLEY
¼ POUND CHOCOLATE MALT
¼ POUND BLACKSTRAP MOLASSES

1 TABLESPOON GYPSUM
4 OUNCES NORTHERN BREWER HOPS (BITTERING)
2 OUNCES FUGGLES HOPS (AROMA)
½ TEASPOON IRISH MOSS
1 PACKAGE WHITBREAD ALE YEAST
1¼ CUPS DRY MALT EXTRACT (PRIMING)

Mash crushed grains with gypsum for 60 to 90 minutes. Collect 6 gallons of wort and add light malt extract. Bring to a boil and add Northern Brewer hops. Boil for 1 hour. Add Fuggles hops 30 minutes into the boil. Cool wort and pitch yeast. Ferment 10 to 14 days. Transfer to secondary fermenter and ferment an additional 3 to 4 weeks. Bottle, using dry malt extract. Age at least 2 weeks. Flavor will continue to improve as this beer ages. After 3 months, you should notice a distinct mellowing, and we recommend setting aside a few bottles to keep for 1 year.

OG: 1.095

Beer isn't just beer. . . . Beer needs a home.
—*DIE WELT* (GERMAN NATIONAL NEWSPAPER)

Thatched Roof Ale

THIS SCOTTISH ALE IS AUTHENTICALLY flavored with a small amount of peated malt. The result is as pleasant as a stroll in the green Scottish countryside.

6⅔ POUNDS AMBER MALT EXTRACT
3⅓ POUNDS LIGHT MALT EXTRACT
½ POUND CRYSTAL MALT (40L)
¼ POUND ROASTED BARLEY
¼ POUND PEATED MALT
2 OUNCES CASCADE HOPS
  (BITTERING)
½ OUNCE NORTHERN BREWER HOPS
  (FLAVORING)
1 PACKAGE SCOTTISH ALE YEAST
½ CUP MOLASSES (PRIMING)
½ CUP HONEY (PRIMING)

Steep crushed grains at 155 degrees for 30 minutes. Remove spent grains. Add malt extracts and Cascade hops and boil for 1 hour, adding Northern Brewer hops after 30 minutes. Cool wort and pitch yeast. Ferment for 10 to 14 days. Bottle, using molasses and honey. Age in bottle 1 to 3 months.

OG: 1.065

Ye Olde Ale

OLD ALES BENEFIT FROM AGING, hence the name. The high starting gravity and resulting alcohol content make it difficult for the yeast to stay active, therefore a starter is recommended.

9 POUNDS PALE MALT EXTRACT
1 POUND CRYSTAL MALT (60L)
1 POUND CHOCOLATE MALT
¼ POUND BLACK PATENT MALT
1 TABLESPOON GYPSUM
1½ OUNCES NORTHERN BREWER
  HOPS (BITTERING)
1 OUNCE KENT GOLDINGS HOPS
  (FLAVORING)
1½ OUNCES KENT GOLDINGS HOPS
  (DRY HOP)
1 PACKAGE BRITISH ALE YEAST
1 CUP MOLASSES (PRIMING)

Place crushed grains and gypsum in water and steep at 155 degrees for 30 minutes. Remove spent grains and add malt extract. Bring to a boil and add Northern Brewer hops. Add 1 ounce of Kent Goldings hops 30 minutes into the boil. Cool wort and pitch yeast. Ferment 10 to 14 days. Transfer to secondary fermenter, add 1½ ounces Kent Goldings hops, and ferment an additional 10 to 14 days. Bottle, using molasses. Age at least 1 month. Flavor will peak in 6 to 12 months.

OG: 1.070

I throw a little dry malt, which is left of purpose, on top of the mash, with a handful of salt, to keep the witches from it, and then cover it up.
—INSTRUCTIONS FOR BREWING SCOTCH ALE, 1793

Macbeth's Scotch MacAle

"WHEN SHALL WE THREE MEET again? In thunder, lightning, or in rain?" Or maybe just as soon as we brew up another batch of this beer, that's when!

10 POUNDS LIGHT MALT EXTRACT
1 POUND CRYSTAL MALT (40L)
2 OUNCES CHOCOLATE MALT
1 CUP LIGHT BROWN SUGAR
2 OUNCES WILLAMETTE HOPS
   (BITTERING)

½ TEASPOON GYPSUM
1 TEASPOON IRISH MOSS
1 PACKAGE SCOTTISH ALE YEAST
¾ CUP CORN SUGAR (PRIMING)

Steep crushed crystal malt and chocolate malt at 155 degrees for 30 minutes. Remove spent grains and add malt extract, brown sugar, gypsum, and Willamette hops. Boil for 1 hour, adding the Irish moss during the last 10 minutes. Cool wort and pitch yeast. Ferment for 10 to 14 days. Transfer to secondary fermenter and ferment an additional 7 to 10 days. Bottle, using corn sugar. Age in bottle 10 to 14 days.

OG: 1.072

Sow Your Wild Oats Strong Ale

THE ADDITION OF ROLLED OATS smooths out the characteristics of this strong ale. Take it from us, after a few of these you'll be primed and ready to sow your wild oats, if you get our drift.

9 POUNDS PALE 2-ROW MALT
1 POUND FLAKED BARLEY
1 POUND MUNICH MALT
1 POUND ROLLED OATS
½ POUND TORREFIED WHEAT
2 OUNCES PROGRESS HOPS
  (BITTERING)

1 OUNCE CHALLENGER HOPS
  (AROMA)
1 PACKAGE LONDON ALE YEAST
1 CUP BUCKWHEAT HONEY (PRIMING)

Mash crushed grains for 60 to 90 minutes. Collect 6 gallons of wort and add Progress hops. Boil for 1 hour, adding the Challenger hops during the last 5 minutes. Cool wort and pitch yeast. Ferment 7 to 10 days. Transfer to secondary fermenter and ferment an additional 14 to 21 days. Bottle, using honey. Age in bottle 10 to 14 days.

OG: 1.071

I wish we could all have good luck, all the time!
I wish we had wings!
I wish rain water was beer!
ROBERT BOLT, *A MAN FOR ALL SEASONS*

Coming on a Little Strong

THIS ENGLISH-STYLE STRONG ALE possesses the maltiness associated with the style but is balanced with moderate hop bitterness and aroma. Aroma hops can be increased and the ale will still remain within the style.

10 POUNDS BRITISH 2-ROW MALT
1 POUND CRYSTAL MALT (40L)
1 POUND DEXTRINE MALT
¼ POUND FLAKED BARLEY
1 OUNCE FUGGLES HOPS
  (BITTERING)
½ OUNCE KENT GOLDINGS HOPS
  (BITTERING)

½ OUNCE FUGGLES HOPS
  (FLAVORING)
1 OUNCE FUGGLES HOPS (AROMA)
1 PACKAGE LONDON ALE YEAST
1 CUP MOLASSES (PRIMING)

Mash crushed grains for 60 to 90 minutes. Collect 6 gallons of wort, add 1 ounce Fuggles hops and the Kent Goldings, and boil for 1 hour, adding ½ ounce Fuggles after 30 minutes. Remove from heat, add 1 ounce Fuggles, and steep for 10 minutes. Cool wort and pitch yeast. Ferment for 7 to 10 days. Transfer to secondary fermenter and ferment an additional 10 to 14 days. Bottle, using molasses. Age in bottle 14 to 21 days.

OG: 1.069

Fruit, Herb,
and
Smoked Beers

A Pint of Plain Is Your Only Man
by Flann O'Brien

When things go wrong and will not come right,
Though you do the best you can,
When life looks black as the hour of night—
A pint of plain is your only man.

When money's tight and is hard to get
And your horse has also ran,
When all you have is a heap of debt—
A pint of plain is your only man.

When health is bad and your heart feels strange,
And your face is pale and wan,
When doctors say that you need a change—
A pint of plain is your only man.

When food is scarce and your larder bare
And no rasher grease your pan,
When hunger grows as your meals are rare—
A pint of plain is your only man.

In time of trouble and lousy strife,
You have still got a darlint plan,
You still can turn to a brighter life—
A pint of plain is your only man.

Life, alas,
Is very drear.
Up with the glass
Down with the beer!
—LOUIS UNTERMEYER

Lemon Coriander Weiss

THE LIGHT TASTE OF WHEAT beer lends itself perfectly to the addition of lemon and coriander, making this a perfect summer brew.

6 POUNDS IREKS WEIZENBIER
  EXTRACT (100 PERCENT WHEAT)
3 POUNDS LIGHT MALT EXTRACT
1 OUNCE SAAZ HOPS (BITTERING)
1 PACKAGE WEIHENSTEPHAN WHEAT
  YEAST

1 OUNCE CRUSHED CORIANDER SEED
ZEST OF 1 LEMON
¾ CUP CORN SUGAR (PRIMING)

Combine extracts and hops in water and boil for 1 hour. Transfer to primary fermenter. Cool wort and pitch yeast. Allow to ferment for 5 to 7 days. Transfer to secondary fermenter. Add crushed coriander seed and lemon zest and allow to ferment an additional 5 to 7 days. Bottle, using corn sugar. Age in bottle for 10 days.

OG: 1.044

Tea for Brew, and Brew for Tea

THE ADDITION OF HERBAL TEA can lend some wonderful flavors to your beer. There are lots of great teas available, so experiment and find your favorite.

8 POUNDS ALEXANDER'S PALE MALT
  EXTRACT
1 OUNCE SAAZ HOPS (BITTERING)
½ OUNCE SAAZ HOPS (AROMA)

8 RED ZINGER TEA BAGS
1 TEASPOON IRISH MOSS
1 PACKAGE AMERICAN LAGER YEAST
¾ CUP CORN SUGAR (PRIMING)

Combine malt extract and 1 ounce Saaz hops in water and boil for 1 hour. Remove from heat, add Red Zinger tea bags, and steep for 20 to 30 minutes, adding ½ ounce Saaz hops and Irish moss during the last 5 minutes. Cool wort and pitch yeast. Primary-ferment at 50 to 55 degrees for 5 to 7 days. Transfer to secondary fermenter. Lager 3 to 4 weeks. Bottle, using corn sugar. Age in bottle 7 to 10 days.

OG: 1.046

Some Like It Hot

WE CAME UP WITH THE name for this beer because we like to cross-dress when we brew it. No, just kidding. The name refers to the hot, spicy flavor of this rich, and very drinkable, hot pepper beer. Once the peppers are added to the secondary, be sure to taste the beer every day to make sure you don't overshoot the heat level you're going for. Substitute Anaheim peppers for a milder pepper flavor, and, if you would like to cross-dress while you brew it, be our guest.

6⅔ POUNDS AMBER MALT EXTRACT
1 POUND CRYSTAL MALT
½ POUND TORREFIED WHEAT
2 OUNCES CHOCOLATE MALT
1½ OUNCES SAAZ HOPS (BITTERING)

1 PACKAGE AMERICAN ALE YEAST
¼ POUND DRIED SZECHUAN
   PEPPERS
¾ CUP CORN SUGAR (PRIMING)

Place crushed crystal malt, torrefied wheat, and chocolate malt in water and steep at 155 degrees for 30 minutes. Remove spent grains, add malt extract and Saaz hops, and boil for 1 hour. Cool wort and pitch yeast. Ferment 10 to 14 days. Transfer to secondary fermenter and add peppers. Taste wort after 1 day to check for amount of spice. Bottle, using corn sugar, when desired amount of spice has been achieved. Age in bottle 7 to 10 days.

OG: 1.042

The immense importance of a pint of ale to a common person should never be overlooked.
— FROM THE CANON OF ST. PAUL'S CATHEDRAL

Jammin' Jamaican Jingered Ale

FRESH JAMAICAN GINGERROOT WILL really make this ale special—the dark malt, hop bitterness, and ginger zing. The spice adds a third dimension to the usual malt sweetness–hop bitterness balance. This dark amber beer is not as heavy as it looks, despite the addition of molasses. The original recipe used Venezuelan brown sugar in place of the molasses. If you can come by it, we recommend using it.

3 POUNDS DARK DRY MALT EXTRACT
3⅓ POUNDS DARK MALT EXTRACT
¾ POUND CRYSTAL MALT (40L OR HIGHER)
½ POUND CHOCOLATE MALT
2 OUNCES CASCADE HOPS (BITTERING)
1 OUNCE WILLAMETTE HOPS (AROMA)
¾ CUP DARK MOLASSES
3 OUNCES GRATED FRESH GINGER
2 PACKAGES DRIED ALE YEAST
¾ CUP CORN SUGAR (PRIMING)

Place grains in water and steep at 155 degrees for 30 minutes. Remove spent grains and add malt extracts and molasses. Bring to a boil and add Cascade hops. Add Willamette hops and ginger during the last 15 minutes of the boil. Transfer to fermenter when cool and add enough cold water to make 5 gallons. Cool wort and pitch both yeasts. Ferment for 7 days and transfer to secondary fermenter. Ferment an additional 7 to 10 days. Bottle, using corn sugar. Age 7 to 10 days.

OG: 1.055

Berry Garcia

WE WERE GETTING READY TO brew on the morning of August 9, 1995, when a friend called and told us that Jerry Garcia had died. While none of us would consider ourselves Deadheads, we were universal in our admiration of Jerry Garcia as an artist and humanitarian. We decided to brew something in his honor. We concocted this recipe, went to the homebrew shop that morning, and brewed that afternoon. It turned out to be one of the finest fruit beers we have ever had. Who knows, maybe a little divine intervention.

6 POUNDS IREKS WEIZENBIER EXTRACT (100 PERCENT WHEAT)
3 POUNDS LIGHT MALT EXTRACT
1 OUNCE TETTNANGER HOPS (BITTERING)
1 PACKAGE WEIHENSTEPHAN WHEAT YEAST (#3068)

8 POUNDS ASSORTED BERRIES (SOUR CHERRIES, SWEET CHERRIES, BLUEBERRIES, RASPBERRIES, OR YOUR PERSONAL FAVORITE)
¾ CUP CORN SUGAR (PRIMING)

Add extracts and Tettnanger hops to boiling water. Boil for 1 hour. Cool wort and pitch yeast. Ferment for 7 days. Transfer to secondary fermenter. Steep fruit in enough 150-degree water to cover for 20 minutes. Add fruit and water to fermenter. Ferment an additional 10 to 14 days. Rack to tertiary fermenter, and let sit for 2 to 3 days. Bottle, using corn sugar. Age in bottle for 10 days.

OG: 1.049

Using Fruit in Beer

Fruit beers are fun to create, but the use of fruit entails some practical considerations.

As in cooking, certain flavors don't hold up well to being cooked down. So we like to add our fruit to the secondary fermenter. As with dry hopping, we feel you also get more fruit aroma by adding fruit to the secondary. If your fruit is washed well, you stand little chance of contamination, since the alcohol in the beer should kill any wild beasties that might be lingering. But to be on the safe side, pasteurize by steeping your fruit in 150-degree water for 20 minutes. We like to use the steeping water, too, because some of the juices inevitably mix with it.

Also, to get your beer as clear as possible and to prevent excess sediment from collecting in the bottom of your bottles, transfer the beer from your secondary into a tertiary fermenter for 2 to 3 days to let it settle out, and then bottle as usual. Adding a clarifying agent to the tertiary fermenter is sometimes advisable, depending on the fruit used.

However, if you'd rather place the fruit in the primary, that's fine too. If you do choose this method, do not boil the fruit in the beer, as it will bring out the pectin and you will end up with perpetually cloudy beer. As with adding fruit to the secondary fermenter, allow the wort to cool to 150 degrees and steep the fruit for 20 minutes.

When adding the fruited wort to the primary fermenter, *never, ever* fill it to the top. Unless, of course, it's always been your dream to recreate Old Faithful in your kitchen. Either divide the batch into two 5-gallon fermenters, or place the wort in a 6-gallon fermenter, allowing plenty of headroom. A 6-gallon plastic bucket is preferable, since even a 6-gallon carboy may clog at the neck.

Murph's Cranberry Wheat

AS A SAILOR, OUR FRIEND Murph had the opportunity to travel to all corners of the globe and try all sorts of beers. But as a brewer Murph came home to New England to create this great holiday refresher. The key, as he tells it, is to use fresh cranberries that you picked yourself. Since you may not have access to a local cranberry bog, you may substitute the store-bought variety. As the cranberry season falls in September, this is a great beer to serve with Thanksgiving dinner. You better stash a six-pack if you expect any to last till Christmas.

6⅔ POUNDS IREKS WHEAT MALT EXTRACT (100 PERCENT WHEAT)
1 OUNCE HALLERTAUER HOPS (BITTERING)
1 OUNCE TETTNANGER HOPS (BITTERING)

2 POUNDS CRANBERRIES
1 TABLESPOON IRISH MOSS
1 PACKAGE BAVARIAN WHEAT ALE YEAST
¾ CUP CORN SUGAR (PRIMING)

Combine extract and hops with water and boil for 1 hour. After 15 minutes add both the Hallertauer and Tettnanger hops and boil for another 45 minutes. Puree cranberries in a food processor or blender and add during the last 30 minutes of the boil. Add the Irish moss during the last 15 minutes. Cool wort and pitch yeast. Ferment for 7 days and transfer to secondary fermenter. Ferment an addtitional 7 to 10 days. Bottle, using corn sugar. Age for at least 7 days.

OG: 1.062

Sweet Woodruff

THE ADDITION OF SWEET WOODRUFF syrup is traditional with the Berliner Weiss style and is an essential ingredient in May wine. Its addition to this light lager imparts a wonderful herbal aroma and flavor.

4 POUNDS ALEXANDER'S PALE MALT
  EXTRACT
2 POUNDS LIGHT DRY MALT EXTRACT
1½ OUNCES HALLERTAUER HOPS
  (BITTERING)

½ OUNCE SAAZ HOPS (AROMA)
4–5 SPRIGS FRESH SWEET
  WOODRUFF
1 PACKAGE PILSEN LAGER YEAST
¾ CUP CORN SUGAR (PRIMING)

Combine malt extracts and Hallertauer hops in water and boil for 1 hour, adding Saaz hops during the last 5 minutes. Cool wort and pitch yeast. Primary-ferment at 50 to 55 degrees for 5 to 7 days. Transfer to secondary fermenter. Lager 3 to 4 weeks. Place sprigs of sweet woodruff in 1 pint of 150-degree water and steep for 15 to 20 minutes. Remove sweet woodruff sprigs and bottle, using corn sugar. Age in bottle 7 to 10 days.

OG: 1.045

Pineapple Pale Ale

UNTIL HAWAII PASSED A LAW legalizing brewpubs in 1993, all beer was imported. This recipe was created in an attempt to capture the feeling of paradise in a beer. It's not exactly as pleasant as a Maui sunset, but the tropical flavor is rather refreshing. A nice summer beer. Hawaiian pineapple is used for the freshest flavor, but in a pinch canned pineapple can be used.

5 POUNDS EXTRA-PALE MALT
  EXTRACT
1 POUND CRYSTAL MALT
2 OUNCES CASCADE HOPS
  (BITTERING)
1 OUNCE HALLERTAUER HOPS
  (AROMA)

1 OUNCE HALLERTAUER HOPS
  (DRY HOP)
1 TEASPOON GYPSUM
1 PACKAGE BELGIAN ALE YEAST
4 POUNDS FRESH HAWAIIAN
  PINEAPPLE
¾ CUP CORN SUGAR (PRIMING)

Place cracked crystal malt in water and steep at 155 degrees for 30 minutes. Remove the spent grains and add malt extract, gypsum, and 2 ounces Cascade hops. Boil for 1 hour. Add 1 ounce Hallertauer hops during the last 15 minutes of the boil. Cool wort and pitch yeast. Ferment for 5 to 7 days. Transfer to secondary fermenter, add pasteurized pineapple (see Brewer's Tip, p. 118) and 1 ounce Hallertauer hops. Ferment for an additional 10 days. Rack beer to a tertiary fermenter and allow to sit for an additional 3 days. Bottle, using corn sugar. Age in bottle 7 to 10 days.

OG: 1.035

*I would give all my fame
for a pot of ale, and safety.*
—WILLIAM SHAKESPEARE, *HENRY V*

Aplomb of an Ale

THE LIGHT, CLEAR FLAVORS OF plum make this mild ale a summer favorite. It is soft and refreshing, like biting into the real thing.

4 POUNDS ALEXANDER'S PALE MALT
  EXTRACT
1 POUND DRY MALT EXTRACT
2 OUNCES CRYSTAL MALT (40L)
½ POUND FLAKED WHEAT
1 OUNCE CASCADE HOPS
  (BITTERING)

1 PACKAGE BRITISH ALE YEAST
6 POUNDS PLUMS, PITTED AND
  HALVED
¾ CUP CORN SUGAR (PRIMING)

Steep grains at 155 degrees for 30 minutes. Remove spent grains. Add extracts and Cascade hops, and boil for 1 hour. Cool wort and pitch yeast. Ferment in primary fermenter for 5 to 7 days. Transfer to secondary fermenter. Lightly mash the plums with a fork or the back of a spoon and steep in 150-degree water for 20 minutes. Add plums and water to secondary and ferment 7 days. Rack to tertiary fermenter, straining out fruit, and let sit for 2 to 3 days. Bottle, using corn sugar. Age in bottle 10 to 14 days.

OG: 1.035

On Top of Old Smoky

WHILE RAUCHBIER IS TRADITIONALLY A lager style, smoked beer can certainly be made as an ale. The top fermenting ale yeast adds esters, which mix with the smoky flavor to produce an interesting and unusual flavor. We recommend apple or peach wood for the sweet character they contribute.

6²/₃ POUNDS LIGHT MALT EXTRACT

1½ POUNDS SMOKED KLAGES MALT
  (SEE BREWERS TIP, P. 123)

½ POUND CHOCOLATE MALT

1 OUNCE PERLE HOPS (BITTERING)

1 PACKAGE AMERICAN ALE YEAST

¾ CUP CORN SUGAR (PRIMING)

Place crushed smoked Klages malt and chocolate malt in water and steep at 155 degrees for 30 minutes. Remove spent grains, bring water to a boil, and add malt extract and Perle hops. Boil for 1 hour. Cool wort and pitch yeast. Ferment for 10 to 14 days. Bottle, using corn sugar. Age in bottle for 10 to 14 days. Beer will mellow with age.

OG: 1.044

Smoked Malt

An easy way to recreate authentic smoked beers requires no more than a small barbecue grill, a clean piece of metal wire mesh, and some wood chips (we like hickory or apple wood). Soak the chips in water or beer. Ignite a small amount of charcoal in your grill. When the coals are almost ready to cook on (i.e., gray ashen-colored with a red glow), crush your grains and soak them in water for 5 to 10 minutes. Spread the wood chips on the coals. Spread the grains on the window screen and place it on the rack over the coals. Cover and let smoke for 15 to 20 minutes. Check the grains occasionally, mixing if they seem to be smoking unevenly. Keep a water spray bottle handy to spray the grains if they seem to be burning. Use the grains as with any other specialty grain.

Blue Devil Brew

IN CELEBRATION OF DUKE UNIVERSITY'S back-to-back NCAA Basketball Championships in 1991 and 1992, some alumni created this recipe. The blueberries did not impart the desired color, but the flavor came through like an in-your-face slam dunk. It is not a very heavy beer, and the relatively low alcohol content makes it quite drinkable. Brew this beer in mid-February to enjoy during March Madness.

6²/₃ POUNDS AMBER MALT EXTRACT
½ POUND CRYSTAL MALT (20L)
½ POUND MALTED WHEAT
1½ OUNCES CASCADE HOPS
  (BITTERING)
½ OUNCE CASCADE HOPS (AROMA)

1 OUNCE TETTNANGER HOPS
  (DRY HOP)
7 POUNDS FROZEN BLUEBERRIES
1 PACKAGE BRITISH ALE YEAST
¾ CUP CORN SUGAR (PRIMING)

Place crushed crystal malt and wheat in water and steep at 155 degrees for 30 minutes. Remove spent grains, add malt extract, and bring to a boil. Add 1½ ounces of Cascade 15 minutes into the boil. Add last ½ ounce of Cascade during the last 5 minutes of the boil. Cool wort and pitch yeast. Ferment for 3 days, and add Tettnanger hops. Ferment an additional 5 to 7 days. Transfer to secondary fermenter and add pasteurized blueberries (see Brewer's Tip, p. 118). Ferment an additional 7 to 10 days. Bottle, using corn sugar. Age for at least 7 days.

OG: 1.036

*Oh, I have been to Ludlow fair
And left my necktie God knows where,
And carried halfway home, or near,
Pints and quarts of Ludlow beer.*

—A. E. HOUSMAN

Cardamom Stout

STOUT HAS A BAD REPUTATION as a heavy, cloying, bitter brew. Though it will never enjoy the role of thirst quencher on a hot summer day, it is definitely underrated as beverages go. Whole cardamom seed (not powdered) adds a cola-like flavor to this stout that makes it seem a little lighter, a little fresher. Sounds yummy, doesn't it? It is.

4 POUNDS PALE MALT EXTRACT

1 POUND CRYSTAL MALT (60L)

½ POUND BRITISH PALE 2-ROW MALT

½ POUND ROASTED BARLEY

½ POUND BLACK PATENT MALT

1 TEASPOON GYPSUM

1½ OUNCES WILLAMETTE HOPS (BITTERING)

½ OUNCE WILLAMETTE HOPS (FLAVORING)

½ TEASPOON WHOLE CARDAMOM SEED

½ TEASPOON CRUSHED CARDAMOM SEED

1 PACKAGE IRISH ALE YEAST

⅔ CUP LIGHT OR DARK BROWN SUGAR (PRIMING)

Place crushed grains and gypsum in water and steep at 155 degrees for 30 minutes. Remove spent grains and add malt extract. Bring to a boil, add 1½ ounces Willamette hops and whole cardamom seed. Add ½ ounce Willamette hops 30 minutes into the boil. Cool wort and pitch yeast. Ferment 7 to 10 days. Transfer to secondary fermenter and add crushed cardamom seed. Ferment an additional 7 to 10 days. Bottle, using brown sugar. Age 1 week.

OG: 1.040

New England Cranberry Ale

WE ARE BIG FANS OF fruit beers. Although many fruits make excellent beers, the tartness of cranberries adds a terrific zing. In addition, the wonderful deep ruby color makes this beer as attractive in the glass as it is tasty out of it.

6⅔ POUNDS LIGHT MALT EXTRACT
1 POUND CRYSTAL MALT (40L)
2 OUNCES ROASTED BARLEY
1½ OUNCES CASCADE HOPS
  (BITTERING)
½ OUNCE MOUNT HOOD HOPS
  (AROMA)

1 TEASPOON GYPSUM
1 TEASPOON IRISH MOSS
1 PACKAGE EUROPEAN ALE YEAST
6 POUNDS CRANBERRIES
1 CUP CORN SUGAR
¾ CUP CORN SUGAR (PRIMING)

Place cracked crystal malt and roasted barley in water and steep at 155 degrees for 30 minutes. Remove the spent grains and add malt extract, gypsum, and Cascade hops. Boil for 1 hour, adding Mount Hood hops and Irish moss during the last 10 minutes of the boil. Cool wort and pitch yeast. Ferment 5 to 7 days. Place cranberries in a food processor and crush, then steep cranberries with 1 cup corn sugar in 150-degree water for 10 minutes. Place the cranberries in the secondary fermenter and rack beer into the secondary fermenter. Ferment an additional 10 to 14 days. Rack to tertiary fermenter and let sit for 3 days. Bottle, using corn sugar. Age in bottle 7 to 10 days.

OG: 1.043

Smoke It If You Got It

THE FIRST RAUCHBIER WAS PROBABLY created thanks to a maltster who didn't pay quite enough attention as he dried his malt over an open fire. The city of Bamberg in Germany is the source of most Rauchbiers, but they are quickly gaining popularity with microbreweries and brewpubs as well.

3⅓ POUNDS AMBER MALT EXTRACT
4 POUNDS ALEXANDER'S PALE MALT
  EXTRACT
½ POUND SMOKED CRYSTAL MALT
  (SEE BREWER'S TIP, P. 123)
½ POUND SMOKED MUNICH MALT
  (SEE BREWER'S TIP, P. 123)
1 OUNCE HALLERTAUER HOPS
  (BITTERING)

1 OUNCE TETTNANGER HOPS
  (FLAVORING)
1 OUNCE TETTNANGER HOPS
  (AROMA)
1 PACKAGE MUNICH LAGER YEAST
¾ CUP CORN SUGAR (PRIMING)

Place crushed, smoked crystal malt and Munich malt in water, and steep at 155 degrees for 30 minutes. Remove spent grains, add malt extracts and Hallertauer hops, and boil for 1 hour, adding 1 ounce Tettnanger hops after 30 minutes and 1 ounce Tettnanger after 50 minutes. Cool wort and pitch yeast. Primary-ferment at 50 to 55 degrees for 5 to 7 days. Transfer to secondary fermenter. Lager for 3 to 4 weeks. Bottle, using corn sugar. Age in bottle 7 to 10 days.

OG: 1.041

Cherries Jubilee

THIS LOVELY AND COMPLEX OLD ale is reminiscent of the brandied dessert. It is an elegant aperitif or after-dinner drink.

10 POUNDS PALE MALT EXTRACT
1 POUND CRYSTAL MALT (40L)
½ POUND FLAKED BARLEY
¼ POUND CHOCOLATE MALT
2 OUNCES ROASTED BARLEY
2 POUNDS HONEY
2 OUNCES FUGGLES HOPS
    (BITTERING)

½ OUNCE WILLAMETTE HOPS
    (AROMA)
1 PACKAGE LONDON ESB YEAST
12 POUNDS PITTED CHERRIES
    (PREFERABLY 6 POUNDS OF SOUR
    AND 6 OF SWEET)
1 ¼ CUPS DRY MALT EXTRACT
    (PRIMING)

Steep crushed grains at 155 degrees for 30 minutes. Remove spent grains. Add malt extract, honey, and Fuggles hops. Boil for 1 hour, adding Willamette hops for the last 15 minutes. Cool wort and pitch yeast. Ferment for 10 to 14 days. Transfer to secondary fermenter. For 20 minutes, steep cherries in enough 150-degree water to cover. Add cherries and water to fermenter. Ferment for 7 to 10 days. Rack to tertiary fermenter and let sit 2 to 3 days. Bottle, using dry malt extract. Age in bottle for 1 to 3 months, but it will improve with age—we recommend 6 months if possible.

OG: 1.071

Washing Yeast

Though it's not necessary, washing your yeast a couple of times before repitching will help to improve the quality. To wash your yeast, first allow the jar of slurry to settle in the refrigerator for 24 hours. Then remove the lid; pour off and discard the top layer of beer. Add 1 cup of cool sterilized water to the jar and replace the lid. Swirl around the contents of the jar for a couple of minutes and then place it back in the refrigerator. Allow it to settle for 24 hours. Pour off the top layer of liquid and then repeat the procedure once more.

On the Chest of a barmaid in Sale
Were tattooed the prices of ale,
And on her behind
For the sake of the blind
Was the same information in Braille.
—ANONYMOUS

Peachy Keen

THE WINE-LIKE MALT FLAVOR OF the barleywine style is perfectly balanced by the sweet, round flavor of peach. If you can't find fresh or frozen peaches, 2 or 3 ounces of peach extract added at bottling will work as well.

14 POUNDS PALE 2-ROW MALT
1 POUND DEXTRINE MALT
4 OUNCES CHINOOK HOPS
   (BITTERING)
2 OUNCES SAAZ HOPS (AROMA)

8 POUNDS PEACHES (PEELED,
   PITTED, AND SLICED)
1 PACKAGE IRISH ALE YEAST
   (STARTER RECOMMENDED)
3/4 CUP CORN SUGAR (PRIMING)

Mash grains for 60 to 90 minutes. Collect 6 gallons of wort. Add Chinook hops and boil for 1 hour, adding the Saaz hops for the last 10 minutes. Cool wort and pitch yeast. Ferment for 10 to 14 days. Transfer to secondary fermenter. For 20 minutes, steep peaches in enough 150-degree water to cover. Add peaches and water to fermenter. Ferment an additional 14 to 21 days. Rack to tertiary fermenter, straining out fruit, and let sit 2 to 3 days. Bottle, using corn sugar. Age in bottle 3 to 4 weeks. Beer will improve with age.

OG: 1.092

Smoky IPA

THIS IS A VERY BIG beer—lots of malt, lots of hops, and a strong, sweet smoky taste. It certainly isn't a beer for everyone, as is the case with most smoked beers, so you may want to make this one in a smaller batch the first time out.

7 POUNDS PALE 2-ROW MALT
1 POUND CRYSTAL MALT (40L)
1 POUND SMOKED MUNICH MALT
   (SEE BREWER'S TIP, P. 123)
1/2 POUND DEXTRINE MALT
2 OUNCES LIBERTY HOPS
   (BITTERING)

1 OUNCE TETTNANGER HOPS
   (FLAVORING)
1 OUNCE CASCADE HOPS (AROMA)
1 OUNCE CASCADE HOPS (DRY HOP)
1 PACKAGE AMERICAN ALE YEAST
3/4 CUP CORN SUGAR (PRIMING)

Mash crushed grains for 60 to 90 minutes. Collect 6 gallons of wort. Add Liberty hops and boil for 1 hour, adding the Tettnanger hops after 30 minutes and 1 ounce Cascade hops after 50 minutes. Cool wort and pitch yeast. Ferment for 5 to 7 days. Transfer to secondary fermenter and add 1 ounce Cascade hops. Ferment an additional 7 to 10 days. Bottle, using corn sugar. Age in bottle 7 to 10 days.

OG: 1.046

Cobbler Lager

THE WARM, BROWN-SUGARY FLAVORS of a homebaked cobbler inspired this recipe. The combination of apples and pears really shines through in this crisp lager.

6 POUNDS PILSNER MALT
1 POUND MUNICH MALT
1 POUND TORREFIED WHEAT
1 OUNCE TETTNANGER HOPS
  (BITTERING)
2 CUPS LIGHT BROWN SUGAR
2 POUNDS MUTSU APPLES (PEELED,
  CORED, AND QUARTERED)

2 POUNDS GRANNY SMITH APPLES
  (PEELED, CORED, AND QUARTERED)
3 POUNDS PEARS (PEELED, CORED,
  AND QUARTERED)
3 CINNAMON STICKS
1 PACKAGE AMERICAN LAGER YEAST
3/4 CUP CORN SUGAR (PRIMING)

Mash crushed grains for 60 to 90 minutes. Collect 6 gallons of wort. Add Tettnanger hops, brown sugar, and cinnamon sticks, and boil for 1 hour. Cool wort and pitch yeast. Primary-ferment at 50 to 55 degrees for 5 to 7 days. Transfer to secondary fermenter. Lager for 2 to 3 weeks. For 20 minutes, steep apples and pears in enough 150-degree water to cover. Remove fruit from heat and add to fermenter. Lager an additional 7 to 10 days. Rack to tertiary fermenter and let sit 2 to 3 days. Bottle, using corn sugar. Age in bottle 7 to 10 days.

OG: 1.043

Mother's in the kitchen washing out the jugs,
Sister's in the pantry bottling the suds,
Father's in the cellar mixing up the hops,
Johnny's on the front porch watching for the cops.
—PROHIBITION SONG

Jimmy Carter's Peach Wit

MANY PEOPLE MAY THINK THAT Jimmy Carter's greatest accomplishment in political life was the peace accord he negotiated between Begin and Sadat. Or perhaps his work in Haiti, or his work with the underprivileged. While we agree that those were wonderful accomplishments, we have a different opinion as to which was his greatest. During Prohibition, Congress had passed a law to allow wine and beer making at home. However, by a clerical error, the words "and beer" after the word "wine" were omitted from the final document, thus rendering homebrewing illegal. In February of 1979, President Jimmy Carter corrected the mistake and made homebrewing legal. For this fact alone they should clear a spot on Mount Rushmore.

5 POUNDS PALE 2-ROW BARLEY
3 POUNDS MALTED WHEAT
1 POUND FLAKED WHEAT
1 OUNCE SAAZ HOPS (BITTERING)

8 POUNDS FRESH PEACHES (PITTED, SLICED, AND PEELED)
1 PACKAGE BELGIAN WHITE YEAST
3/4 CUP CORN SUGAR (PRIMING)

Mash crushed grains for 60 to 90 minutes. Collect 6 gallons of wort and add Saaz hops. Boil for 1 hour. Cool wort and pitch yeast. Ferment for 7 days. Transfer to a secondary fermenter. For 20 minutes, steep peaches in enough 150-degree water to cover. Add peaches and water to fermenter. Ferment an additional 10 days. Rack to tertiary fermenter for 2 to 3 days. Bottle, using corn sugar. Age in bottle for 7 to 10 days.

OG: 1.043

Pumpernickel Rye

EVOKING THE SUBTLE FLAVORS OF our favorite loaf, this lager is crisp and dry, with a hint of rye and caraway. Like pumpernickel bread, it uses molasses to help achieve its characteristic color.

6 POUNDS AMERICAN 6-ROW MALT
1 POUND FLAKED RYE
2 OUNCES CRYSTAL MALT (60L)
2 OUNCES CHOCOLATE MALT
1 CUP MOLASSES
1 OUNCE HALLERTAUER HOPS
  (BITTERING)

1 PACKAGE AMERICAN ALE YEAST
2 TABLESPOONS CARAWAY SEEDS,
  LIGHTLY CRUSHED
1¼ CUPS DRY MALT EXTRACT
  (PRIMING)

Mash crushed grains for 60 to 90 minutes (a protein rest is advisable, because of the rye). Collect 6 gallons of wort. Add molasses and Hallertauer hops and boil for 1 hour. Cool wort and pitch yeast. Ferment for 7 to 10 days. Transfer to secondary fermenter, adding caraway seeds, and ferment for an additional 14 to 21 days. Bottle, using dry malt extract. Age in bottle for 10 to 14 days.

OG: 1.045

Holiday
and
Seasonal Beers

From *A Drinking Life by Pete Hamill*

After that late Sunday breakfast, after the talk, after the reading of the Irish letter, my father would go out, down the dark linoleum-covered hallway, into the street. He'd turn left outside of the areaway, and walk up the block, saying hello to people. Sometimes I'd watch him from the stoop. He'd step hard on the good right leg and swing the wooden left leg behind him, and I thought that being a cripple wasn't such a terrible thing; he walked in his own special way, and that made him different from other men. Along the way, most of the Sunday people smiled at him. He was off to Mass. Or so he said.

And then one Sunday when I was almost eight, he said to me, Come on, McGee. I walked with him up to the corner and for the first time entered the tight, dark, amber-colored, wool-smelling world of a saloon. This one was called Gallagher's.

In I went behind him, to stand among the stools and the gigantic men, overwhelmed at first by the sour smell of dried beer, then inhaling tobacco smells, the toilet smell, the smell of men. The place had been a speakeasy during Prohibition, and the men still entered through the back door. There was a front entrance too, opening into a large dim room with booths and tables; it was supposed to be a restaurant, but the kitchen was dusty and dark and nobody was ever there, except a few quiet women, who could not get service in the barroom proper. In that room, the men were jammed together at a high three-sided bar, talking, smoking, singing, laughing and drinking. They drank beer. They drank whiskey. There was no television then, so they made their own entertainments.

Hey, Billy, give us a song! someone yelled. And then he started.

> Mister Patrick McGinty
> An Irishman of note,
> He fell into a fortune
> And bought himself a goat.
> A goat's milk, said Paddy,
> Of that I'll have me fill,
> But when he got the nanny home
> He found it was a bill.

Laughter and cheers and off he went, verse after verse, even one about Hitler, added to help the war effort. Then everyone in the bar joined him for the song's final lines:

> And we'll leave the rest to Providence—
> And Paddy McGinty's goat!

They cheered and hooted and asked for another, and my father raised his glass to his lips, beaming, delighted with himself, took a long drink, and gave them what they wanted. From where I was huddled against the wall, he was the star of the place, ignoring the stools that the other men used, standing almost defiantly with one hand on the lip of the bar for balance, his face all curves, clearly the center of attention. Even the portrait of Franklin Delano Roosevelt, hanging in the dim light above the cash register, seemed to approve.

This is where men go, I thought; this is what men do. When he was finished, they bought him drinks and then someone else began to sing and then Bing Crosby was singing on the jukebox. One of my father's friends slipped me a nickel, another gave me a dime, and Dick the Bartender, a mysterious shiny-faced man in *starched collar, passed me some saltine crackers in cellophane and a ginger ale with a cherry in it. Strangers rubbed my blond head. They told me I was getting bigger. And then my father said, Go on now, go along home.*

As for drinks, we shall have to make some beer.
—FATHER LEJEUNE, 1634

New Year's Lambic

THIS BEER IS THE ULTIMATE in brewing tradition. The first batch is created on New Year's Day, and is ready to enjoy on the following New Year's Eve. Drink this sweet concoction as you and your loved ones ring in the new year, but make sure you save a six-pack for the next day. Five to help cure that hangover, and one to add to next year's batch. This is truly a brew that embodies the spirit of each passing year and will remind you of where you've been, where you are, and where you're going.

6 POUNDS IREKS WHEAT MALT
  EXTRACT (100 PERCENT WHEAT)
3⅓ POUNDS LIGHT MALT EXTRACT
1½ OUNCES CASCADE HOPS
  (BITTERING)
½ OUNCE CASCADE HOPS (AROMA)
8 POUNDS CRANBERRIES (FRESH)

1 BOTTLE PREVIOUS YEAR'S NEW
  YEAR'S LAMBIC
1 CUP CORN SUGAR
1 PACKAGE BELGIAN WHITE YEAST
1 PACKAGE BRETTANOMYCES
  BRUXELLENSIS YEAST
¾ CUP CORN SUGAR (PRIMING)

Dissolve malt extracts in water and cool to 125 degrees. Sour wort (see Brewer's Tip, p. 181). Add wort to brew pot, add 1½ ounces Cascade hops, and boil for 1 hour, adding ½ ounce Cascade hops for the last 10 minutes. Cool wort and pitch Belgian White yeast. Ferment 7 to 10 days. Transfer to secondary fermenter and pitch Brettanomyces bruxellensis yeast culture. Ferment an additional 10 to 14 days. Place crushed cranberries in 2 cups water and add 1 cup corn sugar. Steep at 150 degrees for 20 minutes. Add to secondary fermenter and ferment an additional 5 to 7 days. Rack to tertiary fermenter and let sit for 2 to 3 days.

Bottle, using ¾ cup corn sugar that has been boiled in 1 bottle of previous year's batch for 5 minutes. Age in bottle for 2 to 3 months. Best after 1 year.

OG: 1.051

All the buildup and hype, everything else, is foam. The game is the beer.

—MARV LEVY, BUFFALO BILLS HEAD COACH

Super Bowl Sunday Pale Ale

WHILE NOT AN "OFFICIAL HOLIDAY," Super Bowl Sunday could be the most fervently observed day in America. Around the country, Super Bowl parties abound with chicken wings, pizza, nachos, and of course—beer. This pale ale has taken all of the elements of Super Bowl Sunday into account. In short, it's great with all of your typical Super Bowl food, but light enough to drink all day, which is what the Super Bowl seems to take.

5 POUNDS PALE 2-ROW MALT
1 POUND CRYSTAL MALT (40L)
1 POUND WHEAT MALT
½ POUND FLAKED BARLEY
½ POUND FLAKED MAIZE
2 OUNCES KENT GOLDINGS HOPS
  (BITTERING)

1½ OUNCES CASCADE HOPS
  (AROMA)
1 TEASPOON IRISH MOSS
1 PACKAGE AMERICAN ALE YEAST
¾ CUP CORN SUGAR (PRIMING)

Mash crushed grains for 60 to 90 minutes. Collect 6 gallons of wort. Add Kent Goldings hops and boil for 1 hour, adding Irish moss for the last 10 minutes. Remove from heat, add Cascade hops, and steep for 15 minutes. Cool wort and pitch yeast. Ferment for 5 to 7 days. Transfer to secondary fermenter and ferment an additional 7 to 10 days. Bottle, using corn sugar. Age in bottle 10 to 14 days.

OG: 1.038

Fat Tuesday's Cajun Pepper Ale

THERE IS NOTHING QUITE LIKE Mardi Gras. What better way to prepare for the most revered Christian holiday season than with a week of drunken debauchery in New Orleans? We brewed this beer with the New Orleans feel in mind. If you're one of those people that just haven't developed a taste for pepper beers, brew this up in a three- or one-gallon batch and use it to cook with. It makes a wonderful addition to a pot of chili or a spicy tomato sauce.

6⅔ POUNDS LIGHT MALT EXTRACT
½ POUND CRYSTAL MALT
1½ OUNCES FUGGLES HOPS
 (BITTERING)
½ OUNCE SAAZ HOPS (AROMA)

1 TEASPOON IRISH MOSS
¼ POUND CAYENNE PEPPERS
 (HALVED AND SEEDED)
1 PACKAGE EUROPEAN ALE YEAST
¾ CUP CORN SUGAR (PRIMING)

Place crushed crystal malt in water and steep at 155 degrees for 30 minutes. Remove spent grains and add malt extract and Fuggles hops and boil for 60 minutes, adding the Irish moss during the last 10 minutes and the Saaz hops during the last 5 minutes. Cool wort and pitch yeast. Ferment for 5 to 7 days. Transfer to secondary fermenter with peppers. Ferment for 7 to 10 days. Bottle, using corn sugar. Age in bottle for 7 to 10 days.

OG: 1.044

Do not cease to drink beer, to eat, to intoxicate thyself, to make love and celebrate the good days.
—EGYPTIAN PROVERB

Lover's Lane Valentine Stout

THIS CHOCOLATE-CHERRY STOUT IS a perfect way to counteract the midwinter chill. Its rich, frothy character is especially satisfying when shared with a loved one in front of a warm fire. So pour a pint and snuggle up.

6⅔ POUNDS DARK MALT EXTRACT
3 POUNDS AMBER MALT EXTRACT
½ POUND CHOCOLATE MALT
½ POUND BLACK PATENT MALT
½ POUND ROASTED BARLEY
1½ OUNCES CASCADE HOPS
   (BITTERING)
½ POUND SEMISWEET BAKING
   CHOCOLATE

6 POUNDS SWEET DARK CHERRIES
   (STEMMED AND LIGHTLY CRUSHED)
2 TEASPOONS IRISH MOSS
1 PACKAGE IRISH ALE YEAST
1¼ CUPS DRY MALT EXTRACT
   (PRIMING)

Place crushed chocolate malt, roasted barley, and black patent malt in water and steep at 155 degrees for 30 minutes. Remove spent grains, and add dark and amber malt extracts, Cascade hops, and melted chocolate (melting in a bowl in the microwave has been the best method that we've found). Boil for 1 hour, adding the Irish moss for the last 10 minutes. Cool wort and pitch yeast. Ferment for 7 to 10 days and then transfer to a secondary fermenter. For 20 minutes, steep the cherries in enough 150-degree water to cover. Add the cherries and the water to the fermenter. Ferment an additional 7 to 10 days. Bottle, using dry malt extract. Age in bottle for 10 days.

OG: 1.064

St. Patrick's Day Irish Cream Stout

SAINT PATRICK'S DAY IS WITHOUT a doubt the greatest of all the drinking holidays. Established to commemorate the driving of the snakes out of Ireland by Saint Patrick, it has become a vast celebration of the Irish heritage. And if there is one aspect of the Irish heritage that is eternal, it is the great love of drink. Shlonta!

4 POUNDS ALEXANDER'S PALE MALT EXTRACT	½ POUND BLACK PATENT MALT
3⅓ POUNDS DARK MALT EXTRACT	2 OUNCES WILLAMETTE HOPS (BITTERING)
1 POUND DARK DRY MALT EXTRACT	1 PACKAGE IRISH ALE YEAST
¾ POUND CRYSTAL MALT (120L)	4 OUNCES IRISH CREAM EXTRACT
½ POUND ROASTED BARLEY	1¼ CUPS DRY MALT EXTRACT (PRIMING)
½ POUND CHOCOLATE MALT	

Place crushed crystal malt, chocolate malt, roasted barley, and black patent malt in water and steep at 155 degrees for 30 minutes. Remove spent grains, and add Alexander's pale malt extract, dark malt extract, dark dry malt extract, and Willamette hops. Boil for 1 hour. Cool wort and pitch yeast. Ferment for 10 to 14 days. Transfer to secondary fermenter and add the Irish cream extract. Ferment an additional 5 to 7 days. Bottle, using 1¼ cups dry malt extract. Age in bottle for 10 to 14 days.

OG: 1.058

Labeling

Many homebrewers like to label their beers for presentation. This extension of the creative process is really quite fun, and here are some tips to make it easier.

The first step is getting suitable bottles to put your beer in. Twelve-ounce bottles are the most common, and are easily obtained at recycling centers and bars, or you can save all your empties. You will quickly realize that the labels are notoriously difficult to get off. We have found that soaking the bottles in a bathtub with enough water to cover bottles and 1 cup ammonia will dissolve most label adhesives used by commercial brewers.

Better yet, seek out imported beer bottles, particularly Bass and Guinness, whose brewers never intended them to soak in an ice bath at the local pub as do their American counterparts. You will find that the labels of these bottles fall right off after a short soak in warm water. Add some bleach, and you have just sanitized the bottles and removed labels at the same time.

The best way to create labels is with a computer drawing program and a laser printer. The images are reproducible and easily stored. Creating them by hand is just as practical, using a photocopier to mass-produce them.

Amazingly, the best adhesive we have found yet is milk. Brush milk on the back of your label and stick it to your clean, dry bottle of homebrew. Allow it to dry and you will have a personalized beer until you soak it in water, when it will fall off like a Bass label.

It is my design to die in a brewhouse; let ale be placed to my mouth when I am expiring, that when the choir of angels come, they may say, "Be God propitious to this drinker."

—SAINT COLOMBANUS

Easter Sunday Bitter (ESB)

IN CHRISTIANITY, THE FORTY DAYS prior to Easter Sunday are a time of fasting. If you choose to give up beer for that time (God forbid), this is a great one to break the fast with. It is a smooth bitter that you can share with the whole family while the kids search for Easter eggs on a beautiful spring afternoon. It even goes well with chocolate bunnies. Well, maybe not.

5½ POUNDS BRITISH PALE 2-ROW MALT
1 POUND CRYSTAL MALT (10L)
¼ POUND CHOCOLATE MALT
1 TABLESPOON GYPSUM
2 CUPS BREWER'S CORN SYRUP
1 OUNCE NORTHERN BREWER HOPS (BITTERING)
1½ OUNCES KENT GOLDINGS HOPS (FLAVORING)
1 OUNCE KENT GOLDINGS HOPS (DRY HOP)
1 TEASPOON IRISH MOSS
1 PACKAGE BRITISH ALE YEAST
¾ CUP CORN SUGAR (PRIMING)

Mash crushed grains with gypsum for 90 minutes. Collect 6 gallons of wort and add corn syrup. Bring to a boil, and add Northern Brewer hops. Boil 1 hour, adding 1½ ounces Kent Goldings hops after 30 minutes. Add Irish moss during final 10 minutes of boil. Cool wort and pitch yeast. Ferment 7 to 10 days. Transfer to secondary fermenter, add 1 ounce Kent Goldings hops, and ferment an additional 7 to 10 days. Bottle, using corn sugar. Age for 40 days, naturally.

OG: 1.045

May Day Maibock

MAI BOCK IS TRADITIONALLY BREWED FOR consumption on the first of May, or May Day—a holiday similar to Labor Day in the U.S. The celebration coincides with the coming of spring and the reappearance of flowers. Participants dance around the maypole holding streamers attached to the pole. We like to think they tried it without the streamers, but because of the Mai bock, it wasn't possible.

10 POUNDS AMBER MALT EXTRACT
1 POUND CRYSTAL MALT (20L)
½ POUND GERMAN PALE 2-ROW
  MALT
½ POUND CHOCOLATE MALT

1 OUNCE PERLE HOPS (BITTERING)
1 OUNCE HALLERTAUER HOPS
  (AROMA)
1 PACKAGE BAVARIAN LAGER YEAST
¾ CUP CORN SUGAR (PRIMING)

Place crushed grains in water and steep at 155 degrees for 30 minutes. Remove spent grains and add malt extract. Boil 1 hour, adding Perle hops after 15 minutes. Add Hallertauer hops 45 minutes into the boil. Cool wort and pitch yeast. Ferment at 50 to 55 degrees for 5 days. Transfer to secondary fermenter and lager 3 to 4 weeks. Bottle, using corn sugar, and age 1 week.

OG: 1.072

I have total irreverence for anything connected with society, except that which makes the road safer, the beer stronger, and the old men and women warmer in the winter and happier in the summer.

—BRENDAN BEHAN

Watermelon Summer Lager

FEW THINGS SAY SUMMER LIKE the sweet, juicy taste of watermelon. Its light, clean sweetness has made this a favorite for Fourth of

July barbecues and beach parties. Its cool, refreshing taste is guaranteed to create memories of the good old summertime.

5½ POUNDS ALEXANDER'S PALE   1 PACKAGE AMERICAN LAGER YEAST
MALT EXTRACT   8 POUNDS WATERMELON (CUBED)
1 OUNCE SAAZ HOPS (AROMA)   ¾ CUP CORN SUGAR (PRIMING)
1 TEASPOON IRISH MOSS

Place malt extract in water and boil for 1 hour, adding Saaz hops and Irish moss duing the last 5 minutes. Cool wort and pitch yeast. Primary-ferment at 50 to 55 degrees for 5 to 7 days. Transfer to secondary fermenter. Lager for 2 to 3 weeks. For 20 minutes, steep watermelon in enough 150-degree water to cover. Add watermelon and water to fermenter. Ferment an additional 5 to 7 days. Bottle, using corn sugar. Age in bottle for 5 to 7 days.

OG: 1.033

Firecracker Red

ALTHOUGH SUMMER IS NOT THE ideal time to be brewing, we can't imagine a Fourth of July picnic without homebrew. The red-hots add a cinnamon spice and an interesting color.

6⅔ POUNDS LIGHT MALT EXTRACT   1½ OUNCES LIBERTY HOPS
1 POUND CRYSTAL MALT (20L)   (FLAVORING)
2 OUNCES ROASTED BARLEY   1 TEASPOON IRISH MOSS
½ POUND TORREFIED WHEAT   1 PACKAGE AMERICAN ALE YEAST
1 POUND RED-HOTS CANDIES   ¾ CUP CORN SUGAR (PRIMING)
1 OUNCE CENTENNIAL HOPS
(BITTERING)

Place the crushed grains in water and steep at 155 degrees for 30 minutes. Remove the grains and add the malt extract, red-hots, and Centennial hops. Boil for 1 hour. Add Liberty hops for the last 20 minutes of the boil. Add the Irish moss for the last 10 minutes. Cool wort and pitch yeast. Ferment for 1 week, then transfer to a secondary fermenter. Ferment for 1 week in secondary fermenter. Bottle, using corn sugar. Beer should be ready within 7 days.

OG: 1.045

Apple Brown Betty Fall Ale

FARM-FRESH APPLES MAKE THIS a special brew. There is no fruit that embodies the crisp character of autumn like orchard apples. The tartness of Granny Smith, the sweetness of Red Delicious—they each impart their own personalities to this savory ale. Cinnamon and brown sugar add a quality reminiscent of apple cobbler cooling on the windowsill.

6⅔ POUNDS LIGHT MALT EXTRACT
1 POUND DRY MALT EXTRACT
½ POUND CHOCOLATE MALT
1 CUP DARK BROWN SUGAR
8 POUNDS APPLES (HALF GRANNY
  SMITH, HALF RED DELICIOUS)
2 TEASPOONS GROUND CINNAMON
1½ OUNCES FUGGLES HOPS
  (BITTERING)

½ OUNCE HALLERTAUER HOPS
  (AROMA)
1 TEASPOON IRISH MOSS
1 PACKAGE BRITISH ALE YEAST
1 STICK CINNAMON
1¼ CUPS DRY MALT EXTRACT
  (PRIMING)

Add crushed chocolate malt to water and steep at 155 degrees for 30 minutes. Remove spent grains and add light malt extract and 1 pound dry malt extract, brown sugar, and Fuggles hops. Boil for 1 hour. During the boil, peel, core and dice half the apples (2 pounds of each) making sure to discard the seeds. Remove wort from heat and add the diced apples, ground cinnamon, Hallertauer hops, and Irish moss, and steep for 30 minutes. Strain out apples and set aside for Malted Applesauce. Cool wort and pitch yeast. Ferment for 5 to 7 days. Transfer to secondary fermenter. Peel, slice and core the rest of the apples and puree in a food processor. Steep apple puree in 150-degree water for 20 minutes and add the puree and a cinnamon stick to secondary fermenter. Ferment for an additional 7 to 10 days. Rack to tertiary fermenter and let sit 2 to 3 days. Bottle, using 1¼ cups dry malt extract. Age in bottle for 5 to 7 days, and then enjoy after a rosy afternoon of raking leaves.

OG: 1.053

Falling Leaves Autumn Cider

FRESH APPLE CIDER IS ONE of the most eagerly awaited aspects of the fall. The champagne yeast really allows the taste of the apples to shine and creates smaller bubbles, which provide more of the sparkle we prefer in cider. The brown sugar and vanilla provide a sweet counterpart to the tang of the apples. It's a taste of fall we look forward to every year.

5 GALLONS FRESH APPLE CIDER

1 CUP CORN SUGAR

1 CUP DARK BROWN SUGAR

3 TABLESPOONS VANILLA EXTRACT

2 TEASPOONS PECTIN ENZYME

1 TO 2 PACKAGES CHAMPAGNE
   YEAST

¾ CUP CORN SUGAR (OPTIONAL)

Place 4 gallons of the apple cider in the fermenter. Dissolve 1 cup corn sugar, brown sugar, vanilla extract, and pectin enzyme in 1 gallon of cider. Add to fermenter with cider. Allow to sit for 24 to 36 hours. Pitch champagne yeast (using 2 packages of yeast will provide a drier cider). Allow to ferment for 7 to 10 days. Bottle, using ¾ cup corn sugar for a sparkling cider or no corn sugar for a flat cider. Age in bottle for 7 days.

*They who have drunk beer . . . fall on their back
. . . but there is peculiarity in the effects of the
drink made from barley . . . for they that get drunk
on other intoxicating liquors fall on all parts of
their body, they fall on the left side, on the right
side, on their faces, and on their backs. But it is
only those who get drunk on beer that
fall on their backs with their faces upward.*

—ARISTOTLE

Slidin'-on-Your-Back Oktoberfest Lager

OUR FAVORITE MOMENT OF THE 1992 Winter Olympics occurred during a profile of a German luger. "There are only two things that this man does well," the narrator stated, "slide down a hill on his back and drink beer." In an instant, he became our hero. We brewed this Oktoberfest lager in his honor. We think he would appove.

6²/₃ POUNDS AMBER MALT EXTRACT
2 POUNDS DRY LIGHT MALT EXTRACT
1 POUND CRYSTAL MALT (40L)
2 OUNCES SAAZ HOPS (BITTERING)
1 OUNCE HALLERTAUER MITTELFRÜH
  HOPS (AROMA)

1 TEASPOON IRISH MOSS
1 PACKAGE MUNICH LAGER YEAST
³/₄ CUP CORN SUGAR (PRIMING)

Place crushed crystal malt in water and steep at 155 degrees for 30 minutes. Remove spent grains, add malt extracts and Saaz hops, and boil for 1 hour, adding the Hallertauer hops and Irish moss during the last 5 minutes. Cool wort and pitch yeast. Primary-ferment at 50 to 55 degrees for 5 to 7 days. Transfer to secondary fermenter. Lager 3 to 4 weeks. Bottle, using corn sugar. Age in bottle for 14 days.

OG: 1.061

Drunk-in-the-Streets-of-Cologne Oktoberfest Lager

ANY HOLIDAY WHERE PEOPLE STOP working and just drink beer is our kind of holiday. Witness the glory of Oktoberfest! While no homebrew can replicate the essence of sitting in a German Fest Haus on a chilly September day, this one comes close. Raise a stein of this German-style brew come September and salute the Germans.

6⅔ POUNDS WHEAT MALT EXTRACT
  (55/45 BLEND)
3 POUNDS AMBER MALT EXTRACT
2½ OUNCES SAAZ HOPS (BITTERING)
1 OUNCE MOUNT HOOD HOPS
  (AROMA)

1 TEASPOON IRISH MOSS
1 PACKAGE BAVARIAN LAGER YEAST
¾ CUP CORN SUGAR (PRIMING)

Place malt extract and Saaz hops in water and boil for 1 hour, adding Mount Hood hops and Irish moss during the last 5 minutes. Cool wort and pitch yeast. Primary-ferment at 50 to 55 degrees for 5 to 7 days. Transfer to secondary fermenter. Lager for 3 to 4 weeks. Bottle, using corn sugar. Age in bottle for 14 days.

OG: 1.053

Filled with mingled cream and amber
I will drain that glass again.
Such hilarious visions clamber
Through the chamber of my brain —
Quaintest thoughts — queerest fancies
Come to life and fade away:
What care I how time advances?
I am drinking ale today

—EDGAR ALLAN POE

Black Cat Halloween Porter

TIRED OF GETTING UP TO answer the door fifty times every October 31? Tired of cleaning the eggs off your front door and the toilet paper out of the trees? Have a batch of this brew ready next year. You'll be amazed how much more pleasant things will be.

3⅓ POUNDS DARK MALT EXTRACT
3⅓ POUNDS AMBER MALT EXTRACT
½ POUND CHOCOLATE MALT
½ POUND BLACK PATENT MALT
1 CUP MOLASSES
3 TABLESPOONS VANILLA EXTRACT
1½ OUNCES FUGGLES HOPS
 (BITTERING)

1 OUNCE TETTNANGER HOPS
 (AROMA)
1 PACKAGE IRISH ALE YEAST
1¼ CUPS DRY MALT EXTRACT
 (PRIMING)

Place crushed chocolate malt and black patent malt in water and steep at 155 degrees for 30 minutes. Remove spent grains, add dark and amber malt extracts, molasses, and Fuggles hops, and boil for 1 hour, adding the Tettnanger hops for the last 5 minutes of the boil. Cool wort and pitch yeast. Ferment for 7 to 10 days. Transfer to secondary fermenter and add vanilla extract. Ferment an additional 5 to 7 days. Bottle, using 1¼ cups dry malt extract. Age in bottle for 7 to 10 days.

OG: 1.044

The Great Pumpkin Ale

THE TRADITION OF USING PUMPKIN in beer is as old as the first Thanksgiving itself. Since barley was at times quite scarce, the pilgrims would use pumpkin as the fermentable base in many of their beers. This is one of our favorite recipes in the book. It has a smooth, rich taste with a hint of pumpkin flavor and a wonderful spicy aftertaste. Our friends and relatives look forward to it each and every Thanksgiving.

3 POUNDS AMBER MALT EXTRACT
3 POUNDS LIGHT DRY MALT EXTRACT
1 POUND CRYSTAL MALT
½ POUND CHOCOLATE MALT
1 TEASPOON GYPSUM
2 OUNCES KENT GOLDINGS HOPS
  (BITTERING)
1 OUNCE FUGGLES HOPS (AROMA)
1 TEASPOON IRISH MOSS

8 POUNDS PUMPKIN (FRESH,
  NOT CANNED)
1 PACKAGE PUMPKIN PIE SPICE
4 CINNAMON STICKS
3 WHOLE NUTMEGS
6 WHOLE ALLSPICE
1 PACKAGE LONDON ALE YEAST
¾ CUP CORN SUGAR (PRIMING)

Quarter the pumpkin and sprinkle with pumpkin pie spice. Bake for 2 hours at 350 degrees, until it is tender. Remove from the oven. Cut the pumpkin into 1-inch cubes, mash slightly, and set aside. Place crushed crystal malt, chocolate malt, and gypsum in water and steep at 155 degrees for 30 minutes. Remove spent grains and add the malt extracts, Kent Goldings hops, pumpkin, cinnamon sticks, nutmeg, and allspice. Boil for 1 hour, adding the Fuggles hops and Irish moss during the last 5 minutes. Remove the whole spices and pumpkin. Cool wort and pitch yeast. Ferment 10 to 14 days. Transfer to secondary fermenter and ferment an additional 5 to 7 days. Bottle, using corn sugar. Age in bottle for 7 to 10 days.

OG: 1.049

Pilgrim Ale

THE ENGLISH SETTLERS WHO ARRIVED in America in 1620, now better known as the Pilgrims, originally intended to follow in the footsteps of the first English colonists and land in Virginia. So why stop in Massachusetts? Simple—beer. As the scribe of the *Mayflower* wrote, "So in the morning, after we had called on God for direction, we came to this resolution—to go presently ashore again and to take a better view of two places which we thought most fitting for us; for we could not take time for further search or consideration, our victual being much spent, especially our beer." Happy Thanksgiving.

7 POUNDS PALE 2-ROW MALT
1 POUND CRYSTAL MALT
½ POUND MUNICH MALT
¼ POUND CHOCOLATE MALT
8 POUNDS FRESH PUMPKIN
1 PACKAGE PUMPKIN PIE SPICE
1 OUNCE MOUNT HOOD HOPS
  (BITTERING)
1 OUNCE LIBERTY HOPS (AROMA)

1 TEASPOON GYPSUM
1 TEASPOON IRISH MOSS
4 CINNAMON STICKS
1½ TABLESPOONS WHOLE ALLSPICE
2 NUTMEGS (CRUSHED)
4 WHOLE CLOVES
1 PACKAGE AMERICAN ALE YEAST
¾ CUP CORN SUGAR (PRIMING)

Quarter the pumpkin and sprinkle with pumpkin pie spice. Bake for 2 hours at 350 degrees, until it is tender. Remove from the oven. Cut the pumpkin into 1-inch cubes, mash slightly, and set aside. Mash grains for 60 to 90 minutes. Collect 6 gallons of wort. Add pumpkin, Mount Hood hops, gypsum, and half of the whole spices, and boil for 1 hour. Add Irish moss for the last 5 minutes. Remove from heat, add Liberty hops, and steep for 5 minutes. Cool wort and pitch yeast. Ferment for 5 to 7 days. Transfer to secondary fermenter and add remaining spices. Ferment an additional 7 to 10 days. Bottle, using corn sugar. Age in bottle 7 to 10 days.

OG: 1.046

Now, thrice welcome Christmas!
which brings us good cheer;
mince pies and plum pudding—
strong Ale and strong Beer.
—CHRISTMAS POEM, 1695

Grandma's House Christmas Chocolate Mint Stout

IF YOU'RE LIKE US, YOU'VE spent many a holiday season going from one relative's house to another, exchanging presents and making small talk. And in every house a big bowl of peppermints and chocolate awaited our eager, grasping fingers. This beer is brewed in that tradition. Have a batch ready for the holiday season and put it out instead of the candy bowl. We guarantee it will make everyone's Yuletide much brighter. The mint and chocolate tastes are very subtle but unmistakable.

6²/₃ POUNDS DARK MALT EXTRACT

2 POUNDS DARK DRY MALT EXTRACT

1 POUND CRYSTAL MALT (60L)

½ POUND ROASTED BARLEY

½ POUND BLACK PATENT MALT

1½ OUNCES CASCADE HOPS (BITTERING)

½ OUNCE HALLERTAUER HOPS (AROMA)

2 TEASPOONS GYPSUM

6 OUNCES SEMISWEET BAKING CHOCOLATE

4 OUNCES FRESH MINT LEAVES

1 PACKAGE IRISH ALE YEAST

1¼ CUPS DRY MALT EXTRACT (PRIMING)

Place the crushed crystal malt, gypsum, roasted barley, and black patent malt in water and steep at 155 degrees for 30 minutes. Remove spent grains and add dark malt extract, dark dry malt extract, and Cascade hops. Boil 30 minutes. Add chocolate. Boil an additional 30 minutes, adding Hallertauer hops during the last 5 minutes. Cool wort and pitch yeast. Ferment for 7 to 10 days. Transfer to secondary fermenter and add crushed mint leaves. Ferment an additional 7 days. Bottle, using 1¼ cups dry malt extract. Age in bottle 14 days.

OG: 1.063

Holiday Prowler Beer

AS A HOMEBREWER, YOU FIND yourself with a lot more beer than you can actually drink. If you are lucky, you can trade homebrew with friends, and treat yourself to a wider variety of beers than those that you brew yourself. But more probably you will end up giving your beer to your non-brewing friends as part of your never-ending mission to increase beer awareness. There is no better time than the winter holidays to spread good cheer. Holiday Prowler is the perfect gift to take to all the parties of the season. Make plenty, because like the holidays this beer will be gone before you know it.

6 POUNDS AMBER DRY MALT
  EXTRACT
1 ½ POUNDS CLOVER HONEY
¾ POUND CRYSTAL MALT
¼ POUND CHOCOLATE MALT
2 OUNCES BLACKSTRAP MOLASSES
1 TABLESPOON GYPSUM
1 OUNCE CLUSTER HOPS
  (BITTERING)
1 OUNCE WILLAMETTE HOPS
  (AROMA)
4 CINNAMON STICKS

½ TEASPOON FRESH-GROUND
  NUTMEG
1 VANILLA BEAN (SPLIT
  LENGTHWISE)
1 ½ TEASPOONS CLOVES
7 WHOLE ALLSPICE
ZEST OF 2 ORANGES
½ TEASPOON IRISH MOSS
1 PACKAGE LONDON ALE YEAST
1 ¼ CUPS DARK DRY MALT EXTRACT
  (PRIMING)

Place crushed grains and gypsum in water and steep at 155 degrees for 30 minutes. Remove spent grains and add amber malt extract and honey. Boil 1 hour. Add the Cluster hops 15 minutes into the boil. Add Irish moss during the final 20 minutes of the boil. Place spices in a permeable bag (a hop bag will do nicely), and add them along with the Willamette hops for the final 15 minutes of the boil. Cool wort and pitch yeast. Ferment 7 to 10 days. Transfer to secondary fermenter and ferment an additional 7 days. Bottle, using dark dry malt extract. Age for 10 to 14 days.

OG: 1.048

There were more dances, and there were forfeits, and more dances, and there was cake, and there was negus, and there was a great piece of Cold Roast, and there was a great piece of Cold Boiled, and there were mince-pies, and plenty of beer.

—CHARLES DICKENS, *A CHRISTMAS CAROL*

Dickens' Strong Christmas Ale

IN A NUMBER OF DICKENS' best works he refers to the joys of brew. The Cratchits celebrated with gin and lemons, but old Fezziwig served up plenty of beer at his Christmas bash. And so, as Tiny Tim said, "Merry Christmas and God bless us, everyone."

6⅔ POUNDS DARK MALT EXTRACT
2 POUNDS DRY DARK MALT EXTRACT
3 POUNDS BUCKWHEAT HONEY
½ POUND CHOCOLATE MALT
½ POUND CRYSTAL MALT (80L)
½ POUND BLACK PATENT MALT
2 OUNCES NORTHERN BREWER HOPS
 (BITTERING)
1 OUNCE CASCADE HOPS (AROMA)
1 OUNCE GINGER, GRATED
3 ORANGES, PEELED AND
 QUARTERED
3 CINNAMON STICKS
2 WHOLE NUTMEGS
6 WHOLE CLOVES
½ TEASPOON IRISH MOSS
1 PACKAGE IRISH ALE YEAST
1¼ CUPS DRY MALT EXTRACT
 (PRIMING)

Place crushed crystal malt, chocolate malt, and black patent malt in water and steep at 155 degrees for 30 minutes. Remove spent grains, add dark and dry dark malt extracts, honey, and Northern Brewer hops, and boil for ½ hour. Add ginger, cinnamon sticks, nutmegs, and cloves, and boil an additional ½ hour. Add the Cascade hops and Irish moss during the last 5 minutes of the boil. Turn off heat and add the oranges. Allow to steep for 30 minutes, then strain. Cool wort and pitch yeast. Ferment for 10 to 14 days and then transfer to a secondary fermenter. Ferment an additional 7 to 10 days. Bottle, using 1¼ cups dry malt extract. Age in bottle for 7 to 10 days.

OG: 1.073

Winter Wonderland

ONE OF OUR FAVORITE STYLES of beer is the winter warmer that now seems to be offered by every good brewery. Our favorite is Samuel Smith's Winter Warmer. This is our own offering.

8 POUNDS ALEXANDER'S PALE MALT EXTRACT

1 POUND CRYSTAL MALT (60L)

1/2 POUND DEXTRINE MALT

1/2 POUND TORREFIED WHEAT

2 OUNCES CHOCOLATE MALT

2 OUNCES ROASTED BARLEY

2 POUNDS BUCKWHEAT HONEY

2 OUNCES CHALLENGER HOPS (BITTERING)

1 OUNCE KENT GOLDINGS HOPS (FLAVORING)

1 OUNCE KENT GOLDINGS HOPS (AROMA)

1 TEASPOON IRISH MOSS

1 OUNCE KENT GOLDINGS HOPS (DRY HOP)

3 CINNAMON STICKS

2 NUTMEGS (CRUSHED)

3 WHOLE CLOVES

2 WHOLE CARDAMOMS (CRUSHED)

1 PACKAGE LONDON ALE YEAST

1 1/2 CUPS MOLASSES (PRIMING)

Place crushed crystal malt, dextrine malt, torrefied wheat, chocolate malt, and roasted barley in water and steep at 155 degrees for 1 hour. Remove spent grains and add malt extract, honey, and Challenger hops. Boil for 1 hour, adding 1 ounce of Kent Goldings hops after 30 minutes and 1 ounce of Kent Goldings and Irish moss after 55 minutes. Cool wort and pitch yeast. Ferment for 7 to 10 days. Transfer to secondary fermenter and add 1 ounce Kent Goldings hops, cinnamon, nutmeg, cloves, and cardamom. Ferment an additional 7 to 10 days. Strain and bottle, using molasses. Age in bottle 10 to 14 days.

OG: 1.048

Of course you'll have another drop of ale.
A man's twice the man afterward.
You feel so warm and glorious.
—THOMAS HARDY, *FAR FROM THE MADDING CROWD*

Fireside Winter Warmer

SURE, EGGNOG IS THE TRADITIONAL beverage of choice while you decorate the tree, but be honest, wouldn't you *really* rather be drinking a beer? Brew up a batch of this winter warmer for next Christmas, and we're sure you'll never go back to eggnog again.

7 POUNDS PALE 2-ROW MALT
1 POUND CARA-PILS MALT
1 POUND MUNICH MALT
1 POUND FLAKED BARLEY
½ POUND LIGHT BROWN SUGAR
1½ OUNCES CASCADE HOPS
 (BITTERING)

1 TEASPOON IRISH MOSS
1½ OUNCES CASCADE HOPS
 (AROMA)
1 PACKAGE AMERICAN ALE YEAST
½ POUND LACTOSE
¾ CUP CORN SUGAR (PRIMING)

Mash crushed grains for 60 to 90 minutes. Collect 6 gallons of wort. Add brown sugar and 1½ ounces Cascade hops, and boil for 1 hour, adding Irish moss for last 10 minutes. Remove from heat and add 1½ ounces Cascade hops. Steep for 10 minutes. Cool wort and pitch yeast. Ferment for 10 to 14 days. Bottle, using corn sugar that has been boiled with lactose. Age in bottle 10 to 14 days.

OG: 1.058

Brewery Copycats

From Autobiography by Benjamin Franklin

At my first admission into this printing-house I took to working at press, imagining I felt a want of the bodily exercise I had been used to in America, where presswork is mixed with composing. I drank only water; the other workmen, near fifty in number, were great guzzlers of beer. On occasion, I carried up and down stairs a large form of types in each hand, when others carried but one in both hands. They wondered to see, from this and several instances, that the Water-American, *as they called me was* stronger than themselves, who drank strong beer! We had an alehouse boy who attended always in the house to supply the workmen. My companion at the press drank every day a pint before breakfast and dinner, a pint at dinner, a pint in the afternoon about six o'clock, and another when he had done his day's work. I thought it a detestable custom; but it was necessary, he supposed, to drink strong beer, that he might be strong to labor. I endeavored to convince him that the bodily strength afforded by beer could only be in proportion to the grain or flour of the barley dissolved in the water of which it was made; that there was more flour in a pennyworth of bread; and therefore, if he would eat that with a pint of water, it would give him more strength than a quart of beer. He drank on, however, and had four or five shillings to pay out of his wages every Saturday night for that muddling liquor; an expense I was free from. And thus these poor devils keep themselves always under.

Watts, after some weeks, desiring to have me in the composing room, I left the pressmen; a new bien venu or sum for drink, being five shillings, was demanded of me by the compositors. I thought it an imposition, as I had paid below; the master thought so too, and forbade my paying it. I stood out two or three weeks, was accordingly considered an excommunicate, and had so many little pieces of private mischief done me, by mixing my sorts, transposing my pages, breaking my matter, etc., etc., if I were ever so little out of the room, and all ascribed to the chappel ghost, which they said ever haunted those not regularly admitted, that, notwithstanding the master's protection, I found myself obliged to comply and pay the money, convinced of the folly of being on ill terms with those one is to live with continually.

I was now on a fair footing with them, and soon acquired considerable influence. I proposed some reasonable alterations in their chappel laws, and carried them against all opposition. From my example, a great part of them left their muddling breakfast of beer, and bread, and cheese, finding they could with me be supplied from a neighboring house with a large porringer of hot water gruel, sprinkled with pepper, crumbed with bread, and a bit of butter in it, for the price of a pint of beer, three half-pence. This was a more comfortable as well as cheaper breakfast, and kept their heads clearer. Those who continued sotting with beer all day, were often, by not paying, out of credit at the alehouse, and used to make interest with me to get beer, their light, as they phrased it, being out. I watched the pay table on Saturday night, and collected what I stood engaged for them, having to pay sometimes nearly thirty shillings a week on their accounts. This, and my being esteemed a pretty good riggite, that is, a jocular verbal satirist, supported my consequence in the society.

California Cascade

PERHAPS NO OTHER BREWERY IS more responsible for the craft brewing explosion in America than Sierra Nevada. Their pale ale is a wonderful balance between the floral quality of Cascade hops and malt sweetness. This is our attempt to duplicate it.

6⅔ POUNDS LIGHT MALT EXTRACT
1 POUND CRYSTAL MALT (20L)
1½ OUNCES PERLE HOPS
  (BITTERING)
1 OUNCE NUGGET HOPS (FLAVORING
  AND AROMA)

1½ OUNCES CASCADE HOPS (DRY
  HOP)
1 TEASPOON IRISH MOSS
1 PACKAGE AMERICAN ALE YEAST
¾ CUP CORN SUGAR (PRIMING)

Add crushed crystal malt to water and steep at 155 degrees for 30 minutes. Remove spent grains and add malt extract and Perle hops. Boil for 1 hour. Add ½ ounce of Nugget hops at 30 minutes and ½ ounce and the Irish moss at 50 minutes. Cool wort and pitch yeast. Ferment for 5 to 7 days. Transfer to secondary fermenter and add Cascade hops. Ferment 7 days. Bottle, using corn sugar. Age in bottle 7 days.

OG: 1.045

I think 49 Guinnesses is piggish.
—DYLAN THOMAS

Dublin's Finest

IN 1759 ARTHUR GUINNESS PURCHASED a little-used brewery in Dublin. And the rest, as they say, is history. While it is served around the world in a number of incarnations, and certainly falls into the category of "megabrewery," they still continue to produce a world-class stout that has come to define the dry stout style. You must add about 3 or 4 percent soured stout to properly recreate Guinness.

6²/₃ POUNDS DARK MALT EXTRACT
24 OUNCES GUINNESS STOUT
  (SOURED) (SEE BREWER'S TIP,
  BELOW)
½ POUND CRYSTAL MALT (80L)
½ POUND ROASTED BARLEY
½ POUND CHOCOLATE MALT

2 OUNCES KENT GOLDINGS HOPS
  (BITTERING)
½ CUP MALTO-DEXTRIN
1 PACKAGE IRISH ALE YEAST
1¼ CUPS DRY MALT EXTRACT
  (PRIMING)

Place crushed crystal malt, chocolate malt, and roasted barley in water and steep at 155 degrees for 30 minutes. Remove spent grains. Add dark malt extract, soured stout, malto-dextrin, and Kent Goldings hops. Boil for 1 hour. Cool wort and pitch yeast. Ferment for 10 to 14 days. Bottle, using dry malt extract. Age in bottle for 10 days.

OG: 1.055

Quick Souring

Certain beers, like Guinness copycats or Weizenbiers, require a certain amount of sourness to replicate the exact style. You can make a small amount of sour beer, which can be added to the wort to achieve the desired effect. However, if you haven't the time or the patience to make your own sour mash, you can simulate the results with a bottle or two of similarly styled beer. Two or three days before you are going to brew, pour the beer into a sanitized vessel that provides a generous exposed surface area, such as a pint glass. Cover with a clean, dry cloth (cheesecloth is ideal) and secure with a rubber band. Allow it to sit in a dark space at room temperature. Add the now-soured beer to your wort and boil for 1 hour. The boil will kill any microorganisms in the soured beer. Another option is to add the soured beer at bottling time. Allow to sour as above, and boil the soured beer for 10 minutes with the priming sugar.

Appliance-on-the-Fritz Pale Ale

WHEN THE TERM "GRANDFATHER OF the craft brewing revolution" is bandied about, the name Fritz Maytag always goes to the top of the list. Gambling a portion of his share of the family appliance fortune, Maytag bought the nearly bankrupt Anchor Brewing Company in the late sixties. While Anchor Brewing Company is best known for its Anchor Steam beer, Anchor Liberty is one of the finest examples of the American Pale Ale style. It possesses a strong hop aroma that is balanced nicely by the malt sweetness. This is our version.

6²/₃ POUNDS LIGHT MALT EXTRACT
¹/₂ POUND CRYSTAL MALT (40L)
1¹/₂ OUNCES WILLAMETTE HOPS
   (BITTERING)
1¹/₂ OUNCES CASCADE HOPS
   (AROMA)
1¹/₂ OUNCES CASCADE HOPS (DRY
   HOP)
2 TEASPOONS GYPSUM
1 TEASPOON IRISH MOSS
1 PACKAGE AMERICAN ALE YEAST
³/₄ CUP CORN SUGAR (PRIMING)

Place crushed crystal malt in water and steep at 155 degrees for 30 minutes. Remove spent grains. Add malt extract, gypsum, and Willamette hops, and boil for 1 hour, adding Irish moss for last 10 minutes. Turn off heat and add 1¹/₂ ounces Cascade hops and let steep for 15 minutes. Cool wort and pitch yeast. Ferment for 5 to 7 days. Transfer to secondary fermenter and add 1¹/₂ ounces Cascade hops. Ferment for 7 days. Bottle, using corn sugar. Age in bottle for 7 days.

OG: 1.051

First Stop Bitter

THE NEXT TIME (OR FIRST TIME) you travel to London via Heathrow airport, you may want to make the Fuller Brewery your first stop. And why not, since it *is* on the way from the airport. We feel that Fuller's is the best example of the extra-special bitter style, though there are many that are terrific. We've bottled with only

½ cup corn sugar in our version in an attempt to duplicate the hand-drawn variety.

6⅔ POUNDS LIGHT MALT EXTRACT
½ POUND CRYSTAL MALT (40L)
½ CUP LIGHT BROWN SUGAR
1 OUNCE KENT GOLDINGS HOPS
  (BITTERING)
½ OUNCE KENT GOLDINGS HOPS
  (AROMA)

1 TEASPOON IRISH MOSS
1 PACKAGE LONDON ESB ALE YEAST
2 TABLESPOONS LACTIC ACID
½ CUP CORN SUGAR (PRIMING)

Place crushed crystal malt in water and steep at 155 degrees for 30 minutes. Remove spent grains and add malt extract, brown sugar, and 1 ounce Kent Goldings hops. Boil for 1 hour, adding Irish moss for last 10 minutes. Turn off heat, add ½ ounce Kent Goldings, and steep for 10 minutes. Cool wort and pitch yeast. Ferment for 7 to 10 days. Bottle, using corn sugar and lactic acid. Age in bottle for 7 to 10 days.

OG: 1.047

He who drinks beer sleeps well. He who sleeps well cannot sin. He who does not sin goes to heaven. Amen.

—MONK, NAME UNKNOWN

Sinner's Salvation

THE ABBEY NOTRE DAME DE Scourmont is the largest and probably best known of the monastic breweries of Belgium. Within its walls the monks create some of the most unusual and extraordinary beers in the world. It is essential to culture the yeast from a bottle of Chimay to create this beer, since there is really no commercially available strain that comes close. After downing a couple of these reproductions, you are sure to begin singing "Cheer, cheer, for old Notre Dame."

6⅔ POUNDS LIGHT MALT EXTRACT
2 POUNDS DRY AMBER EXTRACT
½ POUND CRYSTAL MALT (60L)
¼ POUND CHOCOLATE MALT
1 OUNCE GALENA HOPS (BITTERING)
1 OUNCE TETTNANGER HOPS
   (AROMA)

1 PINT YEAST CULTURED FROM
BOTTLE OF CHIMAY (SEE
BREWER'S TIP, P. 36)
¾ CUP CORN SUGAR (PRIMING)

Place crushed crystal malt and chocolate malt in water and steep at 155 degrees for 30 minutes. Remove spent grains, add malt extracts and Galena hops, and boil for 1 hour. Turn off heat and add Tettnanger hops and steep for 10 minutes. Cool wort and pitch yeast culture. Ferment for 7 to 10 days. Transfer to secondary fermenter and ferment an additional 7 days. Bottle, using corn sugar. Age in bottle for 7 to 10 days.

OG: 1.063

A True American Original

LIKE BASEBALL, COCA-COLA, and the blues, steam beer is a true American original. Fritz Maytag single-handedly revived the Steam Beer style, which he has since trademarked. Just like the real thing, ours is a rich amber beer with a strong hop character.

6⅔ POUNDS LIGHT MALT EXTRACT
1 POUND CRYSTAL MALT (40L)
1½ OUNCES NORTHERN BREWER
   HOPS (BITTERING)
½ OUNCE CASCADE HOPS (AROMA)

1 TEASPOON IRISH MOSS
1 PACKAGE CALIFORNIA LAGER
   YEAST
¾ CUP CORN SUGAR (PRIMING)

Place crushed crystal malt in water and steep at 155 degrees. Remove spent grains, add malt extract and Northern Brewer hops, and boil for 1 hour, adding Cascade hops and Irish moss for the last 5 minutes. Cool wort and pitch yeast. Ferment for 7 to 10 days at 65 to 70 degrees. Transfer to secondary fermenter and ferment an additional 14 days at 45 to 50 degrees. Bottle, using corn sugar. Age in bottle for 7 to 10 days.

OG: 1.045

Strange Brew

BREWED AT THREAKSON'S BREWERY IN Yorkshire, Old Peculier is a dark strong ale with a surprisingly soft character. The addition of molasses is absolutely necessary to mimic the original successfully. When choosing your molasses, make sure to pick up one that is unsulfured.

3⅓ POUNDS LIGHT MALT EXTRACT

3⅓ POUNDS AMBER MALT EXTRACT

½ POUND CRYSTAL MALT (60L)

¼ POUND ROASTED BARLEY

1 CUP BLACKSTRAP MOLASSES

2 TEASPOONS GYPSUM

¼ CUP LACTOSE

1 OUNCE KENT GOLDINGS HOPS
  (BITTERING)

1 PACKAGE BRITISH ALE YEAST

1 CUP MOLASSES (PRIMING)

Place crushed crystal malt and roasted barley in water and steep at 155 degrees for 30 minutes. Remove spent grains, add malt extracts, blackstrap molasses, gypsum, and Kent Goldings hops, and boil for 1 hour. Dissolve lactose in 1 cup of water and add to wort at the end of the boil. Cool wort and pitch yeast. Ferment for 10 to 14 days. Bottle, using 1 cup molasses. Age in bottle 7 to 10 days.

OG: 1.050

Stuck Fermentation

If your fermentation has stopped sooner than you expected, first check your hydrometer: your beer may simply be done earlier than expected. If the reading tells you that it's not done, then you have a problem.

The most common cause is lack of oxygen or lack of nutrients. You can try giving your beer a good shake to rouse the yeast and inject oxygen. Or you can pitch more yeast. Champagne yeast is particularly good for this, since it won't add additional esters to your beer.

If you're making an ale, temperature could be another cause. Make sure you're not fermenting your beer too cold. The ideal temperature range should be between 68 and 72 degrees.

I'm a cheap drunk.
—PETE SLOSBERG

If You're Down with Pete, Then You're Down with Me

THE HARDEST-WORKING EX-HOMEBREWER, Pete Slosberg, is an inspiration to us all. He turned a great homebrew recipe into a beer empire. Pete told us that he is so busy now doing personal appearances to promote his ever-growing line of wicked beers that he is lucky if he gets to drink three beers a week. So much for the glamour of the big brewers. This is our attempt to recreate his breakout brew. We're not worthy!

4 POUNDS AMERICAN PALE 2-ROW
   MALT
4 POUNDS BRITISH PALE 2-ROW
   MALT
3/4 POUND CRYSTAL MALT (40L)
1/8 POUND CHOCOLATE MALT
1 TEASPOON GYPSUM
1 OUNCE BREWER'S GOLD HOPS
   (BITTERING)

1 OUNCE CASCADE HOPS
   (FLAVORING)
1 OUNCE BREWER'S GOLD HOPS
   (DRY HOP)
1/2 TEASPOON IRISH MOSS
1 PACKAGE LONDON ALE YEAST
3/4 CUP CORN SUGAR (PRIMING)

Mash crushed grains with gypsum for 90 minutes. Collect 6 gallons of wort. Bring to a boil, and add 1 ounce Brewer's Gold hops. Boil for 1 hour. Add 1 ounce Cascade hops after 30 minutes. Add Irish moss during final 10 minutes of boil. Cool wort and pitch yeast. Ferment 7 to 10 days. Transfer to secondary fermenter, add 1 ounce Brewer's Gold hops, and ferment an additional 7 to 10 days. Bottle, using corn sugar. Age an additional 7 to 10 days.

OG: 1.052

Slate-Lined Stout

SAMUEL SMITH'S BREWERY IN TADCASTER, England, produces some of the finest beers in the world. Our favorite is their oatmeal stout, which is almost a meal in itself. For lack of the slate-lined fermenter, we haven't been able to get an exact replica, but it's close.

8 POUNDS BRITISH 2-ROW MALT
1 POUND FLAKED BARLEY
1 POUND ROASTED BARLEY
1/2 POUND DEXTRINE MALT
1/4 POUND CHOCOLATE MALT
1/4 POUND CRYSTAL MALT (80L)
2 POUNDS ROLLED OATS

1 1/4 OUNCES BULLION HOPS
   (BITTERING)
1 OUNCE KENT GOLDINGS HOPS
   (AROMA)
1 PACKAGE LONDON ALE YEAST
1 1/4 CUPS DRY MALT EXTRACT
   (PRIMING)

Mash crushed grains for 60 to 90 minutes. Collect 6 gallons of wort. Add Bullion hops and boil for 1 hour, adding the Kent

Goldings hops for the last 10 minutes. Cool wort and pitch yeast. Ferment for 5 to 7 days. Transfer to secondary fermenter and ferment an additional 7 to 10 days. Bottle, using dry malt extract. Age in bottle 10 to 14 days.

OG: 1.056

What two ideas are more inseparable than beer and Britannia?

—REVEREND SIDNEY SMITH

Britain's Favorite Brown

NEWCASTLE BROWN ALE, BREWED AT Newcastle-upon-Tyne, is probably the best-known brown ale. In fact, it is the best-selling bottled beer in England. A blending of a high- and low-gravity beer gives Newcastle its unique quality, and recreating this at home is very simple, provided you have the equipment. And if you don't have the equipment, it may be worth investing in, since this beer is so good.

7 POUNDS PALE 2-ROW MALT
1 POUND CRYSTAL MALT (40L)
1/2 POUND FLAKED BARLEY
1/3 POUND CHOCOLATE MALT
1 1/2 OUNCES KENT GOLDINGS HOPS
   (BITTERING)

1 OUNCE KENT GOLDINGS HOPS
   (AROMA)
2 PACKAGES LONDON ALE YEAST
3/4 CUP CORN SUGAR (PRIMING)

Mash crushed grains for 60 to 90 minutes. Collect the first 3 gallons of wort in one brew pot and the second 3 gallons in another brew pot. Add 1 ounce Kent Goldings to the first pot and 1/2 ounce in the second brew pot. Boil both for 1 hour, adding 1/2 ounce of Kent Goldings to each for the last 5 minutes. Cool both, place in separate fermenters, and pitch 1 packet of yeast to each. Ferment for 5 to 7 days. Combine the 2 batches into a secondary fermenter and ferment an additional 7 to 10 days. Bottle, using corn sugar. Age in bottle 7 to 10 days.

OG: 1.051

Image Is Everything

WHILE RUMMAGING THROUGH HIS GRANDFATHER'S trunk in the attic, lawyer Jim Koch unearthed an old homebrew recipe. He brewed it up, tasted it, liked it, and began to market it, or so the story goes. In any event, the Boston Beer Company was certainly instrumental in the microbrew boom on the East Coast, and eventually across the nation. Here's our version of their Sam Adams Boston Lager.

7 POUNDS 2-ROW AMERICAN
KLAGES MALT
1 POUND CRYSTAL MALT (60L)
1½ OUNCES HALLERTAUER HOPS
(BITTERING)
1 OUNCE TETTNANGER HOPS
(AROMA)

1 OUNCE TETTNANGER HOPS (DRY
HOP)
1 TEASPOON IRISH MOSS
1 PACKAGE AMERICAN LAGER YEAST
¾ CUP CORN SUGAR (PRIMING)

Mash crushed grains for 60 to 90 minutes. Collect 6 gallons of wort. Add Hallertauer hops and boil for 1 hour, adding 1 ounce Tettnanger hops and Irish moss for the last 10 minutes. Cool wort and pitch yeast. Primary-ferment at 50 to 55 degrees for 5 to 7 days. Transfer to secondary fermenter. Lager for 3 weeks, adding 1 ounce Tettnanger hops for the last 7 to 10 days. Bottle, using corn sugar. Age in bottle 7 to 10 days.

OG: 1.048

Merci, Pierre

AFTER SELLING THE HOEGAARDEN BREWERY in Belgium, where he saved and revived the white beer style, Pierre Celis came to America. Specifically, Austin, Texas. There Celis created perhaps the finest example in the world of the white beer style, Celis White. In order to properly recreate this style, it is essential to make an all-grain version, since even the palest extract is too dark.

5 POUNDS PALE 2-ROW MALT
3 POUNDS FLAKED WHEAT
1 POUND ROLLED OATS
1 OUNCE SAAZ HOPS (BITTERING)
½ OUNCE SAAZ HOPS (AROMA)
1 OUNCE CORIANDER SEED

½ OUNCE CURAÇAO ORANGE PEEL
   (BITTER)
½ OUNCE CURAÇAO ORANGE PEEL
   (SWEET)
1 PACKAGE BELGIAN WHITE YEAST
¾ CUP CORN SUGAR (PRIMING)

Mash malt, wheat, and oats for 90 minutes. Collect 6 gallons of wort. Add 1 ounce Saaz hops and boil for 1 hour, adding ½ ounce Saaz for last 5 minutes. Cool wort and pitch yeast. Ferment for 5 to 7 days. Transfer to secondary fermenter and add orange peels and crushed coriander seed. Ferment 7 to 10 days. Bottle, using corn sugar. Age in bottle 7 days.

OG: 1.045

Then we trotted gentle, not to break the bloomin'
   glass
   Though the Arabites 'ad all their ranges
   marked;
But we dursn't 'ardly galloped for the most was
   bottles Bass
An' we'd dreamed of it since we was
   disembarked.

—RUDYARD KIPLING

Trademark Ale

BASS IS A WONDERFUL PALE ale with a rich history. Their logo, the red triangle, was the first registered trademark in history, and their famous Burton Union system of connected wooden vessels was one of the unique ales of the world. And while some people believe that the quality of Bass has declined since the company abandoned the Burton Union system, they still produce some of the finest beers in the world. Here's our attempt to recreate the famous Bass flavor.

7 POUNDS BRITISH 2-ROW MALT
½ POUND CRYSTAL MALT (40L)
1 POUND DARK BROWN SUGAR
2 TEASPOONS GYPSUM
1 TEASPOON IRISH MOSS
1 OUNCE KENT GOLDINGS HOPS
(BITTERING)

1 OUNCE FUGGLES HOPS
(FLAVORING AND AROMA)
1 PACKAGE LONDON ALE YEAST
1¼ CUPS DRY MALT EXTRACT
(PRIMING)

Mash grains for 60 to 90 minutes. Collect 6 gallons of wort. Add brown sugar, gypsum, and Kent Goldings hops. Boil for 1 hour, adding ½ ounce Fuggles hops at 30 minutes and ½ ounce after 50 minutes. Add Irish moss for last 5 minutes. Cool wort and pitch yeast. Ferment for 7 to 10 days. Bottle, using dry malt extract. Age in bottle 7 to 10 days.

OG: 1.046

Meads, Lambics, and Ciders

From Dubliners *by James Joyce*

He stood in a doorway opposite the office, watching to see if the cashier would come out alone. All the clerks passed out and finally the cashier came out with the chief clerk. It was no use trying to say a word to him when he was with the chief clerk. The man felt that his position was bad enough. He had been obliged to offer an abject apology to Mr Alleyne for his impertinence, but he knew what a hornet's nest the office would be for him. He could remember the way in which Mr Alleyne had hounded little Peake out of the office in order to make room for his own nephew. He felt savage and thirsty and revengeful, annoyed with himself and with everyone else. Mr Alleyne would never give him an hour's rest; his life would be a hell to him. He had made a proper fool of himself this time. Could he not keep his tongue in his cheek? But they had never pulled together from the first, he and Mr Alleyne, ever since the day Mr Alleyne had overheard him mimicking his North of Ireland accent to amuse Higgins and Miss Parker; that had been the beginning of it. He might have tried Higgins for the money, but sure Higgins never had anything for himself. A man with two establishments to keep up, of course he couldn't. . . .

He felt his great body again aching for the comfort of the public-house. The fog had begun to chill him and he wondered could he touch Pat in O'Neill's. He could not touch him for more than a bob —and a bob was no use. Yet he must get money somewhere or other: he had spent his last penny for the g.p. and soon it would be too late for getting money anywhere. Suddenly, as he was fingering his watch chain, he thought of Terry Kelly's pawn-office in Fleet Street. That was the dart! Why didn't he think of it sooner?

He went through the narrow alley of Temple Bar quickly, mut-tering to himself that they could all go to hell, because he was going to have a good night of it. The clerk in Terry Kelly's said "A crown" but the consignor held out for six shillings; and in the end the six shillings was allowed him literally. He came out of the pawn-office joyfully, making a little cylinder of the coins between his thumb and fingers. In Westmoreland Street the footpaths were crowded with young men and women returning from business, and ragged urchins ran here and there yelling out the names of the evening editions. The man passed through the crowd, looking on the spectacle generally with proud satisfaction and staring masterfully at the office-girls. His head was full of the noises of tram-gongs and swishing trolleys and his nose already sniffed the curling fumes of punch. As he walked on he preconsidered the terms in which he would narrate the incident to the boys:

"So, I just looked at him—coolly, you know, and looked at her. Then I looked back at him again—taking my time you know. 'I don't think that's a fair question to put to me,' says I."

Nosey Flynn was sitting up in his usual corner of Davy Byrne's and, when he heard the story, he stood Farrington a half-one, saying it was as smart a thing as ever he heard. Farrington stood a drink in his turn. After a while O'Halloran and Paddy Leonard came in and the story was repeated to them. O'Halloran stood tailors of malt, hot, all round and told the story of the retort he had made to the chief clerk when he was in Callan's of Fownes's Street; but, as the retort was after the manner of the liberal shep-herds in the eclogues, he had to admit that it was not as clever as Farrington's retort. At this Farrington told the boys to polish off that and have another.

Just as they were naming their poisons who should come in but Higgins! Of course he had to join in with the others. The men asked him to give his version of it, and he did so with great vivacity, for the sight of five small hot whiskies was very exhilarating. Everyone roared laughing when he showed the way in which Mr Alleyne shook his fist in Farrington's face. Then he imitated Farrington, saying, "And here was my nabs, as cool as you please" while Farrington looked at the company out of his heavy dirty eyes, smiling and at times drawing forth stray drops of liquor from his moustache with the aid of his lower lip.

When that round was over there was a pause. O'Halloran had money, but neither of the other two seemed to have any; so the whole party left the shop somewhat regretfully. At the corner of Duke Street Higgins and Nosey Flynn bevelled off to the left, while the other three turned back towards the city. Rain was drizzling down on the cold streets and, when they reached the Ballast Office, Farrington suggested the Scotch House. The bar was full of men and loud with the noise of tongues and glasses. The three men pushed past the whining match-sellers at the door and formed a little party at the corner of the counter. They began to exchange stories. Leonard introduced them to a young fellow named Weathers who was performing at the Tivoli as an acrobat and knockabout "artiste." Farrington stood a drink all round. Weathers said he would take a small Irish and Apollinaris. Farrington, who had definite notions of what was what, asked the boys would they have an Apollinaris too; but the boys told Tim to make theirs hot. The talk became theatrical. O'Halloran stood a round and then Farrington stood another round, Weathers protesting that the hospitality was too Irish. He promised to get them in behind the scenes and introduce them to some nice girls. O'Halloran said that he and Leonard would go, but that Farrington wouldn't go because he was a married man; and Farrington's heavy dirty eyes leered at the company in token that he understood he was being chaffed. Weathers made them all have just one little tincture at his expense and promised to meet them later on at Mulligan's in Poolbeg Street.

Fermentation and Civilization are inseparable.
—JOHN CIARDI

Temptation Mead

MEAD, IN ITS ENDLESS PERMUTATIONS, can be a daunting undertaking for a homebrewer who has never concocted one, and probably has had few chances to taste one. This recipe, simple and straightforward, is designed to tempt mead novices into their first journey. It is well worth the trip.

10 POUNDS ORANGE BLOSSOM
  HONEY
3 POUNDS BUCKWHEAT HONEY
1 TEASPOON GYPSUM
2 TEASPOONS ACID BLEND

1 TEASPOON IRISH MOSS
⅓ OUNCE YEAST EXTRACT
1 PACKAGE CHAMPAGNE OR MEAD
  YEAST

Add honeys, gypsum, and acid blend to 1½ gallons of water and bring to a boil. Boil for 30 minutes, adding Irish moss for last ten minutes. Place in primary fermenter, add water to fill, and cool to below 80 degrees. Add yeast and yeast extract and aerate well. Ferment 7 days at 72 to 78 degrees. Rack to secondary fermenter. Bottle when clear. Mead is ready to drink when clear, but will mellow and improve with age.

BREWER'S TIP

Honey

Lighter honeys—like orange blossom, clover, and good old supermarket "golden"—are the preferred nectar of many mead makers. These varieties impart less of the strong flavors that darker honeys, like buckwheat or wildflower, contribute. In small quantities, however, dark honeys can add a nice depth and interest to meads. Experiment to find your favorite combinations.

It is not necessary to boil honey when you make mead. You can simply dissolve the honey in hot water. Proponents of this method point out that some of the floral essence of the honey is eliminated in the boiling process. Detractors point out that boiling lowers the risks of contamination and aids in clarificaton. Many mead makers strike a compromise and boil for a short time. The choice is up to you.

Here's Pyment in Your Eye

HERE'S A RECIPE THAT ALLOWS the homebrewer to venture into the neighborhood of the home winemaker with the addition of grape extract. What type of grape extract is really up to you, but remember that a red grape extract will give your pyment a deep ruby color. If, for whatever reason, you can't use grape extract, 4 or 5 cans of frozen concentrated grape juice can be substituted.

10 POUNDS WILDFLOWER HONEY
4 POUNDS CALIFORNIA CHABLIS
  GRAPE EXTRACT
1 TABLESPOON ACID BLEND

1 OUNCE YEAST NUTRIENT
1 PACKAGE CHAMPAGNE OR MEAD
  YEAST

Combine honey, grape extract, and acid blend in 1½ gallons of water and boil for 10 minutes. Transfer to primary fermenter, add water to fill, and cool to below 80 degrees. Pitch yeast and yeast nutrient and aerate very well. Ferment for 14 to 21 days at 72 to 78 degrees. Transfer to secondary fermenter. Bottle when mead is clear. Age in bottle 1 to 3 months.

Mead Me in St. Louis

A LUSCIOUSLY SWEET CONCOCTION CAN be made using maple syrup instead of honey. We make our version using equal parts of maple syrup and honey, with a few spices thrown in for good measure. So what, you're asking, does maple syrup have to do with St. Louis? Well, nothing actually, we just liked the name.

5 POUNDS BUCKWHEAT HONEY
5 POUNDS MAPLE SYRUP
2 TEASPOONS ACID BLEND
3 CINNAMON STICKS
5 WHOLE CLOVES
2 WHOLE NUTMEGS (CRUSHED)

1 OUNCE YEAST NUTRIENT
1 OR 2 PACKAGES CHAMPAGNE OR
   MEAD YEAST
⅔ CUP LIGHT OR DARK BROWN
   SUGAR (PRIMING)

Combine honey, maple syrup, acid blend, and spices in 1½ gallons of water and boil for 10 minutes. Transfer to primary fermenter, straining out whole spices, add cold water to fill, and cool to below 80 degrees. Pitch yeast and yeast nutrient and aerate very well. Ferment for 14 to 21 days at 72 to 78 degrees. Transfer to secondary fermenter and age an additional 2 to 3 months. Bottle, using brown sugar. Age in bottle 1 to 3 months. Mead will improve with age.

Acids in Mead

Acids provide a slightly fruity flavor and balance the strong alcohol flavors of mead. Since honey lacks acidity, acids can be added if these flavors are desired. One to four teaspoons of acid blend—which is 25 percent citric acid, 30 percent malic acid, and 45 percent tartaric acid—or two to three tablespoons of lemon juice work nicely.

God made yeast, as well as dough, and loves fermentation just as dearly as he loves vegetation.
—RALPH WALDO EMERSON

Mead and Mrs. Jones

METHEGLIN. DOESN'T SOUND VERY TEMPTING, does it? Well, it is. Metheglin is nothing more than mead that's been spiced up with herbs or spices.

4 POUNDS ALFALFA HONEY
4 POUNDS WILDFLOWER HONEY
6 SPRIGS FRESH THYME
6 SPRIGS FRESH ROSEMARY
6 SAGE LEAVES

4 BAY LEAVES
1 OUNCE YEAST NUTRIENT
1 PACKAGE CHAMPAGNE OR MEAD
  YEAST

Combine honeys and herbs in 1½ gallons of water and boil for 10 minutes. Remove from heat and steep for 30 minutes. Transfer to primary fermenter, straining out herbs, and add water to fill. Cool to below 80 degrees. Pitch yeast and yeast nutrient and aerate very well. Ferment for 14 to 21 days at 72 to 78 degrees. Transfer to secondary fermenter. Bottle when mead is clear. Age in bottle 1 to 3 months. Mead will improve with age.

Cysing up the Situation

THE BLEND OF APPLE JUICE and honey, or cyser, tickles the tastebuds into a state of near euphoria. Any combination of apple cider and honey will work well.

4 POUNDS CLOVER HONEY
1 POUND BUCKWHEAT HONEY
4 GALLONS FRESH APPLE CIDER
   (NO PRESERVATIVES)
1 CUP LIGHT BROWN SUGAR

1 NUTMEG
1 OUNCE YEAST NUTRIENT
1 PACKAGE CHAMPAGNE OR MEAD
   YEAST
3/4 CUP CORN SUGAR (PRIMING)

Combine honeys, apple cider, brown sugar, and nutmeg in 1½ gallons of water and boil for 20 minutes. Remove nutmeg, transfer to primary fermenter, and add water to fill. Cool to below 80 degrees. Pitch yeast and yeast nutrient, and aerate very well. Ferment for 14 to 21 days at 72 to 78 degrees. Transfer to secondary fermenter. Bottle when mead is clear, using corn sugar. Age in bottle 1 to 3 months. Cyser will improve with aging.

Peach Glitter

THIS DELIGHTFUL PEACH MEAD IS sparkling and delicious. The flavors of the honey, peaches, cinnamon, and hops balance nicely.

10 POUNDS CLOVER HONEY
1 TEASPOON GYPSUM
3 TABLESPOONS LEMON JUICE
2 CINNAMON STICKS
1½ OUNCES CASCADE HOPS
   (BITTERING)

1 TEASPOON IRISH MOSS
6 POUNDS PEACHES
1/3 OUNCE YEAST EXTRACT
1 PACKAGE CHAMPAGNE OR MEAD
   YEAST
2/3 CUP BROWN SUGAR (PRIMING)

Add honey, gypsum, lemon juice, cinnamon sticks, and Cascade hops to 1½ gallons of water and bring to a boil. Boil for 20 minutes, adding Irish moss for last ten minutes. Remove from heat and allow to cool to 160 degrees. Remove cinnamon and hops, add pitted and halved peaches, cover, and steep for 15 minutes. Transfer to primary fermenter, add water to fill. Cool to below 80 degrees. Add yeast and yeast extract and aerate well. Ferment for 14 days at 72 to 78 degrees. Rack off fruit to secondary. Bottle when clear, using brown sugar. Age in bottle 1 to 3 months. Mead is ready to drink when clear, but will mellow and improve with age.

Hippocrasic Oath

SPICE UP YOUR PYMENT WITH this delicious recipe and what do you get? Hippocras—yet another variation on the mead style.

4 POUNDS ORANGE BLOSSOM HONEY
4 POUNDS WILDFLOWER HONEY
4 POUNDS CALIFORNIA RIESLING
  GRAPE EXTRACT
2 CINNAMON STICKS
1 CRUSHED WHOLE NUTMEG
1 TEASPOON CRUSHED WHOLE
  ALLSPICE

1 TEASPOON WHOLE CARDAMOM
1 VANILLA BEAN
1 TABLESPOON ACID BLEND
1 OUNCE YEAST NUTRIENT
1 PACKAGE CHAMPAGNE OR MEAD
  YEAST

Combine honeys, grape extract, acid blend, spices, and vanilla in 1½ gallons of water and boil for 10 minutes. Remove from heat and steep for 30 minutes. Transfer to primary fermenter, straining out whole spices and vanilla bean, and add water to fill. Cool to below 80 degrees. Pitch yeast and yeast nutrient and aerate very well. Ferment for 14 to 21 days at 72 to 78 degrees. Transfer to secondary fermenter. Bottle when mead is clear. Age in bottle 1 to 3 months. Mead will improve with age.

From man's sweat and God's love,
beer came into the world.
                          —SAINT ARNOLDUS

Dirty Sock Gueuze

LAMBICS ARE CERTAINLY AN ACQUIRED taste. And the gueuze style, which contains no fruit to hide the strong, sour flavor and smell, can be a taste that some never acquire. In fact, when gueuze was served at a recent Belgian beer tasting, our friend Pam proclaimed, upon trying the style for the first time, "This tastes like someone soaked their dirty socks in this for a month." Others found it one of the finest and most unusual beers they had ever sampled and demanded more. In short, this is a style you'll simply have to decide upon for yourself.

3⅓ POUNDS WHEAT MALT EXTRACT (55/45 BLEND)

4 POUNDS ALEXANDER'S PALE MALT EXTRACT

1 POUND CRYSTAL MALT (40L)

½ POUND PALE 2-ROW MALT (SOURING)

½ OUNCE WILLAMETTE HOPS (OLD AND STALE, PREFERABLY)

1 PACKAGE AMERICAN ALE YEAST

1 PACKAGE BRETTANOMYCES BRUXELLENSIS YEAST

¾ CUP CORN SUGAR (PRIMING)

Place crushed grains in water and steep at 155 degrees for 30 minutes. Remove spent grains. Add malt extracts and stir until completely dissolved. Stabilize the wort between 125 and 130 degrees, place in plastic fermenting bucket, and sour (see Brewer's Tip, p. 181). When soured, place wort in pot and add Willamette hops. Boil for 1 hour. Cool wort and pitch American ale yeast. Ferment for 10 to 14 days. Transfer to secondary fermenter and add Brettanomyces bruxellensis yeast. Ferment 8 to 10 weeks. Bottle, using corn sugar. Age in bottle a minimum of 3 months. Lambic will be best after 1 year.

OG: 1.042

Full Wort Souring

For lambics and some other styles, a full wort sour is necessary to achieve an authentic version.

Dissolve your malt extract in water, or if you're all-grain brewing, mash grains and draw off 6 gallons of wort. Place the wort in a clean, sanitized plastic bucket, and cool to 125 to 130 degrees. Add ½ pound crushed pale malt and stir well. Seal the lid, and set in a warm place. Let sit for 12 to 24 hours. The longer the wort is allowed to sit, the more sour it will become, so it's up to you to determine the level of sourness. Hold your nose and remove the lid. The overpowering smell of sour milk will hit you, so be warned. Skim off any mold that has formed on the top and then transfer your wort to your brew pot, straining out the grain, and proceed as usual.

Kriek

KRIEK IS A CHERRY-FLAVORED lambic and one of the most popular styles of lambic available. However, any fruit can be used. We've also tasted peach, and—believe it or not—banana.

6 POUNDS IREKS WHEAT MALT
  EXTRACT (100 PERCENT WHEAT)
3⅓ POUNDS LIGHT MALT EXTRACT
½ POUND CRYSTAL MALT (40L)
½ POUND PALE 2-ROW MALT
  (SOURING)
½ OUNCE TETTNANGER HOPS (THE
  OLDER AND STALER THE BETTER)

10 POUNDS FROZEN SWEET
  CHERRIES
1 PACKAGE BELGIAN ALE YEAST
1 PACKAGE BRETTANOMYCES
  BRUXELLENSIS YEAST
¾ CUP CORN SUGAR (PRIMING)

Place cracked crystal malt in water and steep at 155 degrees for 30 minutes. Remove spent grains and add malt extracts. Steep at 155 degrees for 20 to 30 minutes, till all extract is dissolved. Cool wort to 125 to 130 degrees and sour (see Brewer's Tip, p. 181). When soured, place wort in pot and boil with Tettnanger hops for 1 hour. Cool wort and pitch both yeast cultures. Ferment for 10 to 14 days. Transfer to secondary fermenter. For 20 minutes, steep cherries in enough 150-degree water to cover. Add cherries and water to the fermenter. Ferment an additional 6 to 8 weeks. Rack to tertiary fermenter and let sit for 14 to 21 days. Bottle, using corn sugar. Age in bottle a minimum of 3 months.

OG: 1.053

Framboise

ALONG WITH KRIEK, FRAMBOISE, or raspberry, is the most popular style of lambic beer. Raspberries possess a pungent sweetness that makes this a wonderfully complex beer.

6 POUNDS BELGIAN PILS MALT
3 POUNDS WHEAT MALT
1 POUND FLAKED WHEAT
½ POUND PALE 2-ROW MALT
  (SOURING)
½ OUNCE TETTNANGER HOPS

8 POUNDS FROZEN RASPBERRIES
1 PACKAGE EUROPEAN ALE YEAST
1 PACKAGE BRETTANOMYCES
  BRUXELLENSIS YEAST
¾ CUP CORN SUGAR (PRIMING)

Mash grains for 60 to 90 minutes. Collect 6 gallons of wort. Cool to 125 to 130 degrees and sour (see Brewers Tip, p. 181). When wort is soured, place in pot, add Tettnanger hops, and boil for 1 hour. Cool wort and pitch both yeast cultures. Ferment for 10 to 14 days. Transfer to secondary fermenter. For 30 minutes, steep raspberries in enough 150-degree water to cover. Add raspberries and water to fermenter. Ferment an additional 6 to 8 weeks. Rack to tertiary fermenter and let sit an additional 2 to 3 weeks. Bottle, using corn sugar. Age in bottle a minimum of 3 months. Lambic will improve with age and should peak at 1 year.

OG: 1.052

Sunset Cider

THIS IS A WONDERFULLY EASY and sweet cider. Feel free to use either light or dark brown sugar and any type of honey you like. The trick is to use fresh apple cider that contains no preservatives.

5 GALLONS FRESH APPLE CIDER
 (NO PRESERVATIVES)
2 POUNDS LIGHT BROWN SUGAR
1 POUND CLOVER HONEY
1 POUND BUCKWHEAT HONEY

½ POUND LACTOSE
1 OR 2 PACKAGES CHAMPAGNE
 YEAST
¾ CUP CORN SUGAR (PRIMING)

Place 4 gallons of cider in fermenter. Place 1 gallon of cider in a pot with the brown sugar and honeys. Heat until dissolved, stirring to avoid caramelizing. Add to fermenter. Pitch yeast when cider is cool. Ferment for 3 weeks. Bottle, using corn sugar and lactose. Age in bottle 7 to 10 days.

Mankind: The animal that fears the future and desires fermented beverages.
—JEAN-ANTHELME BRILLAT-SAVARIN

Apple-Pear Cider

APPLE JUICE AND PEAR JUICE make a terrific blend and an even better cider. Blend the two juices in whatever proportion you like. We would suggest using a minimum of 1 gallon of either juice to get its particular flavor to come through.

3 GALLONS FRESH APPLE JUICE
2 GALLONS PEAR JUICE
1 POUND LIGHT BROWN SUGAR

1 TO 2 PACKAGES CHAMPAGNE
 YEAST
¾ CUP CORN SUGAR (PRIMING)

Place 4 gallons of juice in fermenter. Dissolve brown sugar in remaining 1 gallon of juice and add to fermenter. Pitch yeast. Ferment for 7 to 10 days. Transfer to secondary fermenter and ferment an additional 14 to 21 days. Bottle, using corn sugar. Age in bottle 7 to 10 days.

Raspberry Cider

ANY FRUIT CAN BE ADDED to cider to give it a unique taste. Our favorite is raspberries, whose tart taste blends perfectly with the sweet apples. We've also had great results with pears, cherries, and blueberries.

5 GALLONS FRESH APPLE CIDER   1 PACKAGE CHAMPAGNE YEAST
  (NO PRESERVATIVES)   ¾ CUP CORN SUGAR (PRIMING)
2 POUNDS FROZEN RASPBERRIES

    Place apple cider in fermenter and pitch yeast. Ferment for 7 to 10 days, then transfer to secondary fermenter. For 20 minutes, steep raspberries in enough 150-degree water to cover. Add raspberries and water to the fermenter. Ferment an additional 2 weeks. Rack to tertiary fermenter and let sit for 3 to 4 days. Bottle, using corn sugar. Age in bottle 7 to 10 days.

Holiday Cheer

FOR THOSE OF YOUR FAMILY and friends that just haven't developed a taste for beer, try brewing up a batch of this cider come holiday time. It is similar in flavor to a mulled cider.

5 GALLONS FRESH APPLE CIDER   ZEST OF 2 ORANGES
2 CUPS BUCKWHEAT HONEY   1 TO 2 PACKAGES CHAMPAGNE
1 CUP MAPLE SYRUP   YEAST
3 CINNAMON STICKS   ½ POUND LACTOSE
2 TEASPOONS WHOLE CLOVES   ¾ CUP CORN SUGAR (PRIMING)
1 WHOLE NUTMEG (CRUSHED)

    Place 4 gallons of cider in fermenter. Dissolve honey and maple syrup in remaining 1 gallon of cider and add to fermenter. Ferment for 14 to 21 days. Transfer to secondary fermenter and add spices and orange zest. Ferment an additional 10 to 14 days. Bottle, using corn sugar and lactose. Age in bottle 21 to 28 days.

Two of a Perfect Pear

APPLE JUICE ISN'T THE ONLY base of fantastic cider. Pear juice can produce a delectable cider that is sure to impress your friends.

5 GALLONS PEAR JUICE	1 OR 2 PACKAGES CHAMPAGNE
2 TEASPOONS PECTIN ENZYME	YEAST
1 CUP LIGHT BROWN SUGAR	3/4 CUP CORN SUGAR (PRIMING)

Place 4 gallons pear juice in fermenter. Combine remaining pear juice, brown sugar, and pectin enzyme together and mix until dissolved. Add to fermenter. Let sit for 24 hours. Add yeast and ferment for 7 to 10 days. Transfer to secondary fermenter and ferment an additional 10 to 14 days. Bottle, using corn sugar. Age in bottle 14 to 21 days.

Food *and* Beer, Beer *and* Food

For many people, beer is an excellent accompaniment to food —if the food is hot dogs, Wienerschnitzel, or potato chips. But for those of us who have discovered the full range of tastes and textures that beer can offer, beer has become the perfect complement to many of our favorite dishes.

The range of beers we now enjoy also lends itself to a broad range of gourmet uses. Elegant dishes like Cornish Game Hens with Blackberry Stout Sauce now join the more familiar traditional favorites, like Beer-Battered Fish and Kickin' Hot Chili. Creative use of the by-products of brewing can also result in dishes as delicious as they are efficient. The Great Pumpkin Pie, which uses the pumpkin that was boiled in the wort for Great Pumpkin Ale, is a tasty example.

And so we offer these recipes. When you've finished crafting your gourmet beer, try crafting one of these gourmet accompaniments.

*Good bread, good cheese and good beer provide
a complete meal which the most elaborate menu
can scarcely better.*

—ANONYMOUS, 1934

Smoky Beer and Cheddar Soup

THIS TASTY CONCOCTION ALWAYS GETS rave reviews. The smoky flavor of the sausage is a wonderful addition to the sharp tanginess
of the cheddar base. For more tangy bite, use extra-sharp cheddar and substitute romano for the parmesan. Serve it with a
crusty loaf of bread for dipping, and of course, several cold bottles of ale. And leave the bottle of hot sauce within reach for
those who enjoy some extra zing.

6 TABLESPOONS BUTTER
1 POUND SMOKED SAUSAGE,
   CHOPPED
8 LARGE SHALLOTS, CHOPPED
   MEDIUM-FINE
1/2 CUP FLOUR
2 (13 1/2-OUNCE) CANS CHICKEN
   BROTH
1 (12-OUNCE) BOTTLE OF ALE
2 CUPS POTATOES, PEELED AND
   CUBED

2 CUPS MILK
1 POUND CHEDDAR CHEESE, GRATED
1 CUP GRATED PARMESAN
1/4 TEASPOON SALT (OR MORE, TO
   TASTE)
1 TABLESPOON PAPRIKA
1/2 TEASPOON DRY MUSTARD
1 TEASPOON THYME
1 TABLESPOON HOT SAUCE
FRESHLY GROUND PEPPER TO TASTE

Melt the butter in a large stockpot or Dutch oven. Add the
sausage and sauté 5 minutes over medium heat, stirring occasionally. Add the chopped shallots and continue to sauté until
shallots are translucent. Add the flour and stir to coat. Slowly
add the chicken broth and ale, stirring well. Bring to a boil, then
reduce heat and simmer for 3 to 4 minutes, stirring occasionally.
When the mixture has thickened slightly, add the potatoes and
continue to simmer, approximately 12 minutes, until potatoes
are cooked through. Add milk, cheeses, salt, and flavorings. Stir
constantly over low heat until cheese is smooth.

Roasted Beer Soup

COUNTRY VEGETABLES, FRESH HERBS, AND pearl barley make this soup really special. The sweet roasted flavor of the vegetables stands up well to the beefy richness of the broth. Serve with a hearty ale.

1 CUP CARROTS, PEELED AND DICED
1 CUP PARSNIPS, PEELED AND DICED
1 CUP SMALL PEARL ONIONS, PEELED
¼ CUP BEER
SALT AND PEPPER TO TASTE
4 TABLESPOONS BUTTER
2 CUPS BEEF, JULIENNED
3 TABLESPOONS FLOUR
4 QUARTS BEEF STOCK
3 QUARTS BEER, FLAT AND WARM

1 CUP CHOPPED SPINACH (FRESH OR FROZEN)
1 CUP TOMATOES, PEELED AND DICED
¾ CUP PEARL BARLEY
1 CUP ITALIAN PARSLEY, CHOPPED
2 TABLESPOONS FRESH THYME LEAVES
4 SPRIGS FRESH ROSEMARY, CHOPPED

Preheat oven. Put carrots, parsnips, and onions in roasting pan with ale. Toss to coat. Season with salt and pepper and dot with 2 tablespoons of the butter. Roast until lightly browned, stirring occasionally, about half an hour. Season beef with salt and pepper and toss in flour. Melt remaining 2 tablespoons of butter in a large stockpot and brown meat over medium heat. Add stock, 1½ quarts beer, spinach, tomatoes, pearl barley, and half the herbs. Bring to a boil. Reduce heat, cover, and simmer for 40 minutes. Add roasted vegetables, remaining beer, and herbs. Heat to a boil, reduce heat, and simmer 5 minutes more.

Oatmeal Beer Bread

THIS SIMPLE, HEARTY LOAF IS a wonderful fresh-from-the-oven accompaniment to a cozy dinner and is also a superb sandwich bread. It takes just minutes to make. Substitute another cup of self-rising flour if you haven't any oats on hand, for a tasty plain white bread.

2 CUPS SELF-RISING FLOUR
1 CUP PLUS 1 TABLESPOON ROLLED
  OATS

2 TABLESPOONS SUGAR
1 (12-OUNCE) BOTTLE OF GOOD
  BEER

Preheat oven to 375 degrees. Grease an 8½- or 9-inch loaf pan. Combine the flour, the cup of oats, and the sugar in a large mixing bowl. Add the beer and mix, taking care not to overmix. Spread the dough in the greased loaf pan. Sprinkle the tablespoon of oats over the top. Bake for 1 hour.

Smoked Basil Shrimp

THIS IS A FAVORITE DISH in the summertime, when it can be grilled outdoors, but it works just as well under the broiler any time of year. The smoky flavors of the marinade are offset by the sweet and pungent flavor of the basil. Try skewering the shrimp with tomatoes, pearl onions, and green and red bell peppers before cooking.

1 POUND LARGE SHRIMP, SHELLED
  AND DEVEINED
12 OUNCES RAUCHBIER OR OTHER
  SMOKED BEER
1 TEASPOON BALSAMIC VINEGAR

½ CUP FRESH BASIL LEAVES, RINSED
  AND COARSELY CHOPPED
1 PINCH SALT
FRESHLY GROUND PEPPER TO TASTE

Place the shrimp, beer, vinegar, basil, salt, and pepper in a large sealable storage bag. Squeeze out as much air as possible and close. Shake bag and work the mixture with your hands until the marinade is distributed thoroughly. Place in the refrigerator for two hours, flipping bag occasionally. Skewer and grill or broil the shrimp, removing from heat as soon as it turns pink, about 4 to 5 minutes, flipping once halfway through. The marinade can be reserved and reduced on the stovetop to make a tasty smoked sauce.

Hop-Spiced Pickled Veggies

SPICY HOPPED VEGETABLES MAKE A great accompaniment to beer. We recommend Saaz, for their citrusy bite, or Cascade, for their floral spice. A healthy and tangy treat.

3 CUPS ASSORTED PICKLING VEGETABLES (CAULIFLOWER, CARROT, PEARL ONIONS, ZUCCHINI, ETC.)	1 TABLESPOON MUSTARD SEED
	1 TABLESPOON CELERY SEED
	1 TABLESPOON KOSHER SALT
	1 TABLESPOON SUGAR
⅔ CUP WATER	1 THIN SLICE OF LEMON
⅔ CUP MALT VINEGAR	1 DRIED CHILI
½ OUNCE HOPS	2 CLOVES GARLIC, PEELED
1 TABLESPOON PEPPERCORNS	

Chop the vegetables into 2-inch pieces. Bring the water, vinegar, hops, peppercorns, mustard seed, celery seed, salt, and sugar to a boil in a nonreactive saucepan. Reduce heat and simmer 10 minutes. Place the lemon slice, chili, and garlic cloves in the bottom of a sterilized 1-quart mason jar. Fill with the vegetables, pour in the brine through a strainer, and seal with a sterilized top. Store upside down for 2 days, then refrigerate for 5 more days. Will last 30 days refrigerated.

Yams à la Belgique

CANDIED YAMS INSPIRED BY THE sweet, malty flavors of St. Sixtus ale. Once you've tried them, holiday dinners will never be the same without them.

5 POUNDS YAMS	3 TABLESPOONS LIGHT OR DARK BROWN SUGAR
¾ CUP ST. SIXTUS OR OTHER TRAPPIST ALE	2 TABLESPOONS BUTTER

Peel and cut up yams. Place in large pot of cold salted water. Bring to a boil. Boil until just tender, 20 minutes. Drain. Combine ale, sugar, and butter in a large skillet. Bring to a boil. Reduce heat. Add yams and stir to coat. Simmer for 15 minutes, stirring occasionally.

Frijoles Borrachos

THE RICH FLAVOR OF A dark ale or stout sets off the sweet, spicy flavors of this classic Mexican dish. We love to include it in a Mexican-style buffet with colorful bowls of taco fixings and yellow rice, and ice buckets full of cold beer. It can be made in advance and reheated when ready to serve.

1 POUND DRIED PINTO BEANS, SOAKED OVERNIGHT	1 ½ TABLESPOONS GROUND CUMIN
½ POUND BACON, CUT INTO 1-INCH PIECES	1 TABLESPOON GROUND CORIANDER
	1 TABLESPOON CHILI POWDER
	1 TABLESPOON SUGAR
4 CUPS WATER	3 OR 4 JALAPEÑO PEPPERS, CHOPPED FINELY
2 LARGE SPANISH ONIONS, CHOPPED	
10 CLOVES GARLIC, MINCED	3 PLUM TOMATOES, CHOPPED
2 (12-OUNCE) BOTTLES DARK BEER	1 CUP FRESH CILANTRO, CHOPPED

Soak beans according to package directions. Cook bacon in large pot until almost crisp. Remove bacon and drain on paper towels. Discard drippings. Place bacon, drained beans, 4 cups water, onions, and garlic in the same pot and bring to a boil. Boil for 15 minutes, then add beer, spices, sugar, and jalapeño peppers. Simmer, covered, for 1 hour. Add tomatoes and continue to simmer covered for 45 minutes. Uncover and simmer for 20 minutes (beans should be tender and sauce thickened). Serve sprinkled with cilantro.

Malted Applesauce

USE THE APPLES BOILED IN the wort in the Apple Brown Betty Fall Ale, or boil half the apples in dried malt and water to cover (2 tablespoons malt per pint of water). This is sweet and unusual, laced with flavors of malt, cinnamon, and vanilla.

1 ½ POUNDS APPLES, MALT-COOKED
(OR WORT-BOILED—SEE ABOVE)
1 ½ POUNDS GRANNY SMITH
APPLES, PEELED CORED, AND
DICED
2 TABLESPOONS LIGHT OR DARK
BROWN SUGAR

2 TABLESPOONS WATER
½ TEASPOON VANILLA EXTRACT
¼ TEASPOON GROUND CINNAMON
¼ TEASPOON GROUND ALLSPICE

Combine all ingredients in a large saucepan. Cover and cook for 15 minutes over medium heat, stirring frequently. Remove from heat and whisk to a smooth consistency. Chill and serve. Will hold refrigerated for at least 1 week.

Fiesta Pork Stew

THIS SPICY ONE-POT MEAL combines all of our favorite tastes from the Southwest. It is a colorful, flavorful, and inexpensive meal that goes well with some crusty sourdough bread and a hearty ale.

1 PORK BUTT OR SHOULDER,
BONE IN
3 CLOVES GARLIC
2 LARGE GREEN PEPPERS
2 LARGE RED PEPPERS
2 BUNCHES OF SCALLIONS
3 TABLESPOONS OIL
½ CUP FLOUR
1 (28-OUNCE) CAN WHOLE
TOMATOES
2 (12-OUNCE) BOTTLES OF ALE
3 CUPS WATER

½ CUP CHOPPED FRESH CILANTRO
2 TABLESPOONS CUMIN
1 TABLESPOON CHILI POWDER
1 ½ TEASPOONS CAYENNE PEPPER
½ TEASPOON SALT
FRESHLY GROUND BLACK PEPPER
RED PEPPER SAUCE TO TASTE
1 ½ CUPS RAW RICE
2 CANS PINTO OR BLACK BEANS,
RINSED
½ POUND SHARP CHEDDAR, GRATED

Preheat oven to 400 degrees. Remove bone from pork, place bone in a shallow roasting pan, add some water to the bottom of the pan, and roast until browned, about 35 minutes. While it's roasting, cube the pork, mince the garlic, and dice the peppers. Slice the scallions, reserving the greens for garnish, and mince the white bulbs. Heat the oil in a large stewpot. Add the peppers and minced scallions. Sauté until tender, 5 to 6 minutes, adding the garlic during the last minute. Lightly flour the pork cubes, add them to the pot and brown. Stir in the tomatoes, ale, water, cilantro, spices, salt, black pepper, and pepper sauce. Add the browned bone, then deglaze the roasting pan with a little water or beer and add that to the stew as well. Bring to a boil, then reduce heat and simmer for 30 minutes. Add the rice and beans and stir well. Cover and simmer for another 25 minutes, stirring once and adding more liquid if necessary. Ladle into bowls and garnish with grated cheese and scallion greens.

Cornish Game Hens in Blackberry Stout Sauce with Baked Apples

THIS ELEGANT DISH IS A favorite for company. The preparation is simple, the flavors are subtle and rich, and the presentation is beautiful. It never fails to impress our guests. If you don't have a stout with berry flavor on hand, you can substitute a regular stout and a few teaspoons of preserves, but you may want to adjust the brown sugar if the preserves are sweetened.

4 GRANNY SMITH APPLES (OR OTHER
  SUITABLE BAKING APPLES)
2 TABLESPOONS BUTTER
4 CORNISH GAME HENS
1 SMALL ONION, CHOPPED
2 TEASPOONS LIGHT OR DARK
  BROWN SUGAR

1 (12-OUNCE) BOTTLE BLACKBERRY
  STOUT
½ CUP CHICKEN STOCK OR CANNED
  BROTH

Preheat the oven to 375 degrees. Peel the apples, halve and core, and cut into thick half-moon slices. Melt the butter over medium heat in a large, ovenproof Dutch oven. Brown the game hens on each side, about 10 minutes. Remove the hens and add the onion. Sauté until translucent. Remove from heat and stir in sugar until dissolved. Arrange hens in pot. Add apples, stout, and stock. Bake uncovered for 30 minutes, basting occasionally. Place each hen in the center of a plate and surround with apple slices. Pour the sauce over the hen and apples and serve immediately. (If necessary, return sauce to stovetop and reduce after removing hens and apples.)

*Come, Sir, you must mend a bad supper
with a glass of good ale.*

—ROBERT DODSLEY

Kickin' Hot Chili

LIKE OUR HOMEBREW, OUR CHILI is seldom made the same way twice. This is a great basic recipe, but feel free to experiment. Adding ground chicken or turkey to the beef imparts an added richness to the chili. And the juice from a jar of sweet or hot pickled peppers adds some zing. If you happen to have a hot pepper beer on hand, this is an excellent place to use it. Serve with a cold, light, and hoppy beer.

2 TABLESPOONS OIL

2 MEDIUM ONIONS, CHOPPED

1 LARGE GREEN PEPPER, CHOPPED

2 JALAPEÑO PEPPERS (OR OTHER HOT PEPPERS), CHOPPED FINE

4 GARLIC CLOVES, MINCED

3 POUNDS GROUND BEEF (OR 1 ½ POUNDS EACH BEEF AND CHICKEN OR TURKEY)

2 (15-OUNCE) CANS PINTO BEANS (KIDNEY OR BLACK BEANS ARE ALSO GOOD)

1 (26-OUNCE) CAN CRUSHED TOMATOES

1 (4-OUNCE) CAN TOMATO PASTE

1 BOTTLE ALE (ALMOST ANY TYPE OF BEER WILL DO HERE)

1 TABLESPOON CUMIN

2 TABLESPOONS CHILI POWDER

2 TEASPOONS OREGANO

1 TEASPOON CAYENNE PEPPER

½ TEASPOON DRY GROUND MUSTARD (OR 1 TEASPOON PREPARED MUSTARD)

½ TEASPOON SALT (OR TO TASTE)

2 BAY LEAVES

LOTS OF FRESHLY GROUND BLACK PEPPER

Heat the oil in a large stockpot. Add the onions and peppers. Sauté until cooked through but not browned, adding the garlic for the last minute or two. Add the ground meat and brown through. Drain off the fat. Add the remaining ingredients, stirring until combined. Bring the mixture to a boil. Reduce heat, cover, and let simmer for several hours, stirring occasionally, until the sauce is thickened and absorbed.

Chili is best when it cooks for a good long time, so add more liquid if it seems to be cooking down too quickly. The flavors are also enhanced if it is made a day or two ahead.

Maruja's Asopado de Pollo con Cerveza

THE SIGNATURE TASTE OF THIS delicious dish is created by adding a beer just before serving. The unique texture of Valencia rice is an important element of this simple, hearty one-pot meal and is worth going out of your way to find. This traditional Cuban recipe comes to us from Maruja Ventura. It has quickly become one of our favorite meals.

4 CHICKEN THIGHS, BONED AND CUT INTO PIECES
1 LARGE YELLOW ONION, CHOPPED
2 CLOVES GARLIC, MINCED
1 GREEN PEPPER, CHOPPED
1 (8-OUNCE) CAN PLAIN TOMATO SAUCE
1 CUP WHITE WINE
PINCH OF SALT

1½ CUPS VALENCIA OR OTHER SHORT-GRAIN RICE, WASHED
1½ CUPS WATER
1 (12-OUNCE) BOTTLE OF BEER
16 THIN STRIPS OF PIMIENTO OR ROASTED RED PEPPER
1 (12-OUNCE) CAN PEAS
½ CUP PITTED SPANISH OLIVES

Combine chicken, onion, garlic, green pepper, tomato sauce, wine, and salt in a deep skillet. Simmer over medium heat for 15 minutes, stirring frequently. Put chicken mixture in a large saucepot. Add the rice and water. Bring to a boil, then cover and reduce heat. Simmer until rice is tender, about 25 minutes. Add the bottle of beer just before serving and heat through. Garnish with red pepper strips, canned peas, and green olives.

Red Lentil Curry

THIS SATISFYING VEGETARIAN DISH IS colorful and flavorful. Serve with Basmati rice and good bread. The curry sauce also goes well with fish or chicken.

¾ CUP RED LENTILS
2½ CUPS BEER
2 TABLESPOONS BUTTER
1 MEDIUM ONION, SLIVERED
2 CLOVES GARLIC, MINCED
3 PLUM TOMATOES, PEELED AND DICED
2 TABLESPOONS GOOD-QUALITY CURRY POWDER
1 TABLESPOON GINGER

1 TABLESPOON BROWN SUGAR
1 LARGE RED PEPPER, CUT INTO BITE-SIZED PIECES
2 SMALL ZUCCHINI, CUT INTO BITE-SIZED PIECES
2 SMALL SUMMER SQUASH, CUT INTO BITE-SIZED PIECES
1 SMALL EGGPLANT, CUT INTO BITE-SIZED PIECES

Bring the lentils and 1½ cups of beer to a boil. Reduce heat, cover, and simmer for 20 minutes, stirring occasionally. Meanwhile, melt the butter in a large skillet. Sauté the onion over medium heat until translucent, adding garlic for the last minute or two. Add the tomatoes, curry powder, ginger, brown sugar, and ½ cup beer. Simmer until reduced and slightly thickened, stirring occasionally. Add the pepper, zucchini, summer squash, eggplant, curry sauce, and remaining ½ cup beer to the lentils. Cover and simmer for 20 minutes longer and serve.

Beer-Battered Fish

CLASSIC BRITISH PUB FARE. We like our batter thin, with a bit of cornmeal for added texture and a dash of spicy red pepper. Serve the fish with thick-cut fries, tartar sauce, and malted vinegar.

1 CUP FLOUR
1/3 CUP CORNMEAL
1 TABLESPOON SALT
1/4 TEASPOON RED PEPPER
2/3 CUP BEER
2 EGG YOLKS

1 TABLESPOON BUTTER, MELTED
VEGETABLE OIL FOR DEEP FRYING
8 MEDIUM-SIZE FIRM WHITE FISH
   FILLETS
SALT AND PEPPER TO TASTE

Combine the flour, cornmeal, salt, and red pepper. Add beer, egg yolks, and melted butter. Mix well. Season the fish fillets with salt and pepper. Heat the oil until a drop of batter dropped in spatters and sizzles. Dip each fillet in batter and drop into oil. Cook until brown and crisp, about 5 minutes. Drain on paper towels and serve immediately.

Spiced Sauerbraten

THIS SWEET-AND-SOUR VERSION of pot roast is enhanced by the addition of savory spices. Although the cooking time is long, the preparation is fairly simple, relying on the long marinade for its complex flavors. The results are superb.

1 TEASPOON WHOLE CLOVES
3 OR 4 WHOLE ALLSPICE
1/4 TEASPOON BLACK PEPPERCORNS
1 TEASPOON SALT
1 TEASPOON PAPRIKA
1/2 TEASPOON GROUND NUTMEG
1/2 TEASPOON GROUND MACE
1/2 TEASPOON GROUND GINGER
3 TO 4 POUNDS BEEF POT ROAST
4 BAY LEAVES

2 TABLESPOONS LIGHT OR DARK
   BROWN SUGAR
1/2 LEMON, SLICED
1 LARGE ONION, SLICED
1 CUP RED WINE VINEGAR
2 CUPS PLUS 1/2 CUP BEER
2 TABLESPOONS OIL
1/4 CUP FLOUR, OR 2/3 CUP CRUSHED
   GINGERSNAP COOKIES

Coarsely grind cloves, allspice, and black pepper. Combine with salt, paprika, nutmeg, mace, and ginger. Rub over meat, pressing in. Combine bay leaves, brown sugar, lemon, onion, vinegar, and 2 cups beer. Pour over roast. Cover and refrigerate for 36 hours, turning meat at least twice daily. Remove meat from marinade and wipe dry. Strain marinade and reserve liquid and onion in separate containers. Heat oil in a large Dutch oven. Add meat and brown on all sides. Add reserved marinade, cover, and simmer until tender, about 2 hours, turning occasionally and adding onion for last 20 minutes. Remove meat. Top with the onion. Remove all but 1½ cups of pan juices (add more beer if there isn't enough). Blend flour or gingersnaps with ½ cup beer. Whisk some of the juices into the flour or gingersnap mix, then slowly whisk the mixture back into the pot. Stir constantly for 2 to 3 minutes, until thick and bubbly.

Carbonnade Flamande

A COUNTRY WITH CENTURIES OF beermaking history, Belgium has a strong tradition of beer in its cuisine. This tasty Belgian classic beautifully demonstrates the intermingling of food and beer that is typically Belgian.

4 SCALLIONS
2 TABLESPOONS BUTTER
3 TABLESPOONS FLOUR
½ TEASPOON SALT
FRESHLY GROUND PEPPER
2 POUNDS BEEF STEW MEAT
2 (16-OUNCE) BOTTLES OF DOPPEL
 OR FLANDERS BROWN
1 (26-OUNCE) CAN WHOLE
 TOMATOES

½ CUP RAISINS
1 TABLESPOON LIGHT OR DARK
 BROWN SUGAR
2 TABLESPOONS FRESH OR
 1 TEASPOON DRY PARSLEY
2 TABLESPOONS FRESH OR
 1 TEASPOON DRY THYME
1 TABLESPOON FRESH OR
 ½ TEASPOON DRY TARRAGON

Chop scallion whites and 1 inch of green. Melt butter over medium heat in large stewpot. Add scallions. Blend flour with salt and pepper. Toss meat in flour to coat. When scallions are translucent, add meat and brown on all sides. Add one bottle of beer, tomatoes, raisins, brown sugar, and herbs. Raise heat and bring to a boil. Reduce heat, cover, and simmer for 2 to 3 hours. Add the second beer for the final 10 minutes. Adjust seasonings and serve.

Chicken with Roasted-Garlic Cream Sauce

BEER MAKES A SURPRISINGLY GOOD cream sauce, especially when paired with roasted garlic and mushrooms. For added flair, use wild mushrooms, but be wary of simmering them in the reducing sauce for too long—the more delicate varieties will not stand up to a long boil.

8–10 CLOVES GARLIC, SEPARATED, BUT WITH THE SKINS ON	4 TABLESPOONS BUTTER
4 WHOLE BONED CHICKEN BREASTS	1 CUP SLICED MUSHROOMS
3 TABLESPOONS FLOUR	⅔ CUP CHICKEN BROTH
SALT AND PEPPER	⅔ CUP BEER
	⅓ CUP MILK

Preheat oven to 375 degrees. Place garlic in a roaster or small covered baking dish. Roast until soft, about 25 minutes. Meanwhile, trim chicken breasts and halve. Remove rib meat and reserve for another use. Place a sheet of wax paper over each half breast and pound (the handle of a large knife works if you don't have a tenderizer). Blend flour with salt and pepper to taste. Heat 2 tablespoons butter in a large skillet. Lightly dredge chicken in the flour and shake off any excess. Brown chicken (in batches if necessary). Set aside. Heat remaining 2 tablespoons butter in same skillet. Add mushrooms and sauté lightly, 2 to 3 minutes. Squeeze garlic from skin and whisk into the chicken broth. Add broth, beer, and milk to skillet and simmer until reduced to about 1 cup. Add chicken and simmer for 2 minutes, stirring well. Salt and pepper to taste.

Erin Go Bragh Stout Pie

THIS RENDITION OF AN IRISH pub classic is enhanced by the use of more spices than are customary to the original. The result is slightly more elegant, but equally satisfying. Add canned or thawed frozen mixed vegetables to turn it into a variation of Shepherd's Pie.

2 TABLESPOONS OIL	½ CUP BEEF STOCK OR BROTH
1 ONION, CHOPPED	1 TEASPOON THYME OR ROSEMARY
2 CLOVES GARLIC, MINCED	6 LARGE POTATOES, PEELED AND
2 POUNDS BEEF STEW MEAT, CUT	CUBED
INTO ½-INCH CUBES	½ CUP MILK
3 TABLESPOONS FLOUR	2 TABLESPOONS BUTTER
1 CUP STOUT	SALT AND PEPPER TO TASTE

Heat oil in a large skillet. Add onion and sauté until translucent, adding garlic for last minute or two. Toss beef cubes in flour, and shake off excess. Add to the skillet and brown on all sides. Add stout, broth, and herb. Bring to a boil, reduce heat, and simmer uncovered until sauce is reduced by a third. Meanwhile, boil potatoes in a large pot until just tender, about 12 minutes. Drain potatoes and mash with milk, butter, and salt to taste. Preheat oven to 375 degrees. Salt and pepper the beef mixture to taste, then spread in a large baking dish. Spread potatoes in an even layer on top. Bake for 30 to 35 minutes, until potatoes begin to brown at the peaks and beef mixture bubbles at the sides.

Wine is but a single broth, ale is meat, drink and cloth.
—SIXTEENTH-CENTURY ENGLISH PROVERB

Homestyle Meatloaf

FEW THINGS IN LIFE RIVAL the homestyle taste of really good meatloaf. For ours, the milk or sauce that our moms and grandmas always used is replaced with what we think is *the* perfect cooking liquid: beer. Serve this with mashed potatoes and creamed corn, the classic comfort food accompaniments. And don't forget to save some for the ultimate leftover sandwiches.

2 POUNDS GROUND MEAT
  (PREFERABLY A MEATLOAF MIX OF
  BEEF, PORK, AND VEAL)
½ CUP BREADCRUMBS
2 TO 3 CLOVES GARLIC, MINCED
½ TEASPOON SALT
½ TEASPOON PARSLEY
½ TEASPOON OREGANO
¼ TEASPOON CUMIN

¼ TEASPOON CHILI POWDER
FRESHLY GROUND PEPPER TO TASTE
1 LARGE ONION
1 EGG
½ CUP PLUS ¼ CUP BEER
1 CUP PLAIN TOMATO SAUCE
A DASH OR TWO EACH OF SALT,
  CUMIN, CHILI POWDER, AND BLACK
  PEPPER

Preheat the oven to 350 degrees. Place meat, breadcrumbs, garlic, salt, and spices in a large mixing bowl. Peel onion and slice off the end opposite the root. Place a grater over the mixing bowl, and holding the onion by the root end, grate into the bowl. Add the egg and ½ cup of the beer and knead thoroughly. Shape into a loaf and place in a shallow roasting pan. In a separate bowl, stir together the tomato sauce, salt, dashes of spices, and remaining beer. Pour the tomato sauce over the meatloaf and bake until cooked through, about 45 minutes, basting with the drippings once or twice.

Ginger-Beer Bratwurst

PAUL FIXED US UP A traditional German meal one night while we were working on this book. One taste of the delicious bratwurst and we knew it had to go in the book. The recipe is borrowed from Paul's mom and has been one of his favorites all his life. We think it may become a favorite of yours as well.

4 BRATWURST
2 TABLESPOONS FLOUR
2 TABLESPOONS BUTTER
1 (12-OUNCE) BOTTLE DARK BEER
3 OR 4 TABLESPOONS GINGERSNAP
  COOKIES, CRUSHED

1 TABLESPOON GRATED ONION
SEVERAL TABLESPOONS
  CONCENTRATED BEEF STOCK
SALT AND FRESHLY GROUND PEPPER
1 TO 2 TABLESPOONS LEMON JUICE

Poke a few holes in each bratwurst to prevent it from bursting. Dredge the bratwurst in the flour. Melt the butter in a skillet and sauté the bratwurst over medium heat until done. Remove and set aside. Add beer and deglaze the skillet. Sprinkle in ginger-snaps and onion. Simmer for 10 minutes. Season to taste with stock, lemon juice, salt, and pepper. Simmer an additional 2 to 3 minutes. Reduce the heat and return the bratwurst to the skillet until heated through and serve.

Red-Hot Rack of Ribs

RIBS COME IN A VARIETY of styles. These are based on our favorite —Memphis ribs—baby back ribs served dry and highly spiced. Serve some good-quality barbecue sauce on the side for dipping.

BRAISING LIQUID:

2 QUARTS BEER

2 QUARTS BEEF STOCK

½ CUP MALT VINEGAR

3 CLOVES GARLIC, COARSELY CHOPPED

2 TABLESPOONS HOT SAUCE

1 TABLESPOON CAYENNE

2 TABLESPOONS CUMIN

2 TABLESPOONS PAPRIKA

2 (6-OUNCE) CANS TOMATO PASTE

½ CUP HONEY

1 TABLESPOON SALT

FRESHLY GROUND BLACK PEPPER

SPICE RUB:

¼ CUP GARLIC POWDER

¼ CUP PAPRIKA

3 TABLESPOONS CUMIN

3 TABLESPOONS CAYENNE

2 TABLESPOONS SALT

BLACK PEPPER

½ CUP BEER

¼ CUP MALT VINEGAR

2 TABLESPOONS PREPARED MUSTARD

2 TABLESPOONS WORCESTERSHIRE SAUCE

2 TABLESPOONS TOMATO PASTE

4 SLABS BABY BACK RIBS

Combine ingredients for braising liquid in a large pot. Bring to a boil. Add ribs. Raise to a boil, reduce heat, and simmer until meat is cooked but not falling off the bone, 1½ to 2 hours. Pre-heat the oven to 375 degrees. Combine the spice-rub ingredients and mix well to form a paste. Rub the spices all over the ribs. (Ribs can be wrapped well and refrigerated at this point until ready to roast—up to several days.) Place the ribs on a cookie sheet or in a shallow roasting pan and roast for 15 minutes. Serve immediately.

Mary Bielawski's Polska Kielbasa

THIS RECIPE IS A FAMILY favorite passed down from Maura's great-grandmother, who immigrated here from Poland when she was sixteen. She and her husband operated a tavern in upstate New York, where she, of course, brewed the beer.

2 POUNDS KIELBASA

2 TABLESPOONS BUTTER

2 POUNDS SAUERKRAUT

2 APPLES, CORED AND DICED

1 (12-OUNCE) BOTTLE BEER

1 TABLESPOON CARAWAY SEEDS

SALT AND PEPPER TO TASTE

Cut the kielbasa on the diagonal into 2-inch-thick slices. Melt the butter in a large skillet over medium heat. Brown the kielbasa. Combine the kielbasa, sauerkraut, apples, beer, caraway seeds, salt, and pepper in a large pot. Bring the liquid to a boil. Reduce heat, cover, and simmer for at least 1 hour, stirring occasionally and adding more beer if necessary.

Poached Pears with Raspberry Sauce

SERVED WARM OR CHILLED, THIS is a fabulous and elegant dessert. Serve alone or with the Lambic Sorbet (see p. 206), a scoop of vanilla ice cream, or a slice of pound cake. A malty brew can be substituted for the poaching liquid, but we recommend a fruity beer for the sauce.

½ CUP RASPBERRIES, FRESH OR
   FROZEN

2 CUPS RASPBERRY LAMBIC

2 TABLESPOONS SUGAR

6 PEARS, PEELED, HALVED AND
   CORED

1 TABLESPOON LEMON JUICE

2 TABLESPOONS HEAVY CREAM

Puree the raspberries and press through a sieve to remove seeds. Bring the lambic and sugar to a boil in a large skillet. Arrange pear halves in the skillet, working in batches if necessary. Reduce heat and simmer the pears until tender and pink, about 5 minutes. Remove pears. Raise the poaching liquid to a boil and reduce by half. Remove from heat, whisk in raspberry puree, lemon juice, and heavy cream. Drizzle over pears and serve.

Chocolate Cream Stout Cake

RICH, MOIST, AND CHOCOLATY, THIS cake is one of our most requested recipes. It has become the traditional birthday cake in our house. What better way to celebrate—lots of birthday homebrew topped off with this delicious homebrew cake!

CAKE:	ICING:
2 TABLESPOONS PLUS 1 ½ CUPS BUTTER	4 TABLESPOONS BUTTER, AT ROOM TEMPERATURE
1 ⅓ CUPS DARK COCOA	½ CUP CONFECTIONERS' SUGAR
1 (12-OUNCE) BOTTLE CREAM STOUT	1 ½ CUPS SEMISWEET CHOCOLATE MORSELS
1 TEASPOON SALT	1 OUNCE GRAND MARNIER
3 CUPS UNBLEACHED FLOUR	¾ CUP CHOPPED WALNUTS
2 CUPS SUGAR	1 TABLESPOON SCALDED MILK
2 TEASPOONS BAKING SODA	
3 EGGS	
¾ CUP SOUR CREAM	

Preheat oven to 350 degrees. Use the 2 tablespoons of butter to grease two 10-inch springform pans. Dust with ⅓ cup cocoa. In a large mixing bowl, sift together the remaining cocoa, salt, flour, and baking soda. Melt 1½ cups butter in a heavy saucepan. Stir in stout. Remove from heat. Beat into dry ingredients a little at a time. Add eggs and sour cream, and mix at medium speed for 2 minutes. Pour batter into pans and bake for 30 to 35 minutes. A toothpick inserted in the center should come out clean. Cool on wire racks 10 minutes, then remove sides and cool completely.

For the icing, cream the butter and sugar and set aside. Melt the chocolate (a few minutes in the microwave works well) and whisk in the Grand Marnier. Mix half of the chocolate mixture into the butter and sugar, then fold in the nuts. Use the creamed nut frosting between the layers. Whisk the scalded milk into the remaining chocolate and pour over the cake.

Lambic Sorbet

THIS TART AND SWEET SORBET takes an interesting twist with the added pungency of the lambic. Raspberry is our favorite, but try it with other flavors as well. It is a sensational palate cleanser or light dessert.

1 CUP RASPBERRIES	1 (12-OUNCE) BOTTLE RASPBERRY
3 CUPS WATER	LAMBIC
½ CUP SUGAR	1 TABLESPOON LEMON JUICE

Puree the raspberries in a blender or food processor. Press through a sieve to remove the seeds. Combine the raspberries, water, sugar, lambic, and lemon juice in a large saucepan over medium heat, stirring until sugar melts. Remove from heat. Pour into a ceramic container (or into a metal loaf pan lined with plastic wrap), cover with plastic wrap, and freeze, stirring a few times during freezing to break up the ice crystals. Or you can use an ice cream machine, following manufacturer's instructions.

The Great Pumpkin Pie

THIS SCRUMPTIOUS PIE MAKES ECONOMICAL use of the pumpkin that has been boiled in the wort for The Great Pumpkin Ale. The malted barley, hops, and spices from the wort give this pie a unique malty taste. Thoroughly draining the pumpkin is the key to a successful pie—if it is too wet, the pie will brown and toughen on top before it can become solid. Serve it with a big dollop of freshly whipped cream.

CRUST:
1 ½ CUPS ALL-PURPOSE FLOUR
½ TEASPOON SALT
½ CUP SHORTENING
4 TO 5 TABLESPOONS WATER

FILLING:
PUMPKIN FROM THE GREAT PUMPKIN
   ALE

1 ½ CUPS EVAPORATED MILK
½ CUP SUGAR
¼ CUP LIGHT OR DARK BROWN
   SUGAR
½ TEASPOON SALT
2 TEASPOONS PUMPKIN PIE SPICE
   (CINNAMON, GINGER, NUTMEG,
   ALLSPICE, AND GROUND CLOVES)
2 EGGS

Stir flour and salt together in a large mixing bowl. Cut in shortening until pieces are pea sized. Sprinkle 1 tablespoon water over the mixture and toss with a fork. Repeat until it is all moistened. Form into a ball and set aside. Preheat oven to 425 degrees.

Remove the skin from the pumpkin and put it in a strainer. Firmly press down on the pumpkin, removing as much water as possible. Place in food processor or blender and puree. Combine 2 cups of the pureed pumpkin and the evaporated milk, sugar, brown sugar, salt, spices, and eggs in a large mixing bowl and mix well.

Roll out the dough and press into a 9-inch pie plate. Pour in the filling. Bake for 15 minutes, then reduce heat to 350 degrees for 45 minutes, or until a knife inserted in the center comes out clean. Cool before serving.

GLOSSARY

adjunct: Anything added to beer other than malt, hops, yeast, and water. Common adjuncts include corn, rice, and sugars.

all-grain: A method of brewing using grains rather than extract syrup; requires mashing the grains and collecting the wort prior to boiling.

attentuation: Fermentation as measured by changes in the specific gravity of the wort. Beer has reached final attenuation when the yeast can no longer ferment any more sugars.

black and tan: A blend of stout and a lighter beer (often a pale ale), usually poured in layers.

California common: A beer that is fermented using lager yeast at ale temperatures. Also known as Steam beer, a name that has been trademarked by Anchor Brewing Company.

conversion: The process by which the starches in grains are converted to fermentable sugars.

cyser: Mead containing apples, apple juice, or apple extract.

dry-hop: To add hops during secondary fermentation. This gives the finished beer a powerful hop aroma without adding bitterness. Historically, this method was used for preservation of beer during long voyages. See India Pale Ale.

extra special bitter, or ESB: This is a stronger version of the classic British bitter, but not too strong. An ordinary bitter has an original gravity of 1.035 to 1.038, whereas an ESB starts around 1.045 to 1.055.

extraction rate: A measure of the amount of starches converted to fermentable sugars during the mash.

finings: Additives that clarify beer by bonding to various solids and then dropping out so that the solids can be left behind when the beer is transferred.

hippocras: A pyment flavored with herbs or spices.

hot break: Solids that separate from the wort as it cools.

India Pale Ale, or IPA: A style of beer having a strong hop profile and high alcohol content. Usually dry-hopped. IPAs originated when British imperialists in India discovered that ales from home could survive the long sea journey if hops were added to the storage vessels and the beers were brewed with a higher alcohol content.

invert sugar: A fermentable sugar, similar to sucrose, made from the acid treatment of raw cane or beet sugar. The acid treatment creates unique flavor characteristics not present in the sugar's raw form. Invert sugar creates complex flavors that cannot be derived from malt sugars.

kraeusen: The unsightly foamy head that develops as a beer begins to ferment. As funky as it looks, this is a good sign!

kraeusening: Priming a beer with unfermented wort. This takes some planning, but is recommended when conforming to the Reinheitsgebot.

mash: To convert the starches from grain (barley, wheat, etc.) into fermentable sugars; the process involves steeping the grains in water, then sparging to collect the wort.

mead: A fermented beverage made from honey.

metheglin: Mead flavored with herbs or spices.

original gravity: A measure of the density of the wort before it is fermented. It indicates the amount of sugars available for conversion to alcohol.

pitching yeast: Adding yeast to the wort.

pyment: A mead containing grapes or grape extracts.

rack: To transfer the beer from one vessel to another, leaving unwanted solids behind.

racking cane: A length of hard plastic tubing that is attached to the flexible siphon hose to facilitate racking.

Reinheitsgebot: The German beer purity law, enacted in 1516, which requires that beer contain only water, hops, yeast, and malt.

secondary fermentation: Following primary fermentation, the beer is racked off of the dead yeast and other solids in the bottom of the vessel and allowed to ferment further. Additional flavorings such as fruits, herbs, and hops (*see* dry-hop) are often added at this stage.

session beer: In British beer terminology, a beer that goes down easily and does not have a high alcohol content. The idea is that you can sit and talk (or have a session) without becoming too inebriated for meaningful conversation.

siphon hose: A length of flexible tubing that is used in racking the beer from one vessel to another.

smack pack: Yeast packaging that contains a small starter. Each package contains an interior packet of yeast within a small amount of wort. By smacking the packet, the brewer allows the yeast to be exposed to the wort without exposing it to the air.

sparge: To run water slowly through the grain bed to gather the fermentable sugars after the mash.

starter: A small amount of wort to which yeast has been added so that it multiplies prior to pitching. Starters provide larger amounts of active yeast to commence fermentation quicker.

steam beer: *See* California common.

tertiary fermentation: Following secondary fermentation, the beer is racked off of the dead yeast and other solids in the bottom of the vessel and allowed to ferment further. This third fermentation is usually reserved for beers that have had fruits or other solids added during secondary fermentation so that they can be further clarified.

wit: A style of beer originating in Belgium and named for its pale color ("white"), which results from the use of pale grains and wheat.

wort: Sweet liquid containing the converted sugars from the malted barley and other grains.

Undoubtedly you have discovered that homebrewing is not for the impatient. Two weeks from stovetop to belly is a long time to wait for your creation. There is very little you can do to encourage yeast to ferment faster (verbal abuse may make you feel better, but it definitely does not work). What you can do, though, is to try to make your microscopic friends as comfortable as possible. After three hours in the kitchen (sometimes over six with all-grain) you want to pitch your yeast and let it get to work while you clean up the mess. But if you don't have a wort chiller, you most likely have to wait another 12 hours before your five gallons are room temperature.

You can buy a wort chiller from your homebrew supplier for $30 or $40. Or you can make one for less than $15. All you need is the following: 25 feet of copper tubing (3/8-inch outside diameter), 3 to 6 feet of plastic tubing (1/2-inch outside diameter), one hose connector (garden hose variety with 3/8-inch male nipple), and three 1/2-inch hose clamps. All these items can be found at your local hardware store, and you may even have the plastic hose around the house (an old racking hose works perfectly).

The copper tubing comes coiled up, so it is easy to form this to fit your brew pot. The hard part is getting the inlet and outlet to hang over the edge of the pot. Use a coffee can or a 2-liter soda bottle filled with water to help you bend the tubing without putting a kink in it. Create a coil that will fit inside your brew pot, leaving about 1 inch between the coil and the walls of the pot (usually a 10-inch-diameter coil will do). Bend the upper end of the tubing so that it hangs over the edge of your pot by 3 inches. Thread the lower end of the tubing up through the center of the coil and hang it over the edge of the pot in a similar manner.

Locate your brew pot near your sink to determine the length of plastic tubing required. Clamp a length of tubing to the inlet of the wort chiller, and cut it at the point where it meets your water faucet. Clamp the other end to the hose connector, and attach the connector to your faucet, using the adapter from your bottle washer (you do have a bottle washer, don't you?). Clamp another length of plastic tubing to the chiller outlet, and let this hose hang into the sink. Turn on the faucet and check for leaks.

When using a wort chiller, you must sterilize it before you use it. No, you don't have to soak it in bleach. During the last fifteen minutes of your boil, put your wort chiller in your brew pot. The boil will sterilize the coil, so that when you are finished all you need to do is carefully move your brew pot near your sink, and hook up your hoses. Turn on the cold water and gently stir your wort. Check the temperature periodically. Once the temperature goes below 100 degrees, stir briskly to aerate the wort for the yeasties (being careful not to spill it all over the counter). When the wort reaches 60 to 70 degrees, transfer it to your fermenter and pitch your yeast. This whole process should take 20 to 30 minutes, depending on how cold your tap water can get. Stir your wort in the opposite direction from that the water in your wort chiller is flowing to speed up the cooling process.

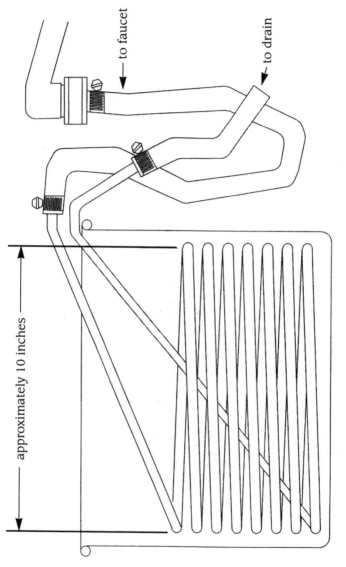

to faucet

to drain

approximately 10 inches

Wort Chiller

WORLD WIDE WEB BEER AND BREWING SITES

The World Wide Web is a wealth of information on beer and brewing. The following are selected sites of general interest. The myriad sites sponsored by commercial breweries, homebrew clubs, retailers, and dedicated individuals are not included, but can easily be accessed from links at many of these sites. Happy surfing.

The Association of Brewers
http://www.aob.org/aob/
AOB home page with links to American Homebrewers Association, Brewers Publications, Great American Beer Festival, etc.

The Beer Hunting Pages
http://www.tiac.net/users/tjd/bier/bier.html
Links to regional beer guides.

The Brewery
http://alpha.rollanet.org
Including Cat's Meow III recipe index and other homebrew information.

CAMpaign for Real Ale
http://www.camra.org.uk/
Official Web site of CAMRA in the UK.

Eric's Beer and Homebrewing Page
http://pekkel.uthscsa.edu/beer.html
Beer information, regional guides, homebrewing links.

The Hop Page
http://realbeer.com/hops/
Hops, hops, hops plus an online IBU calculator.

The MadBrewers
http://www.tezcat.com/~sstrong/madbrewers/titlepage.html
Homebrewing

The Mashtun
http://mashtun.jpl.nasa.gov/yeast.html
Technical homebrew info.

The New York City Beer Guide
http://www.nycbeer.org/
The best of the regional beer guides.

The Real Beer Page ™
http://realbeer.com/RealBeer/
A wealth of information including on-line brewery tours, profiles, and news.

Spencer's Beer Page
http://www-personal.umich.edu/~spencer/beer/
Homebrew-related material.

U.K. Homebrewers Page
http://sun1.bham.ac.uk/GraftonG/homebrew.htm
Homebrewing in the U.K.

The WWW's Virtual Library's Beer & Brewing Index
http://www.mindspring.com/~jlock/wwwbeer.html
A thorough listing of beer resources on the Web.

When entering homebrewing contests, you will be judged on how well you brew a particular style as set down by the American Homebrewers Association, the AHA. Below is a list of the AHA style guidelines to help you in your efforts.

ALE

Ales are distinguished by the use of top-fermenting *Saccharomyces cerevisiae* yeast strains. These strains perform at warmer temperatures, the ferments are faster, and fermentation by-products are generally more evident. Ales tend to have a very pronounced palate where esters and fruity qualities are part of the character.

1. Barleywine

(a) Barleywine

Copper to medium brown. Malty sweetness. Fruity/estery. Low to high bitterness. Medium to full body. Low to high hop aroma and flavor. Alcoholic taste. Low to medium diacetyl O.K.

2. Belgian and French Ale

(a) Flanders Brown

Slight vinegarlike or lactic sourness and spiciness. Light to medium bodied. Deep copper to brown. Fruity/estery. No hop flavor or aroma. Low to medium bitterness. No diacetyl. Low roasted malt character O.K.

(b) Dubbel

Dark amber to brown. Sweet, malty, nutty, chocolate, roast malt aroma O.K. Medium to full body. Low bitterness, very low diacetyl O.K. Low levels of fruity esters (especially banana) O.K.

(c) Tripel

Light, pale color. Light malty and hoppy aroma. Neutral hop/malt balance. Finish may be sweet. Medium to full body. Alcoholic, but best examples do not taste strongly of alcohol. Spicy, phenolic-clove, banana flavors, esters O.K.

(d) Belgian Ale. Golden to deep amber. A Belgian pale ale.
Hop character subdued. Light to medium body. Low malt aroma. Slight acidity O.K. No diacetyl. Low fruity esters in aroma and flavors. Low caramel or toasted malt flavor O.K.

(e) Belgian Strong Ale
Pale to dark brown. Alcoholic. Can be vinous. Darker beers are colored with candi sugar and not so much dark malt. Medium body. Low to high bitterness. Low hop flavor and aroma.

(f) White
Unmalted wheat and malted barley. Oats O.K. Often spiced with coriander seed and dried bitter orange peel. Hop flavor and aroma "noble" type desired. Low to medium bitterness. Low to medium body. Dry. Low diacetyl O.K. Low to medium fruity esters.

(g) Bière de Garde
Deep golden to deep copper/light brown. Medium to high malt flavor. Light to medium body. Medium hop bitterness. Light to medium hop flavor and aroma. May have light to medium fruitiness, esteriness. Lager yeast may be used. Earthy, cellarlike, musty aromas O.K. Traditionally, a French-style beer that improves with some aging.

3. Belgian-Style Lambic

Intensely and cleanly sour. No hop bitterness, flavor, or aroma. Effervescent. Fruity/estery and uniquely aromatic. Malted barley and unmalted wheat. Stale, old hops used. Cloudiness O.K.

(a) Faro
Lambic with sugar and sometimes caramel added. Pale to light amber.

(b) Gueuze
Unflavored blend of old and young lambics, secondarily fermented. Very dry or mildly sweet. Intensely sour and acidic flavor. Fruity/estery. Pale. Light body. Use unmalted wheat, malted barley, and stale aged hops. Very low hop bitterness.

(c) Fruit (framboise, kriek, pêche)
Lambic fermented with fruits such as raspberry, cherry, peach, etc. Fruit flavor, aroma, and color are intense. Sourness predominates. Often very dry.

4. Brown Ale

(a) English Brown
Deep copper to brown. Sweet and malty. Low bitterness. Hop flavor and aroma low. Some fruitiness and esters. Medium body. Low diacetyl O.K.

(b) English Mild
Low alcohol. Light amber to very dark brown. Low hop bitterness, flavor, and aroma. Mild maltiness. Light body. Low esters.

(c) American Brown
Medium to dark brown. High hop bitterness, flavor, and aroma. Medium maltiness and body. Low diacetyl O.K.

5. English-Style Pale Ale

(a) Classic English Pale Ale
Golden to deep amber, copper. Low to medium maltiness. High hop bitterness, flavor, and aroma. Use of English hops such as Goldings, Fuggles, etc. Fruity/estery. Low diacetyl O.K. Medium body. Low caramel character O.K.

(b) India Pale Ale
Golden to deep amber, copper. Medium body. Medium maltiness. High hop bitterness. Hop flavor and aroma medium to high. Fruity/estery. Alcoholic strength evident. Low diacetyl O.K.

6. American-Style Ale

(a) American Pale Ale
Pale to deep amber/red/copper. Low to medium maltiness. High hop bitterness. Use of American hops, such as Cascade, Willamette, Centennial (CFJ-90), etc. Medium body. Low caramel character O.K.

(b) American Wheat
Golden to light amber. Light to medium body. Low to medium bitterness. Low to medium fruitiness and esters. Low diacetyl O.K. Lager or ale yeast O.K.

7. English Bitter

Gold to copper. Low carbonation. Medium to high bitterness. May or may not have hop flavor or aroma. Low to medium maltiness. Light to medium body. Low diacetyl O.K. Fruitiness/esters O.K.

(a) English Ordinary
Mildest form of bitter. Low diacetyl and fruity esters.

(b) English Special
Moderate strength. Maltiness more evident along with increased hop character.

(c) English Extra Special
Strong bitter. Maltiness evident. Hop bitterness flavor and aroma medium to high. Full body.

8. Scottish Ale

(a) Scottish Light
Gold to amber. Low carbonation. Very low bitterness. No hop flavor and aroma. Medium maltiness. Light body. Low to medium diacetyl O.K. Fruitiness/esters O.K. Faint smoky character O.K.

(b) Scottish Heavy
Gold to amber to dark brown. Low carbonation. Low bitterness. May or may not have hop flavor and aroma. Medium to high maltiness. Medium body. Low to medium diacetyl O.K. Low fruitiness/esters O.K. Faint smoky character O.K.

(c) Scottish Export
Gold to amber to dark brown. Low carbonation. Low to medium bitterness. May or may not have hop flavor and aroma. High maltiness. Medium body. Low to medium diacetyl O.K. Fruitiness/esters O.K. Faint smoky character O.K.

9. Porter

(a) Robust Porter
Black. No roast barley character. Sharp bitterness of black malt, without high burnt/charcoal-like flavor. Medium to full bodied. Malty sweet. Hop bitterness medium to high. Hop flavor and aroma: none to medium. Fruitiness/esters O.K. Low diacetyl O.K.

(b) Brown Porter
Medium to dark brown. No roast barley or strong burnt malt character. Light malt sweetness. Medium hop bitterness. Hop flavor and aroma: none to medium diacetyl O.K.

10. English and Scottish Strong Ale

(a) English Old Ale/Strong Ale
Light amber to deep amber/copper. Medium to full body. Malty. Hop bitterness apparent but not aggressive, flavor and aroma can be assertive. Fruitiness/esters high. Alcoholic strength recognizable. Low diacetyl O.K.

(b) Strong Scotch Ale
Similar to English Old/Strong Ale. Overwhelmingly malty. Deep copper to very black. Hop bitterness low. Diacetyl medium to high. Hop flavor and aroma very low or absent. Full bodied. Faint smoky character O.K. Malt character balanced by clean alcohol flavors.

11. Stout

(a) Classic Dry Stout
Black opaque. Medium body. Medium to high hop bitterness. Roasted barley character is required, but can be at low levels. Slight malt sweet-

ness or caramel malt character O.K. No hop flavor or aroma. Slight acidity/sourness O.K. Very low diacetyl O.K.

(b) Foreign Style
Black/opaque. Medium to full body. No hop aroma and flavor. Slight acidity/sourness O.K. Slight malt sweetness or caramel malt character O.K. Very low diacetyl O.K. Low fruity esters O.K.

(c) Sweet Stout/Cream Stout
Overall character sweet. Black opaque. Medium to full body. Hop bitterness low. Roasted barley (coffeelike), character mild. No hop flavor or aroma. Sweet maltiness and caramel flavors evident. Low diacetyl O.K.

(d) Imperial Stout
Dark copper to very black. Hop bitterness, flavor, and aroma medium to high. Alcohol strength evident. Rich maltiness. High fruitiness/esters. Full-bodied. Very low diacetyl O.K.

LAGER
Lagers are produced with bottom-fermenting *Saccharomyces uvarum* (a.k.a. *carlsbergensis*) strains of yeast at colder fermentation temperatures than ales. This cooler environment inhibits the natural production of esters and other fermentation byproducts, creating a cleaner-tasting product.

12. Bock

(a) Traditional German Bock
Deep copper to dark brown. Medium to full body. Malty sweet character predominates in aroma and flavor with some toasted chocolate malt character. Low bitterness. Low hop flavor, "noble" type O.K. No hop aroma. No fruitiness or esters. Low diacetyl O.K.

(b) Helles (light) Bock
Pale to amber. Medium body. Malty sweet character predominates in aroma and malt character. Low bitterness. Low hop flavor, "noble" type O.K. No hop aroma. Low diacetyl O.K.

(c) Doppelbock
Light to very dark; amber to dark brown. Very full body. Malty sweetness predominates in aroma and flavor. High alcoholic flavor. Slight fruitiness/esters O.K., but not desirable. Low hop flavor, "noble" type O.K. No hop aroma. Low bitterness. Low diacetyl O.K.

13. Bavarian Dark

(a) Munich Dunkel
Copper to dark brown. Medium body. Nutty, toasted, chocolatelike malty sweetness in aroma and flavor. Medium bitterness. Low "noble" type hop flavor and aroma. No fruitiness/esters. Low diacetyl O.K.

(b) Schwarzbier
Dark brown to black. Medium body. Roasted malt evident. Low sweetness
in aroma and flavor. Low to medium bitterness. Low bitterness from roast
malt. Hop flavor and aroma, "noble" type O.K. No fruitiness/esters. Low
diacetyl O.K.

14. German Light Lager

(a) Dortmunder/Export
Pale to golden. Medium body. Medium malty sweetness. Medium bitterness. Very low "noble" type hop flavor and aroma. No fruitiness/esters,
or diacetyl. Alcoholic warmth evident.

(b) Munich Helles
Pale to golden. Medium body. Medium malty sweetness. Low bitterness.
"Noble" type hop flavor and aroma O.K. No fruitiness/esters. No diacetyl.

15. Classic Pilsner

(a) German
Pale to golden. Light to medium body. High hop bitterness. Medium hop
"noble" type flavor and aroma. Low maltiness in aroma and flavor. No
fruitiness/esters. Very low diacetyl O.K.

(b) Bohemian
Pale to golden. Light to medium body. Medium to high bitterness. Low to
medium hop "noble" type flavor and aroma. Low to medium maltiness in
aroma and flavor. No fruitiness/esters. Low diacetyl O.K.

16. American Lager

(a) Diet/Lite
Very pale. Light body. Very low bitterness. No malt aroma or flavor. No
hop aroma or flavor. Effervescent. No fruitiness/esters or diacetyl.

(b) American Standard
Very pale. Light body. Very low bitterness. Low malt aroma and flavor. Low
hop aroma and flavor O.K. Effervescent. No fruitiness/esters or diacetyl.

(c) American Premium
Very pale to golden. Light body. Low to medium bitterness. Low malt
aroma and flavor O.K. Low hop flavor or aroma O.K. Effervescent. No
fruitiness/esters or diacetyl.

(d) Dry
Pale to golden. Light body. Low to medium bitterness. Low malt aroma
or flavor. Low hop aroma and flavor. Effervescent. No fruitiness/esters or
diacetyl. No lingering aftertaste or bitterness.

(e) Cream Ale/Lager
Very pale. Effervescent. Light body. Low to medium bitterness. Low hop flavor or aroma O.K. Low fruitiness/ester O.K. Can use ale or lager yeasts or combination.

(f) American Dark
Deep copper to dark brown. Light to medium body. Low bitterness. Low malt aroma or flavor O.K. Low hop flavor or aroma O.K. Effervescent. No fruitiness/esters. Very low diacetyl O.K.

17. Vienna/Oktoberfest/Märzen

(a) Vienna
Amber to deep copper/light brown. Toasted malt aroma and flavor. Low malt sweetness. Light to medium body. Hop bitterness "noble" type low to medium. Low hop flavor and aroma, "noble" type O.K. No fruitiness/esters. Low diacetyl O.K.

(b) Oktoberfest/Märzen
Amber to deep copper/orange. Malty sweetness, toasted malt aroma and flavor dominant. Medium body. Low to medium bitterness. Low hop flavor and aroma, "noble" type O.K. No fruitiness/esters or diacetyl.

MIXED STYLE (LAGER-ALE)
The following beers are fermented or aged with mixed traditions, and could be brewed as ales or lagers.

18. German-Style Ale

(a) Düsseldorf-style Altbier
Copper to dark brown. Medium to high maltiness. Medium to high bitterness. Very low hop flavor. No hop aroma. Light to medium body. Low fruitiness/esters. Traditionally fermented warm but aged at cold temperatures. No diacetyl.

(b) Kölsch
Pale gold. Low hop flavor and aroma. Medium bitterness. Light to medium body. Malted wheat O.K. Lager or ale yeast or combination of yeasts O.K. No fruitiness.

19. Fruit Beer

(a) Fruit Beer
Any ale or lager made with fruit. Character of fruit should be evident in color, aroma, and flavor. Body, color, hop character and strength can vary greatly.

(b) Classic-style Fruit Beer
Any classic style of ale or lager to which fruit has been added. Brewer to specify style.

20. Herb Beer

(a) Herb Beer
Any ale or lager with herbs. Character of herb or spice should be evident in aroma and flavor. Body, color, hop character, and strength can vary greatly.

(b) Classic-style Herb Beer
Any classic style of ale or lager to which herbs have been added. Brewer to specify style.

21. Specialty Beer

Any ale or lager brewed using unusual techniques and/or ingredients other than (or in addition to) malted barley as a unique contribution to the overall character of the beer. Examples of specialty beers include (but are not limited to) beers brewed with honey, maple sap, or syrup; worts heated with white-hot stones (Steinbier); and low or nonalcoholic beers. Examples do not include the use of fruit or herbs, although they can be used to add to the character of other ingredients.

(a) Specialty Beer
Any nonclassic style fitting the above description.

(b) Classic-style Specialty Beer
Any classic ale or lager to which special ingredients have been added or for which a special process has been used, e.g., honey pilsner, maple porter, sorghum stout, pumpkin pale ale. Brewer to specify style.

22. Smoked Beer

(a) Bamberg-style Rauchbier
Oktoberfest style (see Oktoberfest) with a sweet smoky aroma and flavor. Dark amber to dark brown. Intensity of smoke medium to high. Low diacetyl O.K.

(b) Classic-style Smoked Beer
Any beer that is based on a classic-style beer for which smoked characteristics predominate.

(c) Other:
All other beers with smoked characteristics.

23. California Common Beer

(a) California Common Beer
Light amber to copper. Medium body. Toasted or caramel-like maltiness in aroma and flavor. Medium to high hop bitterness. Hop flavor medium to high. Aroma medium. Fruitiness and esters low. Low diacetyl O.K. Lager yeast, fermented warm but aged cold.

24. Wheat Beer

(a) Berliner Weisse
Pale. Light body. Dry. Sharp lactic sourness. Fruity/estery. Between 60 and 70 percent malted wheat. Very low bitterness. No hop flavor or aroma. Effervescent. No diacetyl.

(b) German-style Weizen/Weissbier
Pale to golden. Light to medium body. About 50 percent wheat malt. Clove and slight banana character. Fruity/estery. Clove, vanilla, nutmeg, smoke, and cinnamonlike phenolics permissible. Mild sourness O.K. Highly effervescent. Cloudiness O.K. Low bitterness. Low hop flavor and aroma O.K. No diacetyl.

(c) German-style Dunkelweizen
Deep copper to brown. Dark version of Weizen. Roasted malt and chocolatelike flavors evident. Banana and cloves and other phenolics may still be evident, but to a lesser degree. Stronger than Weizen. Medium body. No diacetyl. Low hop flavor and aroma O.K.

(d) German-style Weizenbock
Usually deep copper to dark brown, but light versions can be amber to copper. Medium to full body. Alcoholic strength evident. Maltiness high. Low bitterness. Hop flavor and aroma absent. Banana and clove character apparent. No diacetyl. Dark versions have a mild roast malt flavor and aroma.

MEAD

Meads are produced by the fermentation of honey, water, yeast, and optional ingredients, such as fruit, herbs, and/or spices. Their final gravity roughly determines whether they are: dry—0.996 to 1.009; medium—1.010 to 1.019; sweet—1.020 to 1.029; or very sweet—1.030 and higher. Wine, champagne, sherry, mead, ale, or lager yeasts may be used.

25. Traditional Mead and Braggot

(a) Sparkling Traditional Mead
Effervescent. Dry, medium, or sweet. Light to medium body. No flavors other than honey. Honey character in aroma and flavor. Low to medium

fruity acidity. Color depends on honey type. Absence of harsh and/or stale character.

(b) Still Traditional Mead
Not effervescent. Dry, medium sweet, or very sweet. Light to full body. Honey character in aroma and flavor. Low to medium fruity acidity. Color depends on honey type. Absence of harsh and/or stale character.

(c) Sparkling Braggot
Effervescent. Made with malt. Dry, medium, or sweet. Light to medium body. Honey flavors predominate.

(d) Still Braggot
Not effervescent. Made with malt. Dry, medium, or sweet. Light to medium body. Honey flavors predominate.

26. Fruit Mead

Melomel is made with any fruit. Cyser is made with apples and/or apple juice; pyment is made with grapes. Ingredients should be expressed in aroma and flavor. Color should represent ingredients. Honey character apparent in aroma and flavor. Absence of harsh and/or stale character.

(a) Sparkling Melomel
Effervescent. Light to medium body. Dry, medium, or sweet.

(b) Still Melomel
Not effervescent. Light to full body. Dry, medium, sweet, or very sweet.

(c) Sparkling Cyser
Effervescent. Light to medium body. Dry, medium, or sweet.

(d) Still Cyser
Not effervescent. Light to full body. Dry, medium, sweet, or very sweet.

(e) Sparkling Pyment
Effervescent. Light to medium body. Dry, medium, or sweet.

(f) Still Pyment
Not effervescent. Light to full body. Dry, medium, sweet, or very sweet.

27. Herb Mead

Metheglin is made with any herbs or spices. Hippocras is made with spices and grapes (spiced pyment). Ingredients should be expressed in aroma and flavor. Color should represent ingredients. Honey character must be apparent in aroma and flavor. Absence of harsh and/or stale character.

(a) Sparkling Metheglin
Effervescent. Light to medium body. Dry, medium, or sweet.

(b) Still Metheglin
Not effervescent. Light to full body. Dry, medium, sweet, or very sweet.

(c) Sparkling Hippocras
Effervescent. Light to medium body. Dry, medium, or sweet.

(d) Still Hippocras
Not effervescent. Light to full body. Dry, medium, sweet, or very sweet.

CIDER

Ciders are produced by the fermentation of apple juices and optional ingredients such as fruits and spices. Wine, champagne, ale, lager, or wild yeasts may be used.

28. Cider

NOTE: Cider made with honey as an adjunct (cyser) should be entered into category 26 for melomel, cyser, and pyment.

(a) Still
Not effervescent. Less than 5.5 percent alcohol by weight (7 percent by volume). Can be dry or sweet. Pale yellow color, must be clear or brilliant. Apple aroma. Light-bodied and crisp apple flavor. Sugar adjuncts may be used.

(b) Sparkling
Effervescent but not foamy. May be force-carbonated. No head. Less than 6.3 percent alcohol by weight (8 percent by volume). Dry or sweet. Pale yellow color, must be clear and brilliant. Light to medium body, crisp apple taste. Sugar adjuncts may be used.

(c) New England–Style
Still or sparkling dry cider. Carbonation must be natural. Between 6.3 and 11 percent alcohol by weight (8 and 14 percent by volume). Pale to medium yellow color. Pronounced apple aroma. Medium to full body. Balanced by drying tannins, but never hot because of excess alcohol. Adjuncts include white and brown sugars, molasses, or raisins. Wild or wine yeasts only.

(d) Specialty Cider
Any and all adjuncts and yeasts may be used. Alcohol content must be below 11 percent alcohol by weight (14 percent by volume). At least 75 percent apple juice must be used in the must.

INDEX OF BEERS BY STYLE

Altbiers
Alt of this World, 13

Barleywines
The Bard's Barleywine, 104
Blue and Gold Barleywine,
 105
John Barleycorn Must Wine,
 107
Pewter Pot Barleywine, 108
Peachy Keen, 128

*Belgian Styles (see also Lambics,
 Wheat Beers, Wit Beers)*
Dubbel, Dubbel, Toil and Trubble,
 18
Ned Flanders Brown, 41
Sinner's Salvation, 162
Trappiste House Brew, 14
Tripel Play, 31

Berliner Weiss
Irving Berliner Weiss, 23

Bitters
Any Pub in London Bitter, 3
Bitter Old Man, 9
Pub Bitter, 24

Bocks (see also Doppelbocks)
American Bock, 95
Basic Helles Bock, 93
Dunkel Bock, 98
Ein Bock, 94
Ides of March Mai Bock, 99
Mai Honey Bock, 99
Tarheel Tarwebok, 97

Brown Ales
Basic American Brown, 40
Basic British Brown, 39
Britain's Favorite Brown, 167
Honey Nut Brown, 42
If You're Down with Pete, Then
 You're Down with Me, 165
Nutty Brown, 44
Oak Leaf Brown Ale, 43
Tuxedo Brown, 44
Uptown Brown, 42

California Common
A True American Original, 163
California Uncommon, 18
Honey Steam, 16
Steamship Porter, 47

Ciders
Apple Pear Cider, 183
Falling Leaves Autumn Cider, 145
Holiday Cheer, 184
Raspberry Cider, 184
Sunset Cider, 183
Two of a Perfect Pear, 185

Cream Ales
American Cream Ale, 73

Cyser
Cysing Up the Situation, 178

Doppelbocks (see also Bocks)
Alligator Doppelbock, 101
Doppel Your Pleasure, 100
Drunk Monk Doppelbock, 101
Masterbator, 103

Dortmunder
Dortmunder, 72

Dunkel Bock
Dunkel Bock, 98

Dunkel Weiss
Slam Dunkelweiss, 12
Uncle Sam's Dark Wheat, 26

Extra Special Bitters
Easter Sunday Bitter, 141
First Stop Bitter, 161
To ESB, or Not to ESB, 12
Too Good to ESB True, 28

French Ales
Louis's French Ale, 34
Ooh La La, Saison, 14

Fruit and Vegetable Beers
Aplomb of an Ale, 121
Apple Brown Betty Fall Ale, 144
Berry Garcia, 117
Blue Devil Brew, 123
Cherries Jubilee, 127
Cobbler Lager, 130
Murph's Cranberry Wheat, 119
Fat Tuesday's Cajun Pepper Ale,
    137
The Great Pumpkin Ale, 149
Holiday Prowler Beer, 152
Jimmy Carter's Peach Wit, 131
Lemon Coriander Weiss, 114
Lover's Lane Valentine Stout, 138
New England Cranberry Ale, 125
New Year's Lambic, 135
Peach Glitter, 178
Peachy Keen, 128
Pilgrim Ale, 150
Pineapple Pale Ale, 120
Some Like It Hot, 115
Watermelon Summer Lager, 142

Helles Bock
Basic Helles Bock, 93

Herb and Spice Beers
Cardamom Stout, 124
Dickens' Strong Christmas Ale, 153
Fat Tuesday's Cajun Pepper Ale,
    137

Grandma's House Christmas
    Chocolate Mint Stout, 151
Holiday Prowler Beer, 152
Jammin' Jamaican Jingered Ale,
    116
Lemon Coriander Weiss, 114
Pumpernickel Rye, 132
Some Like It Hot, 115
Tea for Brew, and Brew for Tea, 114
Winter Wonderland, 154

Hippocras
Hippocrasic Oath, 179

Imperial Stouts
Canadian Imperial Stout, 57
Cool Summer Imperial Stout, 60
Presidential Stout, 59
Russian Imperial Stout, 54

India Pale Ales
Brewtopia IPA, 10
Hophead Lager, 72
Hop on Pop, 32
Oak Tree IPA, 30
Smokey IPA, 129
Yippee IPA, 4

Kölsch
Kölsch, 8

Lagers
Amazing Light Lager, 71
American Cream Ale, 73
Basic Pilsner, 67
Cobbler Lager, 130
Dingo-Ate-My-Baby Lager, 70
Dortmunder, 72
Eat My Schwarzbier, 83
Feels Like the First Time, 82
Fest Haus Märzen, 80
Golden Pils, 76
Great-Grandma's Czech Pilsner, 74
Great White North, 88
Green Meadow Pilsner, 84
Hophead Lager, 72
Image Is Everything, 168
In the Midnight Hour, 77
Maple Leaf, 81
Marvin's Martian Märzen, 85
Märzen Madness, 75
Munich Dunkel, 79

One Helles of a Good Beer, 70
Red Herring, 89
Rice and Easy Does It, 75
Roll-in-the-Hay Wheat Lager, 83
Smoke It If You Got It, 126
Snowball's Chance in Helles, 85
Two Lips, 68
Viva Vienna! 80
Watermelon Summer Lager, 142

Lambics
Dirty Sock Gueuze, 180
Framboise, 182
Kriek, 181
New Year's Lambic, 135

Mai Bock
Ides of March Mai Bock, 99
Mai Honey Bock, 99
May Day Maibock, 141

Märzen/Oktoberfest
Drunk in the Streets of Cologne
    Oktoberfest Lager, 147
Fest Haus Märzen, 80
Marvin's Martian Märzen, 85
Märzen Madness, 75
Slidin On Your Back Oktoberfest
    Lager, 146

Meads
Cysing up the Situation, 178
Here's Pyment in Your Eye, 175
Hippocrasic Oath, 179
Mead and Mrs. Jones, 177
Mead Me in St. Louis, 176
Peach Glitter, 178
Temptation Mead, 174

Metheglin
Mead and Mrs. Jones, 177

Milds
Aplomb of an Ale, 121
Mild-Mannered, 20

Munich Dunkel
Munich Dunkel, 79

Munich Helles
One Helles of a Good Beer, 70
Snowball's Chance in Helles, 85

Oktoberfest (see Märzen/
    Oktoberfest)

Old Ales/Strong Ales
Cherries Jubilee, 127
Coming on a Little Strong, 111
Dickens' Strong Christmas Ale, 153
Macbeth's Scotch MacAle, 110
Sow Your Wild Oats Strong Ale,
    111
Thatched Roof Ale, 109
Ye Olde Ale, 109

Pale Ales
Apple Brown Betty Fall Ale, 144
Appliance-on-the-Fritz Pale Ale,
    161
Baby's Bath Ale, 22
California Cascade, 159
Crimson and Clover Ale, 21
Fireside Winter Warmer, 155
Genuine Stunning Ale, 17
Harvard Crimson, 24
Jack the Ripper British Ale, 6
Maura's Bride Ale, 20
New England Cranberry Ale, 125
Pilgrim Ale, 150
Pineapple Pale Ale, 120
Super Bowl Sunday Pale Ale, 136
The Great Pumpkin Ale, 149
Trademark Ale, 169
Euell Gibbons' Favorite Ale, 28
Vail Pale Ale, 33

Pilsners (see also Lagers)
Basic Pilsner, 67
Feels Like the First Time, 82
Golden Pils, 76
Great-Grandma's Czech Pilsner,
    74
Green Meadow Pilsner, 84

Porters
Basic Porter, 45
Black Cat Halloween Porter, 148
Brown-Sugar Molasses Porter, 46
Chocolate Honey Porter, 48
Hey Porter, 52
Mr. Hare's Porter, 49
Porter #12, 53
Steamship Porter, 47
Viennese Spiced Porter, 50

Pyment
Here's Pyment in Your Eye, 175
Hippocrasic Oath, 179

Rauchbiers (see also Smoked Beers/
Rauchbiers)

Saisons
Ooh La La, Saison, 14

Schwarzbiers
Eat My Schwarzbier, 83
In the Midnight Hour, 77

Scotch Ales
Macbeth's Scotch MacAle, 110
Thatched Roof Ale, 109

Smoked Beers/Rauchbiers
On Top of Old Smokey, 122
Smoke It If You Got It, 126
Smokey IPA, 129

Spiced Beers (see Herb and Spice
Beers)

Stouts (see also Imperial Stouts)
Basic Stout, 54
Cardamom Stout, 124
Dublin's Finest, 159
Ed's Honey Oatmeal Stout, 56
Grandma's House Christmas
Chocolate Mint Stout, 151
Java Stout, 61
Jim and Gill's Barley Stout, 62
Lover's Lane Valentine Stout,
138
Ninepin Stout, 63

Old McDonald Drank a Stout, 58
Slate-Lined Stout, 166
St. Patrick's Day Irish Cream Stout,
139

Strong Ales (see also Old Ales/
Strong Ales)
Tarheel Tarwebok, 97

Vegetable Beers (see Fruit and
Vegetable Beers)

Vienna
Viva Vienna! 80

Wheat Beers
Accident-Prone Wheat, 33
Affengeil Wheat Beer, 7
Belgian White Men Can't Jump, 9
Berry Garcia, 117
Bitchin Belgian White, 15
Murph's Cranberry Wheat, 119
Easy Wheat, 6
Ein Bock, 94
Irving Berliner Weiss, 23
Jimmy Carter's Peach Wit, 131
Lemon Coriander Weiss, 114
Merci, Pierre, 168
Roll-in-the-Hay Wheat Lager, 83
Slam Dunkelweiss, 12
Thomas Jefferson's Ale, 29
Uncle Sam's Dark Wheat, 26

Wit Beers
Belgian White Men Can't Jump, 9
Bitchin' Belgian White, 15
Jimmy Carter's Peach Wit, 131
Merci, Pierre, 168

INDEX

Abbey Notre Dame de Scourmont,
  162
Accident-Prone Wheat, 33
accompaniments:
  Frijoles Borrachos, 192
  Hop-Spiced Pickled Veggies,
    191
  Malted Applesauce, 192
  Yams à la Belgique, 191
aerating wort, 5
aeration stones, 5
Affengeil Wheat Beer, 7
Aharon, Gill, 62
ales, 1–35
  Accident-Prone Wheat, 33
  Alt of this World, 13
  Aplomb of an Ale, 121
  Apple Brown Betty Fall, 144
  Blue Devil Brew, 123
  California Uncommon, 18
  Firecracker Red, 143
  Fireside Winter Warmer, 155
  Holiday Prowler Beer, 152
  Honey Steam, 16
  Kölsch, 8
  Mild-Mannered, 20
  Ooh La La, Saison, 14
  style guidelines for, 219–23
  On Top of Old Smoky, 122
  Trappist House Brew, 14
  Tripel Play, 31
  Uncle Sam's Dark Wheat, 26
  Winter Wonderland, 154

ales (continued)
  see also barleywines; bitters;
    brown ales; extra special
    bitters; imperial stouts; India
    pale ales; lambic(s); old ales/
    strong ales; pale ales; porters;
    stout(s)
all-grain brewing, xxii
  converting recipes between
    extract brewing and, 86–87
Alligator Doppelbock, 101
altbiers:
  Alt of This World, 13
  style guidelines for, 225
Alt of This World, 13
Amazing Light Lager, 71
amber malt, 41
American Bock, 95
American Cream Ale, 73
Anchor Brewing Company, 161
  Liberty, copycat version of, 161
  Steam Beer, copycat version of,
    163
Any Pub in London Bitter, 3
Aplomb of an Ale, 121
apple(s):
  Baked, Cornish Game Hens in
    Blackberry Stout Sauce with,
    194
  Brown Betty Fall Ale, 144
  Cobbler Lager, 130
  Cysing up the Situation, 178
  Falling Leaves Autumn Cider, 145

apple(s) *(continued)*
Holiday Cheer, 184
Pear Cider, 183
Raspberry Cider, 184
Sunset Cider, 183
Applesauce, Malted, 192
Appliance-on-the-Fritz Pale Ale,
161
Aristotle, 146
Arnoldus, Saint, 180
Autobiography (Franklin), 157–58

Baby's Bath Ale, 22
The Bard's Barleywine, 104
Barley Stout, Jim and Gill's, 62
barleywines, 104–8
The Bard's, 104
Blue and Gold, 105
John Barleycorn Must Wine
107
Peachy Keen, 128
Pewter Pot, 108
starters for, 56
style guidelines for, 219
Basic American Brown, 40
Basic British Brown, 39
Basic Helles Bock, 93
Basic Pilsner, 67
Basic Porter, 45
Basic Stout, 54
Bass, copycat version of, 169
batch size, xxi–xxii
beans:
Frijoles Borrachos, 192
Kickin' Hot Chili, 195
Beaux's Stratagem, The (Farquhar),
58
beef:
Carbonnade Flamande, 199
Erin Go Bragh Stout Pie, 200
Kickin' Hot Chili, 195
Red-Hot Rack of Ribs, 203
Spiced Sauerbraten, 198
Behan, Brendan, 142
Belgian foods:
Carbonnade Flamande, 199
Yams à la Belgique, 191
Belgian-style beers:
Belgian White Men Can't Jump, 9
Bitchin' Belgian White, 15
Dubbel, Dubbel, Toil and Trubble,
18

Belgian-style beers *(continued)*
Merci, Pierre, 168
Ned Flanders Brown, 41
Ooh La La, Saison, 14
propagating yeast for, 36
Sinner's Salvation, 162
style guidelines for, 219–20
Trappist House Brew, 14
Tripel Play, 31
see also lambic(s)
Belgian White Men Can't Jump,
9
Berliner weiss:
Irving Berliner Weiss, 23
style guidelines for, 227
Berry, Chuck, 85
berry(ies):
Berry Garcia, 117
Blackberry Stout Sauce, Cornish
Game Hens with Baked Apples
in, 194
Blue Devil Brew, 123
see also cranberry(ies); raspberry
bière de garde, style guidelines for,
220
Bitchin' Belgian White, 15
Bitter Old Man, 9
bitters:
Any Pub in London, 3
Bitter Old Man, 9
Pub, 25
style guidelines for, 221
see also extra special bitters
Blackberry Stout Sauce, Cornish
Game Hens with Baked Apples
in, 194
Black Cat Halloween Porter, 148
Blue and Gold Barleywine, 105
Blue Devil Brew, 123
bocks, 93–100
American, 95
Basic Helles, 93
Dunkel, 98
Ein Bock, 94
Ides of March Mai, 99
Mai Honey, 99
May Day Maibock, 142
style guidelines for, 223
Tarheel Tarwebok, 97
see also doppelbocks
Bolt, Robert, 111
Boston Beer Company, 168

bottles:
  color of, 96
  labeling, 140
braggots, style guidelines for,
  228
Bratwurst, Ginger-Beer, 202
Bread, Oatmeal Beer, 189
brewery copycats, 157–70
  Appliance-on-the-Fritz Pale Ale,
    161
  Britain's Favorite Brown, 167
  California Cascade, 159
  Dublin's Finest, 159
  First Stop Bitter, 161
  If You're Down with Pete, Then
    You're Down with Me, 165
  Image Is Everything, 168
  Merci, Pierre, 168
  Sinner's Salvation, 162
  Slate-Lined Stout, 166
  Strange Brew, 164
  Trademark Ale, 169
  A True American Original, 163
Brewtopia, 10
Bride ale, Maura's, 20
Brillat-Savarin, Jean-Anthelme, 183
Britain's Favorite Brown, 167
brown ales, 39–45
  Basic American, 40
  Basic British, 39
  Britain's Favorite, 167
  Honey Nut, 42
  If You're Down with Pete, Then
    You're Down with Me, 165
  Ned Flanders, 41
  Nutty, 44
  Oak Leaf, 43
  style guidelines for, 219, 220–21
  Tuxedo, 44
  Uptown, 42
Brown-Sugar Molasses Porter, 46

Cajun Pepper Ale, Fat Tuesday's,
  137
Cake, Chocolate Cream Stout, 205
California Cascade, 159
California common beers:
  California Uncommon, 18
  Honey Steam, 16
  Steamship Porter, 47
  style guidelines for, 227
  A True American Original, 163

California Uncommon, 18
Calverley, Charles Stuart, 54
Canadian-style beers:
  Great White North, 88
  Imperial Stout, 57
  Maple Leaf, 81
caps:
  carbonation problems and, 78
  oxygen-absorbent, 96
carbonation, problems with, 78
Carbonnade Flamande, 199
Cardamom Stout, 124
Carpenter, Doctor, 25
Carter, Jimmy, 131
Cash, Johnny, 52
Caxton, J., 39
Celis White, copycat version of, 168
Cheddar and Beer Soup, Smoky, 188
cherry(ies):
  Jubilee, 127
  Kriek, 181
  Lover's Lane Valentine Stout, 138
chicken:
  Kickin' Hot Chili, 195
  Maruja's Asopado de Pollo con
    Cerveza, 196
  with Roasted-Garlic Cream
    Sauce, 200
Chili, Kickin' Hot, 195
chili peppers, see peppers, hot
chill haze, 69
chocolate:
  Cream Stout Cake, 205
  Honey Porter, 48
  Mint Stout, Grandma's House
    Christmas, 151
Christmas beers:
  Dickens' Strong Ale, 153
  Grandma's House Chocolate Mint
    Stout, 151
Christmas Carol, A (Dickens), 153
Ciardi, John, 174
ciders, 183–85
  Apple-Pear, 183
  Falling Leaves Autumn, 145
  Holiday Cheer, 184
  Raspberry, 184
  style guidelines for, 229–30
  Sunset, 183
  Two of a Perfect Pear, 185
clarifying agents, 69
Cobbler Lager, 130

colonial American-style beers:
Baby's Bath Ale, 22
Thomas Jefferson's Ale, 29
Uncle Sam's Dark Wheat, 26
Coming on a Little Strong, 111
conversion rate, 27
Cool Summer Imperial Stout, 60
Coriander Lemon Weiss, 114
Cornish Game Hens in Blackberry
Stout Sauce with Baked Apples,
194
corn sugar, 11
cranberry(ies):
Ale, New England, 125
New Year's Lambic, 135
Wheat, Murph's, 119
cream ales:
American, 73
style guidelines for, 225
Crimson and Clover Ale, 21
Curry, Red Lentil, 197
cysers:
Cysing Up the Situation, 178
style guidelines for, 228
Cysing Up the Situation, 178
Czech-style beers:
Great-Grandma's Pilsner, 74
Green Meadow Pilsner, 84

DaSilva, John, 48
David Copperfield (Dickens), 17
desserts:
Chocolate Cream Stout Cake,
205
The Great Pumpkin Pie, 206
Lambic Sorbet, 206
Poached Pears with Raspberry
Sauce, 204
Dickens, Charles, 17, 47, 60, 153
Dickens' Strong Christmas Ale, 153
Dingo-Ate-My-Baby Lager, 70
Dirty Sock Gueuze, 180
doppelbocks, 100–103
Alligator, 101
Doppel Your Pleasure, 100
Drunk Monk, 101
Masterbator, 103
style guidelines for, 223
Doppel Your Pleasure, 100
Dortmunder, 72
style guidelines for, 224
Dos Equis, 80

Drinking Life, A (Hamill), 133–35
Drunk-in-the-Streets-of-Cologne
Oktoberfest Lager, 147
Drunk Monk Doppelbock, 101
dubbels:
Dubbel, Dubbel, Toil and Trubble,
18
style guidelines for, 219
Dubliners (Joyce), 171–73
Dublin's Finest, 159
dunkel, Munich, see Munich Dunkel
Dunkel Bock, 98
dunkel weiss:
Slam, 12
Uncle Sam's Dark Wheat, 26
Dutch-style beers:
Tarheel Tarwebok, 97
Two Lips, 68

Eames, Alan, 20
Easter Sunday Bitter (ESB), 141
Easy Wheat, 6
Eat My Schwarzbier, 83
Eaton, Nathaniel, 24
Ed's Honey Oatmeal Stout, 56
Ein Bock, 94
eisbocks, style guidelines for, 223
electric stoves, 49
Emerson, Ralph Waldo, 177
England, beer laws in, xx
English-style beers:
The Bard's Barleywine, 104
Basic Brown, 39
Basic Porter, 45
Blue and Gold Barleywine, 105
Britain's Favorite Brown, 167
Coming on a Little Strong, 111
Genuine Stunning Ale, 17
Jack the Ripper British Ale, 6
John Barleycorn Must Wine, 107
Mild-Mannered, 20
Oak Leaf Brown Ale, 43
Old McDonald Drank a Stout, 58
Pewter Pot Barleywine, 108
Sow Your Wild Oats Strong Ale, 111
Strange Brew, 164
style guidelines for, 220–23
Tuxedo Brown, 44
Uptown Brown, 42
Ye Olde Ale, 109
see also bitters; extra special
bitters

entrees:
 Beer-Battered Fish, 197
 Carbonnade Flamande, 199
 Chicken with Roasted-Garlic
  Cream Sauce, 200
 Cornish Game Hens in Blackberry
  Stout Sauce with Baked Apples,
  194
 Erin Go Bragh Stout Pie, 200
 Fiesta Pork Stew, 193
 Ginger-Beer Bratwurst, 202
 Homestyle Meatloaf, 201
 Kickin' Hot Chili, 195
 Maruja's Asopado de Pollo con
  Cerveza, 196
 Mary Bielawski's Polska Kielbasa,
  204
 Red-Hot Rack of Ribs, 203
 Red Lentil Curry, 197
 Smoked Basil Shrimp, 190
 Spiced Sauerbraten, 198
Erin Go Bragh Stout Pie, 200
Euell Gibbons' Favorite Ale, 28
extract brewing, xxii, xxiii
 converting recipes between all-
  grain brewing and, 86–87
extraction rate, 27
extra special bitters (ESB):
 Easter Sunday, 141
 ESB, or Not to ESB, 12
 First Stop Bitter, 161
 style guidelines for, 221
 Too Good to ESB True, 28

Falling Leaves Autumn Cider, 145
Far from the Madding Crowd
 (Hardy), 155
faro, style guidelines for, 220
Farquhar, George, 58
Fat Tuesday's Cajun Pepper Ale, 137
Feels Like the First Time, 82
fermentation:
 stopped sooner than expected,
  165
 temperature for, 19
 times for, xxiv
 vessels for, xxi–xxii
Fest Haus Märzen, 80
Fields, W. C., 73
Fiesta Pork Stew, 193
Firecracker Red, 143
Fireside Winter Warmer, 155

First Stop Bitter, 161
Fish, Beer-Battered, 197
Framboise, 182
 style guidelines for, 220
Franklin, Benjamin, 157–58
French-style beers:
 Louis's French Ale, 34
 Ooh La La, Saison, 14
 style guidelines for, 219–20
Frijoles Borrachos, 192
fruit beers:
 Aplomb of an Ale, 121
 Apple Brown Betty Fall Ale, 144
 Berry Garcia, 117
 Blue Devil Brew, 123
 Cherries Jubilee, 127
 Cobbler Lager, 130
 Framboise, 182
 Holiday Prowler, 152
 Jimmy Carter's Peach Wit, 131
 Kriek, 181
 Lemon Coriander Weiss, 114
 Lover's Lane Valentine Stout, 138
 Murph's Cranberry Wheat, 119
 New England Cranberry Ale, 125
 New Year's Lambic, 135
 Peach Glitter, 178
 Peachy Keen, 128
 Pineapple Pale Ale, 120
 style guidelines for, 226
 tips for, 118
 Watermelon Summer Lager, 142
 see also ciders; meads
Fuller's, copycat version of, 161
full wort boil, xxii–xxiii
full wort souring, 181

Garcia, Jerry, 117
gas stoves, 49
Genuine Stunning Ale, 17
German-style beers:
 Affengeil Wheat, 7
 Alt of this World, 13
 Basic Pilsner, 67
 Dortmunder, 72
 Easy Wheat, 6
 Eat My Schwarzbier, 83
 In the Midnight Hour, 77
 Kölsch, 8
 May Day Maibock, 142
 Munich Dunkel, 79
 One Helles of a Good Beer, 70

German-style beers *(continued)*
Slam Dunkelweiss, 12
Smoke It If You Got It, 126
Snowball's Chance in Helles, 85
style guidelines for, 223–27
see also bocks; doppelbocks;
märzen/Oktoberfest
Germany, beer laws in, xx
ginger:
Beer Bratwurst, 202
Jammin' Jamaican Jingered Ale,
116
"Give Me the Old" (Messenger), 45
Glasheen, Jim, 33, 62
glasses, head retention and, 51
Golden Pils, 76
"gourmet" beer industry, xix
Grandma's House Christmas
Chocolate Mint Stout, 151
Great American Beer Festival, 33
Great Grandma's Czech Pilsner, 74
The Great Pumpkin Pale Ale, 149
The Great Pumpkin Pie, 206
Great White North, 88
Green Meadow Pilsner, 84
"groaning ales," 22
gueuzes:
Dirty Sock, 180
style guidelines for, 220
Guinness, copycat version of, 159

Halloween Porter, Black Cat, 148
Hamill, Pete, 133–35
Hardy, Thomas, 155
Hare, Robert, 49
Harvard Crimson, 24
haziness, 69
head retention, 51
heat, as enemy of beer, 96
heat diffusers, 49
Heineken, 68
helles, Munich, *see* Munich helles
helles bocks:
Basic, 93
style guidelines for, 223
Hemingway, Ernest, 6
Henry V (Shakespeare), 3, 121
Henry VI, Part 2 (Shakespeare), 104
herb and spice beers:
Cardamom Stout, 124
Dickens' Strong Christmas Ale,
153

herb and space beers *(continued)*
Fat Tuesday's Cajun Pepper Ale,
137
Firecracker Red, 143
Grandma's House Christmas
Chocolate Mint Stout, 151
Holiday Prowler, 152
Jammin' Jamaican Jingered Ale,
116
Lemon Coriander Weiss, 114
Mead and Mrs. Jones, 177
Pilgrim Ale, 150
Pumpernickel Rye, 132
Some Like It Hot, 115
style guidelines for, 226, 229
Sweet Woodruff, 119
Tea for Brew, and Brew for Tea,
114
Winter Wonderland, 154
Here's Pyment in Your Eye, 175
Hey Porter, 52
hippocras:
Hippocrasic Oath, 179
style guidelines for, 229
Hippocrasic Oath, 179
Hoegaarden Brewery, 168
holiday beers:
Black Cat Halloween Porter, 148
Dickens' Strong Christmas Ale,
153
Drunk-in-the-Streets-of-Cologne
Oktoberfest Lager, 146
Easter Sunday Bitter (ESB), 141
Fat Tuesday's Cajun Pepper Ale, 137
Firecracker Red, 143
Fireside Winter Warmer, 155
Grandma's House Christmas
Chocolate Mint Stout, 151
Holiday Cheer, 184
Holiday Prowler, 152
Lover's Lane Valentine Stout, 138
May Day Maibock, 142
New Year's Lambic, 135
Pilgrim Ale, 150
St. Patrick's Day Irish Cream
Stout, 139
Slidin'-on-Your-Back Oktoberfest
Lager, 146
see also seasonal beers
homebrewing:
aerating wort in, 5
batch size in, xxi–xxii

homebrewing *(continued)*
  best guide to, xvii
  building your own wort chiller
    for, 213–15
  carbonation problems in, 78
  changes in tastes and, xvi
  clarifying agents in, 69
  conversion rate in, 27
  converting recipes from all-grain
    to extract and vice versa in,
    86–87
  culturing yeast from bottle of
    beer for, 36
  extraction rate in, 27
  extract vs. all-grain, xviii
  fermentation temperature in, 19
  fermentation times in, xx
  full wort boil in, xviii–xix
  full wort souring in, 181
  gas vs. electric stove in, 49
  head retention and, 51
  high-gravity starters in, 56
  history of, xvi
  labeling in, 140
  liquid vs. dry yeast in, xix, 106
  mashing schedule in, xviii
  partial wort boil in, xix
  priming sugar in, 11
  quick souring in, 160
  recipes needed for, xv–xvi
  repitching yeast in, 106
  sanitary conditions essential in,
    xx
  smoking malt in, 123
  storage in, 96
  stuck fermentation in, 165
  toasted or amber malt in, 41
  washing yeast in, 128
  wort chillers in, xix, 69
honey, 11
  Bock, Mai, 99
  Chocolate Porter, 48
  Nut Brown, 42
  Oatmeal Stout, Ed's, 56
  Steam, 16
  see also meads
Hophead Lager, 72
Hop on Pop, 32
Hop on Pop (Seuss), 32
hops, xvi
Hop-Spiced Pickled Veggies, 191
Housman, A. E., 44, 108, 124

Ides of March Mai Bock, 99
If You're Down with Pete,
    Then You're Down with Me,
    165
Image Is Everything, 168
imperial stouts:
  Canadian, 57
  Cool Summer, 60
  Presidential, 59
  Russian, 54
  starters for, 56
  style guidelines for, 223
India pale ales (IPAs):
  Brewtopia, 10
  Hophead Lager, 72
  Hop on Pop, 32
  Oak Tree, 30
  Smokey, 129
  style guidelines for, 221
  Yippee, 4
In the Midnight Hour, 77
Irish moss, 69
Irish-style beers:
  Dublin's Finest, 159
  St. Patrick's Day Irish Cream
    Stout, 139
Irving, Washington, 37–39, 63
Irving Berliner Weiss, 23
isinglass finings, 69

Jack the Ripper British Ale, 6
Jammin' Jamaican Jingered Ale,
    116
Java Stout, 61
Jefferson, Thomas, xviii, 29–30
Jim and Gill's Barley Stout, 62
Jimmy Carter's Peach Wit, 131
John Barleycorn (London), 1–3
John Barleycorn Must Wine,
    107
Joyce, James, 171–73

Kickin' Hot Chili, 195
Kielbasa, Mary Bielawski's Polska,
    204
Kipling, Rudyard, 169
Koch, Jim, 168
Kölsch, 8
  style guidelines for, 225
kraeusening, 11
Kriek, 181
  style guidelines for, 220

labeling, 140
lagers, 65–89
  Amazing Light, 71
  American Cream Ale, 73
  Basic Helles Bock, 93
  Cobbler, 130
  Dingo-Ate-My-Baby, 70
  Dortmunder, 72
  Eat My Schwarzbier, 83
  Great White North, 88
  Hophead, 72
  Image Is Everything, 168
  Maple Leaf, 81
  Midnight Hour, 77
  Munich Dunkel, 79
  One Helles of a Good Beer, 70
  Rice and Easy Does It, 75
  Roll-in-the-Hay Wheat, 83
  Smoke It If You Got It, 126
  Snowball's Chance in Helles, 85
  style guidelines for, 223–25
  Sweet Woodruff, 119
  Two Lips, 68
  Viva Vienna!, 80
  Watermelon Summer, 142
  see also bocks; doppelbocks;
    märzen/Oktoberfest; pilsners
lambic(s), 180–82
  Dirty Sock Gueuze, 180
  Framboise, 182
  full wort sour in, 181
  Kriek, 181
  New Year's, 135
  Sorbet, 206
  style guidelines for, 220
Lee, Ed, 71
LeJeune, Father, 135
Lemon Coriander Weiss, 114
Lentil, Red, Curry, 197
Levy, Marv, 136
Lewis, Jerry Lee, 75
Life of St. Brigid, The, 98
light, as enemy of beer, 96
London, Jack, 1–3
Louis's French Ale, 34
Lover's Lane Valentine Stout, 138

Macbeth's Scotch MacAle, 110
McGill, Eoghan, 105
McSorley's (New York City), 65–
  67
Madison, James, xx, 29–30

Mai bocks (May bocks):
  Honey, 99
  Ides of March, 99
  May Day, 142
main dishes, see entrees
"Make Beer for Man" (Miller), 95
Malted Applesauce, 192
malt:
  smoking, 123
  toasted or amber, 41
malt extract, xxii
  converting between all-grain and
    extract brewing and, 86–87
Man for All Seasons, A (Bolt), 111
Maple Leaf, 81
maple syrup, 11
Maruja's Asopado de Pollo con
  Cerveza, 196
Marvin's Martian Märzen, 85
Mary Bielawski's Polska Kielbasa,
  204
märzen/Oktoberfest:
  Drunk-in-the-Streets-of-Cologne
    Oktoberfest lager, 147
  Fest Haus Märzen, 80
  Marvin's Martian Märzen, 85
  Märzen Madness, 75
  Slidin' on Your Back Oktoberfest
    Lager, 146
  style guidelines for, 225
mashing times and temperatures,
  xxii
Masterbator, 103
Maupassant, Guy de, 34
Maura's Bride Ale, 20
May bocks, see Mai bocks
May Day Maibock, 142
Maynard, Theodore, 93
Maytag, Fritz, 161, 163
Mead and Mrs. Jones, 177
Mead Me in St. Louis, 176
meads, 174–79
  acids in, 177
  Cysing Up the Situation, 178
  Here's Pyment in Your Eye, 175
  Hippocrasic Oath, 179
  honey in, 175
  Mead and Mrs. Jones, 177
  Mead Me in St. Louis, 176
  Peach Glitter, 178
  style guidelines for, 227–29
  Temptation, 174

Meatloaf, Homestyle, 201
melomels, style guidelines for, 228
Merci, Pierre, 168
Messenger, R. H., 45
metheglins:
    Mead and Mrs. Jones, 177
    style guidelines for, 229
microbreweries, xix
Mild-Mannered, 20
milds:
    Aplomb of an Ale, 121
    Mild-Mannered, 20
Miller, Henry, 95
Mint Chocolate Stout, Grandma's
    House Christmas, 151
Mr. Hare's Porter, 49
Mitchell, Joseph, 65–67
molasses, 11
Molson, 88
Moosehead, 88
Munich Dunkel, 79
    style guidelines for, 224
Munich helles:
    One Helles of a Good Beer, 70
    Snowball's Chance in Helles, 85
    style guidelines for, 224
Murph's Cranberry Wheat, 119
Murray, Ross, 88

Ned Flanders Brown, 41
Negra Modelo, 80
Newcastle Brown Ale, copycat
    version of, 167
New Complete Joy of Homebrewing,
    The (Papazian), xvii, xxi
New England Cranberry Ale, 125
New Year's Lambic, 135
Ninepin Stout, 63
1984 (Orwell), 91–93
Nutty Brown, 44

Oak Leaf Brown, 43
Oak Tree IPA, 30
oatmeal:
    Beer Bread, 189
    Honey Stout, Ed's, 56
O'Brien, Flann, 113
Oktoberfest, see märzen/
    Oktoberfest
old ales/strong ales:
    Cherries Jubilee, 127
    Coming on a Little Strong, 111

old ales/strong ales (continued)
    Dickens' Strong Christmas Ale,
        153
    Macbeth's Scotch MacAle, 110
    Sow Your Wild Oats Strong Ale,
        111
    Strange Brew, 164
    style guidelines for, 220, 222
    Tarheel Tarwebok, 97
    Thatched Roof Ale, 109
    Ye Olde Ale, 109
Old House at Home, The (Mitchell),
    65–67
Old McDonald Drank a Stout, 58
One Helles of a Good Beer, 70
On Top of Old Smoky, 122
Ooh La La, Saison, 14
oranges:
    Dickens' Strong Christmas Ale,
        153
    Holiday Prowler Beer, 152
Orwell, George, 80, 91–93
overcarbonation, 78
oxygen:
    as enemy of beer, 96
    injecting into wort, 5

pale ales:
    Apple Brown Betty Fall, 144
    Appliance-on-the-Fritz, 161
    Baby's Bath, 22
    California Cascade, 159
    Crimson and Clover, 21
    Euell Gibbons' Favorite, 28
    Fireside Winter Warmer, 155
    Genuine Stunning, 17
    The Great Pumpkin, 149
    Harvard Crimson, 24
    Jack the Ripper British, 6
    Louis's French, 34
    Maura's Bride, 20
    New England Cranberry, 125
    Pilgrim, 150
    Pineapple, 120
    style guidelines for, 221
    Super Bowl Sunday, 136
    Trademark, 169
    Vail, 33
    see also India pale ales
Papazian, Charlie, xxi
partial wort boil, xxiii
Pasteur, Louis, 34

peach(es):
    Glitter, 178
    Peachy Keen, 128
    Wit, Jimmy Carter's, 131
pear(s):
    Apple Cider, 183
    cider (Two of a Perfect Pear),
        185
    Poached, with Raspberry Sauce,
        204
peppers, hot:
    Fat Tuesday's Cajun Pepper Ale,
        137
    Some Like It Hot, 115
Pewter Pot Barleywine, 108
Pickled Veggies, Hop-Spiced, 191
Pickwick Papers, The (Dickens), 47,
    60
pies:
    Erin Go Bragh Stout, 200
    The Great Pumpkin, 206
Pilgrim Ale, 150
pilsners:
    Basic, 67
    Feels Like the First Time, 82
    Golden Pils, 76
    Great Grandma's Czech, 74
    Green Meadow, 84
    Red Herring, 89
    style guidelines for, 224
    see also lagers
Pineapple Pale Ale, 120
"Pint of Plain Is Your Only Man, A"
    (O'Brien), 113
plums, in Aplomb of an Ale, 121
Poached Pears with Raspberry
    Sauce, 204
Poe, Edgar Allan, 148
Polyclar, 69
Pork Stew, Fiesta, 193
porters, 45–53
    Basic, 45
    Black Cat Halloween, 148
    Brown-Sugar Molasses, 46
    Chocolate Honey, 48
    Hey Porter, 52
    Mr. Hare's, 49
    #12, 53
    Steamship, 47
    style guidelines for, 222
    Viennese Spiced, 50
Presidential Stout, 59

priming sugar, 11
    carbonation problems and, 78
protein haze, 69
Pub Bitter, 25
Pumpernickel Rye, 132
pumpkin:
    Ale, The Great, 149
    Pie, The Great, 206
pyments:
    Here's Pyment in Your Eye, 175
    Hippocrasic Oath, 179
    style guidelines for, 228

raspberry:
    Cider, 184
    Framboise, 182
    Sauce, Poached Pears with, 204
rauchbiers, *see* smoked beers/
    rauchbiers
Red Herring, 89
Red-Hot Rack of Ribs, 203
Red Lentil Curry, 197
Reinheitsgebot, xx
repitching yeast, 106
Ribs, Red-Hot Rack of, 203
Rice and Easy Does It, 75
Rip Van Winkle (Irving), 37–39
Roasted Beer Soup, 189
Rock 'n' Roll Music (Berry), 85
Roll-in-the-Hay Wheat Lager, 83
Roosevelt, Franklin D., 67
Ruggles, Henry, 79
Russian Imperial Stout, 54
Rye, Pumpernickel, 132

St. Patrick's Day Irish Cream Stout,
    139
Saison, Ooh La La, 14
Sam Adams Boston Lager, copycat
    version of, 168
Samuel Smith's, copycat version of,
    166
The Sand Lot Brewery, 33
sanitary conditions, xxiv
    aeration of wort and, 5
    carbonation problems and, 78
Sauerbraten, Spiced, 198
sausages:
    Ginger-Beer Bratwurst, 202
    Mary Bielawski's Polska Kielbasa,
        204
    Smoky Beer and Cheddar Soup, 188

Scherer, Russ, 33
schwarzbiers:
  Eat My Schwarzbier, 83
  In the Midnight Hour, 77
  style guidelines for, 224
Scottish ales:
  Macbeth's Scotch MacAle, 110
  style guidelines for, 222
  Thatched Roof, 109
seasonal beers:
  Apple Brown Betty Fall Ale, 144
  Falling Leaves Autumn Cider, 145
  Watermelon Summer Lager, 142
  Winter Wonderland, 154
  see also holiday beers
Seuss, Dr., 32
Shakespeare, William, 3, 12, 104,
  121
Shrimp, Smoked Basil, 190
Shropshire Lad, A (Housman), 44,
  108
side dishes, see accompaniments
Sierra Nevada, copycat version of,
  159
Simpson, Homer, 82
Sinner's Salvation, 162
Slam Dunkelweiss, 12
Slate-Lined Stout, 166
Slidin' on Your Back Oktoberfest
  Lager, 146
Slosberg, Pete, 165
Smith, Rev. Sidney, 167
Smoked Basil Shrimp, 190
smoked beers/rauchbiers:
  Smoke It If You Got It, 126
  Smokey IPA, 129
  smoking malt for, 123
  style guidelines for, 226–27
  Top of Old Smoky, 122
smoked malt, 123
Smoke It If You Got It, 126
Smokey IPA, 129
Smoky Beer and Cheddar Soup, 188
Snowball's Chance in Helles, 85
Some Like It Hot, 115
Sorbet, Lambic, 206
soups:
  Roasted Beer, 189
  Smoky Beer and Cheddar, 188
souring, full wort, 181
sour mash, simulating effects of,
  160

Sow Your Wild Oats Strong Ale, 111
specialty beers, style guidelines for,
  226
spice beers, see herb and spice
  beers
Spillane, Mickey, 76
starters, for high-gravity beer, 56
Steamship Porter, 47
stews:
  Carbonnade Flamande, 199
  Fiesta Pork, 193
Stone Age, xx
storage, 96
stout(s), 54–63
  Basic, 54
  Blackberry Sauce, Cornish Game
    Hens with Baked Apples in, 194
  Cardamom, 124
  Cream, Chocolate Cake, 205
  Dublin's Finest, 159
  Ed's Honey Oatmeal, 56
  Grandma's House Christmas
    Chocolate Mint, 151
  Java, 61
  Jim and Gill's Barley, 62
  Lover's Lane Valentine, 138
  Ninepin, 63
  Old McDonald Drank a Stout, 58
  Pie, Erin Go Bragh, 200
  St. Patrick's Day Irish Cream, 139
  Slate-Lined, 166
  style guidelines for, 222–23
  see also imperial stouts
strong ales, see old ales/strong ales
style guidelines, 219–30
sugar, priming, see priming sugar
Sunset Cider, 183
Super Bowl Sunday Pale Ale, 136
Svihura, Filomena, 74
Sweet Woodruff, 119

Talmud, 83
Tarheel Tarwebok, 97
Taylor, John, 29
Tea for Brew, and Brew for Tea, 114
Temptation Mead, 174
Thatched Roof Ale, 109
Thomas, Dylan, 159
Thomas Jefferson's Ale, 29
Threakson's Old Peculier, copycat
  version of, 164
toasted malt, 41

To ESB, or Not to ESB, 12
To Have and Have Not (Hemingway), 6
Too Good to ESB True, 28
torrefied wheat, head retention and, 51
Trademark Ale, 169
Trappist ales:
House Brew, 14
propagating yeast for, 36
Tripel Play, 31
tripels:
style guidelines for, 219–20
Tripel Play, 31
A True American Original, 163
Tuxedo Brown, 44
"Twelve Men" (Maupassant), 34
Two Lips, 68
Two of a Perfect Pear, 185

Uncle Sam's Dark Wheat, 26
undercarbonation, 78
Untermeyer, Louis, 114
Uptown Brown, 42

Vail Pale Ale, 33
Valentine Stout, Lover's Lane, 138
vegetable(s):
Hop-Spiced Pickled, 191
Soup, Roasted Beer, 189
Yams à la Belgique, 191
vegetable beers:
Fat Tuesday's Cajun Pepper Ale, 137
The Great Pumpkin Ale, 149
Pilgrim Ale, 150
Some Like It Hot, 115
Ventura, Maruja, 196
Vienna:
style guidelines for, 225
Viva Vienna!, 80
Viennese Spiced Porter, 50
Viva Vienna!, 80

Waananen, Wayne, 33
Washington, George, 49
Watermelon Summer Lager, 142
wheat beers:
Accident-Prone, 33
Affengeil, 7

wheat beers *(continued)*
Belgian White Men Can't Jump, 9
Berry Garcia, 117
Bitchin' Belgian White, 15
Easy, 6
Ein Bock, 94
Irving Berliner Weiss, 23
Jimmy Carter's Peach Wit, 131
Lemon Coriander Weiss, 114
Merci, Pierre, 168
Murph's Cranberry, 119
Roll-in-the-Hay Lager, 83
Slam Dunkelweiss, 12
style guidelines for, 221, 227
Tarheel Tarwebok, 97
Thomas Jefferson's Ale, 29
Uncle Sam's Dark, 26
wheat malt, head retention and, 51
Wilhelm II, Kaiser, 72
Winter's Tale, A (Shakespeare), 12
Winter Wonderland, 154
wit beers:
Belgian White Men Can't Jump, 9
Bitchin' Belgian White, 15
Jimmy Carter's Peach, 131
Merci, Pierre, 168
style guidelines for, 220
World Wide Web beer and brewing sites, 217
wort:
aerating, 5
culturing yeast from bottle of beer in, 36
full, souring, 181
unfermented, priming beer with (kraeusening), 11
wort chillers, xxiii, 69
building, 213–15
Wyncoop Brewing Company, 33

Yams à la Belgique, 191
yeast:
culturing from bottle of beer, 36
liquid vs. dry, xxiii, 106
repitching, 106
suspended, haziness due to, 69
washing, 128
Ye Olde Ale, 109
Yippee IPA, 4